THE POEMS OF

CHARLES CHURCHILL.

IN THREE VOLUMES.

VOLUME II.

THE POETICAL WORKS OF CHARLES CHURCHILL.

WITH COPIOUS NOTES AND A LIFE OF THE AUTHOR,

BY W. TOOKE, F.R.S.

IN THREE VOLUMES.

VOLUME II.

BOSTON:
LITTLE, BROWN AND COMPANY.
NEW YORK: EVANS AND DICKERSON.
PHILADELPHIA: LIPPINCOTT, GRAMBO AND CO.
M.DCCC.LIV.

RIVERSIDE, CAMBRIDGE:
PRINTED BY H. O. HOUGHTON AND COMPANY.

STEREOTYPED BY STONE AND SMART.

CONTENTS.

VOL. II.

THE DUELLIST.

IN THREE BOOKS.

PUBLISHED IN JANUARY, 1764.

THE North Briton, with its usual acrimony of stricture and unrelenting persecution of all the members of administration, had in some of its numbers incidentally introduced some characteristic sketches, supposed to allude to the hero of this poem, Samuel Martin, Esq., M. P. for Camelford, Secretary to the Treasury, and Treasurer to the Princess Dowager of Wales. In that strain of personal abuse, which forms the predominant feature of that scurrilous journal, mention is made in No. 37, published 12 Feb. 1763, of "The secretary of a certain board, a very apt tool of ministerial persecution, who, with a spirit worthy of a Portuguese inquisitor, is hourly looking for carrion in every office to feed the maw of the insatiable vulture. *Imo etiam in senatum venit, notat et designat unumquemque nostrum:* he marks us and all our innocent families for beggary and ruin. Neither the tenderness of age, nor the sacredness of sex is spared by the cruel Scot." And again, in the 40th Number, notice is taken "of the most treacherous, base, selfish, mean, abject, low-lived and dirty fellow that ever wriggled himself into a secretaryship."

Of these passages Mr. Martin took no notice until the first day of the session of the ensuing parliament, when, in the debate * upon the proceedings which had been adopted during

* This debate occasioned the longest sitting which had ever then taken place in the House of Commons. The Speaker was twenty hours in the chair, the House not adjourning until between seven and eight in the morning.

the recess against the persons concerned in the North Briton, he observed, with pointed expression towards Mr. Wilkes, that the author of that paper was a malignant, infamous scoundrel, who had stabbed him in the dark.

On the breaking up of the House, the following letter to Mr. Martin threw the desired light upon the subject of his complaint:

Great George Street, Westminster, Nov. 16, 1763.

SIR,—You complained yesterday, before five hundred gentlemen, that you had been stabbed in the dark by the North Briton, but I have reason to believe you was not so much in the dark as you affected and chose to be. Was the complaint made before so many gentlemen on purpose that they might interpose? To cut off every pretence of ignorance as to the author, I whisper in your ear that every passage in the North Briton, in which you have been named or even alluded to, was written by your humble servant, JOHN WILKES.

To this letter the following answer was returned:—

SIR,—As I said in the House of Commons yesterday, that the writer of the North Briton, who had stabbed me in the dark, was a cowardly as well as a malignant and infamous scoundrel; and your letter of this morning's date acknowledges that every passage of the North Briton, in which I have been named or even alluded to, was written by yourself; I must take the liberty to repeat, that you are a malignant and infamous scoundrel, and that I desire to give you an opportunity of shewing me whether the epithet of cowardly was rightly applied or not.

I desire that you meet me in Hyde Park immediately with a brace of pistols each, to determine our difference.

I shall go to the ring in Hyde Park with my pistols so concealed that nobody may see them, and I will wait in expectation of you one hour. As I shall call in my way at your house to deliver this letter, I propose to go from thence directly to the ring in Hyde Park, from whence we may proceed, if it be necessary, to any more private place, and I mention that I shall wait an hour in order to give you full time to meet me. I am, Sir, your humble servant,

SAMUEL MARTIN.

Mr. Wilkes complied with the appointment, and when he met Mr. Martin at the ring they walked together for a little while to avoid some company who seemed coming up to them. They each brought a pair of pistols. When they were alone, the first fire was from Mr. Martin's pistol, which missed, and the pistol in Mr. Wilkes's hand flashed in the pan. The gentlemen then each took one of Mr. Wilkes's pair of pistols, Mr. Wilkes missed, and the ball of Mr. Martin's pistol lodged in Mr. Wilkes's belly. Mr. Wilkes bled immediately very much; Mr. Martin then came up and desired to give him every assistance in his power. Mr. Wilkes replied that Mr. Martin had behaved like a man of honour, that he was killed, and insisted on Mr. Martin's making his immediate escape, that no creature should know from Mr. Wilkes how the affair happened. Upon this they parted, but Mr. Martin came up again in two or three minutes to Mr. Wilkes, offering him a second time his assistance, but Mr. Wilkes again insisted on his going off. Mr. Martin expressed his concern for Mr. Wilkes, said the thing was too well known by several people who came up almost directly, and then went away. Mr. Wilkes, was carried home, but would not tell any circumstance of the case till he found it so much known. He only said to the surgeon that it was an affair of honour.

The day following, Mr. Wilkes, imagining himself in the greatest danger, returned Mr. Martin his letter, that no evidence might appear against him, and insisted upon it, with his relations, that in case of his death no trouble should be given Mr. Martin, for he had behaved like a man of honour.

The wound Mr. Wilkes had received prevented his obeying an order made by the House of Commons for his attendance, upon which the time was enlarged for a week, and by a vote of the 16th of December, Dr. Heberden, and Mr. Hawkins the surgeon, were directed to attend Mr. Wilkes to observe the progress of his cure, and report the same to the House. Mr. Wilkes, in a very humourous letter to Dr. Brocklesby, professed himself perfectly satisfied with his attentions, and those of Mr. Graves, his own surgeon, and declined the proffered aid of the physicians appointed by the House. As soon as his health would permit, Mr. Wilkes withdrew to Paris, where Mr. Martin also was on a visit; they had a conciliatory interview, and Mr. Martin, in a very handsome note, declared his intention not to take any part in the proceedings of the House of Commons against Mr. Wilkes.

Mr. Martin's conduct, in this transaction, appears to have been highly honourable; but the public mind was so exasperated at the danger to which Wilkes had been exposed, that no credit was given to the spirit which his antagonist had displayed.

It was remarked that Mr. Martin took no notice of the objectionable passages in the North Briton, until above eight months after their publication, and that in so public a manner before the House of Commons as almost to invite its interference; he was also charged with having, during that period, every day practised at a target, Sundays not excepted, and with not returning Mr. Wilkes's letter until a month after the duel, with a view, as it was suggested, had Mr. Wilkes speedily recovered, of making use of it in evidence of his being concerned in the North Briton.

We have, as briefly as we could, given a summary account of the transaction which gave birth to the following poem, and can only regret that Churchill could bestow such strength of colouring, and power of imagery upon subjects which at the time were too insignificant to create an interest in any but the slaves of prejudice and party, and which, though now obscure, are too unimportant in their consequences to excite curiosity.

In 1772 Mr. Martin declined an Alderman's gown. He was a frequent speaker in Parliament between the years 1782 and 1786, and died in 1788. A good engraving from the last portrait painted by Hogarth for himself, and bequeathed by him in his will to Mr. Martin, will be found in the Gentleman's Magazine for Feb. 1805.

The first book, which is the best of the three, opens with some pretty allegorical imagery, but the poem as a whole has less of that fine poetical colouring and seasoning of wit and humour which in most of Churchill's other works relieve his rancorous acrimony of party rage, and though it bears evident marks throughout of carelessness and precipitation, yet at the same time many passages sufficiently point out the hand of the master, and will redeem it from that oblivion which has already overwhelmed the subject and its hero.

We are enabled to subjoin the letters, above alluded to, as having been addressed by Mr. Wilkes to Drs. Heberden and Brocklesby, in consequence of the report required by the House of Commons as to the state of his health.

A Card from Mr. Wilkes to Dr. Heberden.

Monday, December 19.

Mr. Wilkes presents his compliments to Dr. Heberden, and is duly sensible of the kind care and concern of the House of Commons not only for his health but for his speedy recovery. He is attended by Dr. Brocklesby, of whose integrity and ability he has had the experience of many years, and on whose skill he has the most perfect reliance. Mr. Wilkes cannot but still be of opinion that there is a peculiar propriety in the choice he at first made of Dr. Brocklesby for the cure of what is called a gun-shot wound, from the circumstance of the doctor's having been many years physician to the army; but at the same time entertains a real esteem for Dr. Heberden's great merit, and though he cannot say that he wishes to see the doctor at present, he hopes that when he shall be well enough to beg that honour, the Doctor will eat a bit of mutton with him in Great George Street.

Letter from Mr. Wilkes to Dr. Brocklesby.

Great George Street, Monday, Dec. 19, 1763.

Dear sir—I have the favour of your letter and of the papers inclosed. I think you are rather deficient in politeness that you do not congratulate your friend on the new and singular honour done him by the House of Commons, in appointing a physician and surgeon to attend him. The Lords set them such an example, by ordering the physician and surgeon of a member of the other house to their bar, to be examined concerning his state of health. I had before received other unmerited obligations from their Lordships, and the old friendships of Lord Sandwich, though I own I was rather put to the blush by their publishing to the world what they pretended was found (perhaps put) among the things stolen from me. If a man writes a private essay on woman, should all the world see it? Is a treatise against the spleen or the tædium vitæ, so dangerous as now to become a state crime for the cognizance of our present ——l rulers, or rather In—s? Has the nasty, gummy, blubbering, overgrown body of a lord, as barbarous and blustering as the north, has he likewise received his orders to denounce to the Commons a laughable poem, as a horrid crime to make all good Christians shudder? Are the most wretched and impious lines to be forged, that a work which idolizes the sex may be brought into judgment before the crafty Scot, who never loved any woman, and who—

This last act of the Commons seems almost to perfect the scene, and quite overwhelms me with gratitude. Yet though I am a young member, I cannot but observe and lament, that the ancient established forms of Parliament have in the present case been laid aside, as if order had taken leave of the House with old good Onslow. The course of business has always been, that business of importance should previously go to a committee. The affair you have mentioned is of so much real consequence, that it should (in my opinion) have been referred to two Committees. First, it should have gone to the Committee of ways and means, to contrive how the state physician and surgeon can get into my house. Secondly, to the Committee of Supply, to vote the fees due to the gentlemen for their attendance. But I have public economy so much at heart, (though I make no parade of it) that I will save the nation that expense; for I will not suffer either of them to enter my doors.

The Commons, like true country people, seem to have an overflowing of kindness for me, which is very apt to surfeit; and yet, like the others, sometimes in the same moment, they fail in a point of good breeding, even to one of their own members. The House desires Dr. Heberden and Mr. Hawkins to come to me, but forgot to desire me to receive them, and I most certainly will not.

Surely, my dear Sir, this matter has been too lightly determined upon by the honourable House. It is pretty well known that I have already a physician and surgeon, whose characters the foul breath of slander never reached, and whom I confide in and love. Why should I admit any others? Am I to consent to an unjust slur upon gentlemen, with whom I have all the reason in the world to be satisfied? Shall I concur in suffering party madness to fix a vile suspicion, where I know that it ought not to rest? I will never countenance so shameful a proceeding. Honour, justice, gratitude, private friendship, equally forbid it.

My brother members seem quite wild in their rage. They would force a physician and surgeon upon me, when I have one of each already, and they forget that my dear friend and chaplain Churchill has left me for sometime. Would it not therefore have looked better, if these obliging friends had shewn some regard to my spiritual concerns, and had ordered their own Chaplain, the very learned brother of the very conscientious merchant, and of the very acute Secretary to attend me; or they might perhaps have prevailed on the good Mr. Kidgell. He is so ready at every laudable and lucrative work, he would not, I believe, have hesitated. You might in time have had observations on my conversion and apostleship, though I hope not in a way to make you doubt of the whole; at least you would have been sure of a series of letters in the ledger, the profits to be divided between the said Kidgell and his partner Mac-Faden, according to the said Kidgell's former plan. I think the Lords too ought to have considered this important point, chaplainship, and Lord Sandwich or Lord Despencer, or some other pious Lord, should have moved to send me a divine legation of the Bishop of Gloucester. I have been said to have doubts. I really have none. If I had, that orthodox bishop would surely be able to remove them; only I should fear that for every one of mine he carried away he would leave ten of his own behind with me. I might likewise be treated with quaint persuasives to continence. It could never come more á propos, nor with a greater probability of success, for that cold, frozen virtue of chastity, the virtue of age, not of youth, seems likely to be as much my portion this year as it has been the pedant's through every year of his life. His virtue is fixed as in a frost, beyond all the powers of genial spring, or a most lovely wife; mine, I trust, will thaw, melt, and resolve itself to sprightly dew long before the first breath of zephyr.

After all, my dear Doctor, I might, I believe, admit the state-physician and surgeon without any danger of a Russian hœmorrhoidal cholic,* but I will not do any thing on compulsion, Hal. I do not suspect either of them in the least to resemble a Talbot, a Martin, a Forbes, or a Dun. On the contrary, they are both amiable men, and therefore I wish you would bring them here to dinner as soon as I shall get a little better; for, at present, if they come, I should fear they would place themselves by authority, one on the right, and the other on the left hand of their poor patient, and, like Sancho's doctor with his wand, forbid my tasting any thing I ogled, or rather squinted at.

I am alone; if you are disengaged, I wish you to come here at four, and I will give you half of my boiled chicken. We never can want food for laughter, while in the phrase of the sly Fox,† George Grenville has the conduct of the House of Commons. I am ever, my dear Sir, your affectionate humble servant,

JOHN WILKES.

---

* A complaint which has proved fatal to several heirs apparent and princes of the imperial house of Romanoff; of later years an apoplectic fit, occasioned by an awkward adjustment of the cravat, has proved equally efficacious, and quite as satisfactory to the sovereign de facto.

† Henry Fox, afterwards Lord Holland, on his first taking office with the implied management of the House of Commons, was so elated by his position, that, inconsistently with his habitual prudence, he, in his first circular addressed to the ministerial adherents previous to the commencement of the session, was incautious enough to preface it with these words, "His Majesty having been pleased to confide to me the conduct of the House of Commons;" this gave much offence, and one or two members severely animadverted on this improper allusion to the crown, but all farther consequence was averted by an adroit and crafty, although evasive apology on the part of the Fox.

THE DUELLIST.

BOOK I.

THE clock struck twelve; o'er half the globe
Darkness had spread her pitchy robe:
Morpheus, his feet with velvet shod,
Treading as if in fear he trod,
Gentle as dews at even-tide,
Distill'd his poppies far and wide.
  Ambition, who, when waking, dreams
Of mighty, but fantastic schemes,
Who, when asleep, ne'er knows that rest
With which the humbler soul is blest,
Was building castles in the air,
Goodly to look upon and fair,
But on a bad foundation laid,
Doom'd at return of morn to fade.
  Pale Study, by the taper's light,
Wearing away the watch of night,
Sat reading, but with o'ercharged head,
Remember'd nothing that he read.
Starving midst plenty, with a face
Which might the court of Famine grace,
Ragged, and filthy to behold,
Gray Avarice nodded o'er his gold.

Jealousy, his quick eye half-closed
With watchings worn, reluctant dozed:
And, mean distrust not quite forgot,
Slumber'd as if he slumber'd not.
Stretch'd at his length on the bare ground,
His hardy offspring sleeping round,
Snored restless Labour; by his side
Lay Health, a coarse but comely bride.
Virtue, without the doctor's aid,
In the soft arms of sleep was laid;
Whilst Vice, within the guilty breast,
Could not be physic'd into rest.
Thou bloody Man! whose ruffian knife
Is drawn against thy neighbour's life,
And never scruples to descend
Into the bosom of a friend;
A firm, fast friend, by vice allied,
And to thy secret service tied,
In whom ten murders breed no awe,
If properly secured from law:
Thou man of Lust! whom passion fires
To foulest deeds, whose hot desires
O'er honest bars with ease make way,
Whilst idiot Beauty falls a prey,
And to indulge thy brutal flame
A Lucrece must be brought to shame;
Who dost a brave, bold sinner, bear
Rank incest to the open air,
And rapes, full blown upon thy crown,
Enough to weigh a nation down:
Thou simular of Lust! vain man,

Whose restless thoughts still form the plan
Of guilt, which, wither'd to the root,
Thy lifeless nerves can't execute,
Whilst in thy marrowless, dry bones
Desire without enjoyment groans;
Thou perjur'd Wretch! whom falsehood clothes
E'en like a garment, who with oaths
Dost trifle, as with brokers, meant
To serve thy every vile intent,
In the day's broad and searching eye
Making God witness to a lie,
Blaspheming heaven and earth for pelf,
And hanging friends to save thyself:
Thou son of Chance! whose glorious soul,
On the four aces doom'd to roll,
Was never yet with honour caught,
Nor on poor virtue lost one thought;
Who dost thy wife, thy children set,
Thy all, upon a single bet.
Risking, the desperate stake to try,
Here and hereafter on a die;
Who, thy own private fortune lost,
Dost game on at thy country's cost,
And, grown expert in sharping rules,
First fool'd thyself, now prey'st on fools:
Thou noble Gamester! whose high place
Gives too much credit to disgrace,

66 Another allusion to the execution of Ayliffe, and the popular imputations it gave rise to. See note on v. 140 of the Epistle to Hogarth.

Who, with the motion of a die,
Dost make a mighty island fly,
The sums, I mean, of good French gold
For which a mighty island sold;
Who dost betray intelligence,
Abuse the dearest confidence,
And, private fortune to create,
Most falsely play the game of state;
Who dost within the Alley sport
Sums, which might beggar a whole court,
And make us bankrupts all, if Care,
With good Earl Talbot, was not there:
Thou daring Infidel! whom pride
And sin have drawn from Reason's side;
Who, fearing his avengeful rod,
Dost wish not to believe a God;
Whose hope is founded on a plan
Which should distract the soul of man,
And make him curse his abject birth;
Whose hope is, once return'd to earth,
There to lie down, for worms a feast,
To rot and perish like a beast;
Who dost, of punishment afraid,

92 Earl Talbot, Lord Steward of the King's Household from 1761 to 1782. On his first appointment to the office, his lordship proposed some economical reforms in the palace, but the clamour excited among some of the retainers of the court, together with his lordship's want of resolution, induced him to desist from carrying them into execution. In a future page we shall have occasion to notice his lordship's rencontre with Mr. Wilkes at Bagshot.

And by thy crimes a coward made,
To every generous soul a curse,
Than hell and all her torments worse,
When crawling to thy latter end,
Call on destruction as a friend,
Choosing to crumble into dust
Rather than rise, though rise you must:
Thou Hypocrite! who dost profane,
And take the patriot's name in vain;
Then most thy country's foe when most
Of love and loyalty you boast;
Who for the filthy love of gold
Thy friend, thy king, thy God, hast sold,
And, mocking the just claim of Hell,
Were bidders found, thyself wouldst sell.

118 The colouring of these portraits is rather too high, though the general resemblance is preserved. Had Churchill confined his muse to the exposure of such characters only, and not been biased by party prejudice, few of his own friends would have escaped his lash, and an impartial condemnation of profligacy, whether in or out of office, would have been of essential service to the cause of virtue. Mr. Gray's muse appears to have been equally indignant as regards one of these noble worthies, in the following very severe verses written on viewing the grotesque pile of buildings raised at Kingsgate, in the Isle of Thanet, and which were visited by the Bard soon after their erection:

Old and abandon'd by each venal friend,
Here Holland form'd the pious resolution
To smuggle some few years, and strive to mend
A broken character and constitution.
On this congenial spot he fix'd his choice,
(Earl Goodwin trembled for his neighbouring sand)
Here sea-gulls scream and cormorants rejoice,

Ye Villians! of whatever name,
Whatever rank, to whom the claim
Of Hell is certain, on whose lids
That worm, which never dies, forbids
Sweet sleep to fall, come, and behold,
Whilst envy makes your blood run cold,

And mariners, though shipwreck'd, dread to land.
Here reigns the blustering North and blighting East;
No tree is heard to whisper, bird to sing,
Yet nature cannot furnish out the feast:
Art he invokes new horrors still to bring.
Now mould'ring fanes and battlements arise,
Arches and turrets nodding to their fall,
Unpeopled palaces delude his eyes,
And mimic desolation covers all.
"Ah! (said the sighing Peer) had Bute been true,
Nor Rigby's, Calcraft's, Shelburne's friendship vain,
Far other scenes than these had crown'd our view,
And realized the ruins that we feign.
Purged by the sword, and beautified by fire,
Then had we seen proud London's hated walls;
Owls might have hooted in St. Peter's choir,
And Foxes stunk and litter'd in St. Paul's."

Lord Holland was the last! with the exception of Lord Melville, of that class of officials, who from the period of Danby under Charles II. to the close of the reign of George II. carried on the business of government by the means of direct corruption, and during the greater part of which period each of the members of the House of Commons habitually voting with ministers, received a douceur of one hundred guineas, exclusive of all occasional bribes and jobs.

"Once we confess beneath the patriot's cloak,
From the crack'd bag the dropping guinea spoke,
And gingling down the back stairs told the crew,
Old Cato is as great a rogue as you."

Behold, by pitiless Conscience led,
So Justice wills, that holy bed
Where Peace her full dominion keeps,
And Innocence with Holland sleeps.
  Bid Terror, posting on the wind,

Great indignation was expressed throughout the country at the gross peculations of Lord Holland and his associates; the City of London petitioned the King for the redress of various grievances, the removal of evil counsellors, particularly adverting to Lord Holland's defalcations, and the dissolution of parliament: no satisfactory notice being taken of that petition, the Livery, at a special meeting convened for that purpose in October, 1769, unanimously adopted the following resolutions.

Resolved, That Henry Lord Holland was the Paymaster whom we, the Livery of London, in our late petition to the throne for the redress of grievances, &c. affirmed to be the public defaulter of unaccounted millions.

Resolved, That it is the duty of our representatives to obtain, if possible, an honest and proper parliamentary inquiry into the conduct and accounts of Henry Lord Holland.

And, when it shall appear on such inquiry that Henry Lord Holland has, by unnecessary delays, detained the public money for years in his hands, and appropriated the interest thereof to his own use, and has also, by various pretences, interposed repeated impediments to public justice, and by various misrepresentations induced our sovereign to stay the legal proceedings against him, thereby endeavouring to lessen that respect that is due to his majesty, and introduce a power superior to that of law, the use and durance of which create the distinction between monarchy and tyranny—

Resolved, That then it will become in the highest degree, the duty of our representatives in parliament, to endeavour that Henry Lord Holland be impeached, that he may be an example to all future ministers, and shew them how dangerous it is to enrich themselves with the public treasure, and sport with the rights of a free people.

Affray the spirits of mankind;
Bid Earthquakes, heaving for a vent,
Rive their concealing continent,
And, forcing an untimely birth
Through the vast bowels of the earth,

Resolved, That these resolutions be entered by the town-clerk in the record books of this city, as part of the proceedings of the Livery at the election of a Lord Mayor of this city for the year 1770; and that a copy of these resolutions, signed by the sheriffs, be delivered to each of our representatives in parliament.

The universal clamour thus excited had the effect of inducing Lord Holland to withdraw from public observation; but the ministers, who were themselves deeply implicated in similar abuses, would not institute any prosecution against him in his lifetime, but after his death proceedings for restitution were taken in the exchequer against Mr. John Powell, his only acting executor, who was compelled to pay a sum of £232,515 *4s. 8d.* in discharge of some ascertained balances due from Lord Holland as Paymaster-General of his Majesty's Forces, but which was far short of the claim made, or of the actual deficit.

Lord Holland's private were as loose as his public morals; he gambled, and by his example while abroad initiated his son in a love of play and of irregular habits and society, which formed a drawback from his otherwise high and noble qualities, and precluded his conciliating that esteem and confidence of the respectable portion of the public, by means of which his great rival Pitt acquired and secured his ascendency.

Mr. Horne (afterwards Tooke) in the early period of his reform coadjutorship with Mr. Pitt, published a pamphlet, now very scarce, entitled Two Pair of Portraits, exhibiting, in striking contrast, the characters moral and political, of Lord Holland and his son Charles James Fox, as compared with the lofty bearing and purity of conduct, private as well as public, of the Earl of Chatham and his son William Pitt.

Endeavour, in her monstrous womb,
At once all nature to entomb;
Bid all that's horrible and dire,
All that man hates and fears, conspire
To make night hideous as they can,
Still is thy sleep, thou virtuous Man!
Pure as the thoughts which in thy breast
Inhabit, and insure thy rest;
Still shall thy Ayliff, taught, though late,
Thy friendly justice in his fate,
Turn'd to a guardian angel, spread
Sweet dreams of comfort round thy head.
Dark was the night, by Fate decreed
For the contrivance of a deed
More black than common, which might make
This land from her foundations shake,
Might tear up Freedom by the root,
Destroy a Wilkes, and fix a Bute.
Deep Horror held her wide domain;
The sky in sullen drops of rain
Forewept the morn, and through the air,
Which, opening, laid its bosom bare,
Loud thunders roll'd, and lightning stream'd;
The owl at Freedom's window scream'd,
The screech-owl, prophet dire, whose breath
Brings sickness, and whose note is death;
The churchyard teem'd, and from the tomb,
All sad and silent, through the gloom
The ghosts of men, in former times,
Whose public virtues were their crimes,

Indignant stalk'd; sorrow and rage
Blank'd their pale cheeks; in his own age
The prop of Freedom, Hampden there
Felt after death the generous care;
Sidney, by grief, from heaven was kept,
And for his brother patriot wept:
All friends of Liberty, when Fate
Prepared to shorten Wilkes's date,
Heaved, deeply hurt, the heart-felt groan,
And knew that wound to be their own.
  Hail, Liberty! a glorious word,
In other countries scarcely heard,
Or heard but as a thing of course,
Without or energy or force:
Here felt, enjoy'd, adored, she springs,
Far, far beyond the reach of kings;
Fresh blooming from our mother Earth,
With pride and joy she owns her birth
Derived from us, and in return
Bids in our breasts her genius burn;
Bids us with all those blessings live
Which Liberty alone can give,
Or nobly with that spirit die
Which makes death more than victory.
  Hail those old patriots, on whose tongue
Persuasion in the senate hung,
Whilst they the sacred cause maintain'd!
Hail those old chiefs, to honour train'd,
Who spread, when other methods fail'd,
War's bloody banner, and prevail'd!

Shall men like these unmention'd sleep
Promiscuous with the common heap,
And (Gratitude forbid the crime!)
Be carried down the stream of time
In shoals, unnoticed and forgot,
On Lethe's stream, like flags, to rot?
No—they shall live, and each fair name,
Recorded in the book of Fame,
Founded on honour's basis, fast
As the round earth to ages last.
Some virtues vanish with our breath;
Virtue like this lives after death.
Old Time himself, his scythe thrown by,
Himself lost in eternity,
An everlasting crown shall twine
To make a Wilkes and Sidney join.
  But should some slave-got villain dare
Chains for his country to prepare,
And, by his birth to slavery broke,
Make her, too, feel the galling yoke,
May he be evermore accurst,
Amongst bad men be rank'd the worst;
May he be still himself, and still
Go on in vice, and perfect ill;
May his broad crimes each day increase,
Till he can't live nor die in peace;
May he be plung'd so deep in shame,
That Satan mayn't endure his name,
And hear, scarce crawling on the earth,
His children curse him for their birth;

May Liberty, beyond the grave,
Ordain him to be still a slave,
Grant him what here he most requires,
And damn him with his own desires!
  But should some villain, in support
And zeal for a despairing court,
Placing in craft his confidence,
And making honour a pretence
To do a deed of deepest shame,
Whilst filthy lucre is his aim;
Should such a wretch, with sword or knife
Contrive to practise 'gainst the life
Of one who, honour'd through the land,
For Freedom made a glorious stand,
Whose chief, perhaps his only, crime
Is, (if plain Truth at such a time
May dare her sentiments to tell)
That he his country loves too well:
May he—but words are all too weak
The feelings of my heart to speak—
May he—O for a noble curse
Which might his very marrow pierce—
The general contempt engage,
And be the Martin of his age.

THE DUELLIST.

BOOK II.

DEEP in the bosom of a wood,
Out of the road, a temple stood;
Ancient, and much the worse for wear,
It called aloud for quick repair,
And, tottering from side to side,
Menaced destruction far and wide,
Nor able seem'd, unless made stronger,
To hold out four or five years longer.
Four hundred pillars, from the ground
Rising in order, most unsound;
Some rotten to the heart, aloof,
Seemed to support the tottering roof,
But to inspection nearer laid,
Instead of giving, wanted aid.
The structure, rare and curious, made
By men most famous in their trade,
A work of years, admired by all,
Was suffer'd into dust to fall,

[2] Churchill, according to the approved model of patriotic zeal, under this metaphorical picture of the ancient British Constitution, deplores the state of corruption and decay to which it was in his time reduced, and expatiates in glowing verse on its former benefits and blessings. This has with each succeeding generation been a favourite topic of declamation, though the perpetual recurrence of the same complaint, in the same comparative terms, demonstrates its fallacy.

Or, just to make it hang together,
And keep off the effects of weather,
Was patch'd and patch'd from time to time
By wretches, whom it were a crime,
A crime, which Art would treason hold
To mention with those names of old.
Builders, who had the pile survey'd,
And those not Flitcrofts in their trade,
Doubted (the wise hand in a doubt
Merely sometimes to hand her out)
Whether (like churches in a brief,
Taught wisely to obtain relief

26 Henry Flitcroft, an architect of some eminence, was in 1738 appointed comptroller and afterwards Master Mason to the Board of Works. He was one of the numerous school to which the genius of Sir Christopher Wren gave rise; but without possessing the invention or skill of the master, or the originality and daring of Vanbrugh, Hawksmore, or Archer, who were his contemporaries. He was contented to follow in the quiet stream of the school, without the boldness to think for himself or to choose for his prototypes the more elevated productions of the nobler periods of the art. Consequently, his church of St. Giles in the Fields, London, and of St. Olaves, Southwark, although they may not err against the elementary canons of the art, are alike deficient in originality, as in appropriate and impressive effect.

He died at Teddington, Middlesex, in 1769, and was buried in the church there.

29 The system of obtaining eleemosynary contributions by reading briefs in churches, chiefly for the repair and rebuilding of churches and colleges, and other public purposes, but occasionally for the relief of individuals suffering by fire, tempest, and other casualties, was abolished in the year 1828 by act of 9 Geo. IV. c. 42. When the practice commenced is uncertain, but probably in the reign of Queen Elizabeth; for in

Through Chancery, who gives her fees
To this and other charities)
It must not, in all parts unsound,
Be ripp'd, and pull'd down to the ground;
Whether (though after ages ne'er
Shall raise a building to compare)
Art, if they should their art employ,
Meant to preserve, might not destroy,
As human bodies, worn away,
Batter'd and hasting to decay,

the year 1600, one was issued for Richard Grafton, as appears by a printed copy sold at Sotheby's auction rooms on 13 August, 1840, and in 1604, John Stowe, the historian, obtained one in consideration of his merit and distressed circumstances. In 1623 one was issued for repairing a church at St. Alban's, after which the entries are frequent in parish registers of sums collected after briefs being read. The first mention of them in the statutes was in 9 W. III. c. 25, by which they were exempted from stamp duty. In 1705, an act, passed 4 and 5 Anne, for the better collecting charity money on briefs by letters-patent, and preventing abuses in relation to such charities.

Such letters-patent were issued by the Lord High Chancellor upon a certificate from the quarter sessions, and had ever since the year 1799 been delivered to John Stevenson Salt, Esq. of the firm of Messrs. Stevenson and Salt, bankers in Lombard Street. Mr. Salt was from that period exclusively employed as undertaker for the purpose of dispersing copies of the briefs and receiving the collections; but still it was always competent for any person to whom, or for whose benefit a brief was granted, to appoint his own undertaker, Mr. Salt holding no office or permanent appointment.

Upon receipt of the letters-patent the undertaker provided 10,800 printed copies of church briefs, and 11,500 fire briefs, which he caused to be delivered to the churchwardens of the several parishes in England, and a part of Wales, and upon

Bidding the power of Art despair,
Cannot those very medicines bear
Which, and which only, can restore,
And make them healthy as before.
To Liberty, whose gracious smile
Shed peace and plenty o'er the Isle,
Our grateful ancestors, her plain
But faithful children, raised this fane.
Full in the front, stretch'd out in length,
Where Nature put forth all her strength

their return being obtained, the undertaker accounted to the claimants for the sums collected, after deducting the expenses of obtaining the brief, and his charges of collection.

Throughout the 18th century, and up to the time of their abolition in 1828, they averaged about eight or ten in number every year. The net sum received from each brief, after payment of all expenses, ranged about £200; in some extraordinary cases, however, much larger amounts were realized; and on one brief, in 1759, for founding and erecting colleges in New York and Philadelphia, a sum of nearly £10,000 was collected.

The fees on soliciting a church brief, were—

	£.	s.	d.
Fiat	10	5	6
Patent	22	11	6
Paper and Printing	22	10	0
Stamping	13	10	0
Canvas, Carriage, Portages, &c.	15	3	0
	£84	0	0
Undertakers' salary at 4*d.* each for 10,340 country briefs	172	6	8
Ditto for 460 in London, and Bills of Mortality at 8*d.*	15	13	4
	£272	0	0

The undertaker charged double salary for fire and other briefs, his charge therefore, in such cases, was above £500.

In spring eternal, lay a plain
Where our brave fathers used to train
Their sons to arms, to teach the art
Of war, and steel the infant heart;
Labour, their hardy nurse, when young,
Their joints had knit, their nerves had strung;
Abstinence, foe declared to death,
Had, from the time they first drew breath,
The best of doctors, with plain food;
Kept pure the channel of their blood;
Health in their cheeks bade colour rise,
And Glory sparkled in their eyes.
The instruments of husbandry,

The undertaker was responsible for every agent and collector throughout the kingdom, and his salary was latterly quite inadequate to the trouble and risk attending the business.

This plan of raising money gradually fell into disrepute, and consequent unproductiveness, from an almost universal idea that the briefs were formed by the undertaker, he agreeing to pay the petitioners a certain sum, reserving the benefit of the surplus for himself; so that whatever sum might be collected on a brief over and above such supposed payment, was imagined to be paid to him, and therefore, that he and not the petitioners would really profit by any extra benevolence on the part of the public.

This prevailing opinion, though wholly unfounded, operated most powerfully against briefs on the minds of the clergy, the churchwardens, and the public; inducing the clergy in some cases not to read the brief, the churchwardens to be negligent in collecting, and the public to be averse from contributing.

On the passing of the bill abolishing the issue of briefs, a vast number of small balances, some of very old standing, in Mr. Salt's hands, were found in the aggregate to amount to a sum of about £2,000, which by arrangement was appropriately paid over to the Commissioners for building new churches.

As in contempt, were all thrown by,
And, flattering a manly pride,
War's keener tools their place supplied.
Their arrows to the head they drew;
Swift to the point their javelins flew;
They grasp'd the sword, they shook the spear;
Their fathers felt a pleasing fear,
And even Courage, standing by,
Scarcely beheld with steady eye.
Each stripling, lesson'd by his sire,
Knew when to close, when to retire;
When near at hand, when from afar
To fight, and was himself a war.
  Their wives, their mothers, all around,
Careless of order, on the ground,
Breathed forth to Heaven the pious vow,
And for a son's or husband's brow,
With eager fingers, laurel wove;
Laurel which in the sacred grove,
Planted by Liberty, they find,
The brows of conquerors to bind,
To give them pride and spirits, fit
To make a world in arms submit.
  What raptures did the bosom fire
Of the young, rugged, peasant sire,
When, from the toil of mimic fight,
Returning with return of night,
He saw his babe resign the breast,
And, smiling, stroke those arms in jest,
With which hereafter he shall make
The proudest heart in Gallia quake!

Gods! with what joy, what honest pride,
Did each fond, wishing, rustic bride,
Behold her manly swain return!
How did her love-sick bosom burn,
Though on parades he was not bred,
Nor wore the livery of red,
When, Pleasure heightening all her charms,
She strain'd her warrior in her arms,
And begg'd, whilst love and glory fire,
A son, a son just like his sire!
Such were the men in former times,
Ere luxury had made our crimes
Our bitter punishment, who bore
Their terrors to a foreign shore;
Such were the men who, free from dread,
By Edwards and by Henries led,
Spread, like a torrent swell'd with rains,
O'er haughty Gallia's trembling plains:
Such were the men, when lust of power,
To work him woe, in evil hour
Debauch'd the tyrant from those ways
On which a king should found his praise;
When stern Oppression, hand in hand
With Pride, stalk'd proudly through the land;
When weeping Justice was misled
From her fair course, and Mercy dead:
Such were the men, in virtue strong,
Who dared not see their country's wrong,
Who left the mattock and the spade,
And, in the robes of War array'd,
In their rough arms, departing, took

Their helpless babes, and with a look
Stern and determined, swore to see
Those babes no more, or see them free:
Such were the men whom tyrant Pride
Could never fasten to his side
By threats or bribes, who, freemen born,
Chains, though of gold, beheld with scorn;
Who, free from every servile awe,
Could never be divorced from law,
From that broad general law which Sense
Made for the general defence;
Could never yield to partial ties
Which from dependant stations rise:
Could never be to slavery led,
For Property was at their head:
Such were the men, in days of yore,
Who, call'd by Liberty, before
Her temple on the sacred green,
In martial pastimes oft were seen—
Now seen no longer—in their stead,
To laziness and vermin bred,
A race who, strangers to the cause
Of Freedom, live by other laws,
On other motives fight, a prey
To interest, and slaves for pay.
Valour, how glorious on a plan
Of honour founded! leads their van;
Discretion, free from taint of fear,
Cool, but resolved, brings up their rear;
Discretion, Valour's better half;
Dependance holds the general's staff.

In plain and home-spun garb array'd,
Not for vain shew, but service, made,
In a green flourishing old age,
Not damn'd yet with an equipage
In rules of Porterage untaught,
Simplicity, not worth a groat,
For years had kept the temple-door;
Full on his breast a glass he wore,
Through which his bosom open lay
To every one who pass'd that way:
Now turn'd adrift—with humbler face,
But prouder heart, his vacant place
Corruption fills, and bears the key;
No entrance now without a fee.
With belly round, and full fat face,
Which on the house reflected grace,
Full of good fare, and honest glee,
The steward Hospitality;
Old Welcome smiling by his side
A good old servant, often tried
And faithful found, who kept in view
His lady's fame and interest too,
Who made each heart with joy rebound,
Yet never run her state aground,
Was turn'd off, or (which word I find
Is more in modern use) resign'd.

182 The Dukes of Newcastle and Devonshire, Lord Temple, &c., resigned their offices in 1762. The ground on which their successors founded their claim to popularity was the stale pretence of economy, in their zeal for which the pension list was increased beyond all former precedent.

Half-starved, half-starving others, bred
In beggary, with carrion fed,
Detested, and detesting all,
Made up of avarice and gall,
Boasting great thrift, yet wasting more
Than ever steward did before,
Succeeded one, who to engage
The praise of an exhausted age
Assumed a name of high degree,
And call'd himself Economy.

Within the temple, full in sight,
Where without ceasing day and night
The workman toil'd; where Labour bared
His brawny arm; where art prepared,
In regular and even rows,
Her types, a Printing press arose;
Each workman knew his task, and each
Was honest and expert as Leach.

198 Wilkes had a private printing press at his house in Great George Street, Westminster. The uses to which it might have been put, the poet well describes; of the uses to which it was put, the infamous Essay on Woman was a specimen.

200 Dryden Leach was a printer in Crane Court, Fleet Street: he was one of the first who introduced a taste for the embellishments of typography. Some elegant productions from the Parma and Paris presses had a little before this time awakened the attention of the London printers, particularly of Leach, who may be styled the Father of fine printing in this country, but his editions have been since eclipsed by the superior splendor of those of Baskerville, Bensley, and others.

Under the celebrated General Warrant, Nathan Carrington, with his gang of King's messengers, took Leach, with all

Hence Learning struck a deeper root,
And Science brought forth riper fruit;
Hence Loyalty received support,
Even when banish'd from the court;
Hence Government gain'd strength, and hence
Religion sought and found defence;
Hence England's fairest fame arose,
And Liberty subdued her foes.
On a low, simple, turf-made throne,
Raised by Allegiance, scarcely known
From her attendants, glad to be
Pattern of that equality
She wish'd to all, so far as could
Safely consist with social good,
The goddess sat; around her head
A cheerful radiance Glory spread:

his journeymen and servants, into custody; and though it clearly appeared that the North Briton was printed by Balfe, in the Old Bailey, Mr. Leach was detained in confinement several days. For this illegal outrage and imprisonment, Leach brought an action against the messengers, and recovered £400 damages; fourteen journeymen printers also obtained verdicts, and were prevailed on to compromise them with Carrington and Blackmore, two of the messengers, in manner following: thirteen of them, who had £200 damages awarded them, accepted £120 each, and one of them who had £300 accepted £175, and all agreed to pay their own costs.

Earl Temple, with a nobility of spirit peculiar to himself, stood forth at that critical and alarming juncture as the defender of the liberties of his countrymen. His public-spirited liberality supported the printers in their prosecutions, and at length succeeded in obtaining a complete triumph over the violent and oppressive exertions of arbitrary power.

Courage, a youth of royal race,
Lovelily stern, possess'd a place
On her left hand, and on her right
Sat Honour, clothed with robes of light;
Before her Magna Charta lay,
Which some great lawyer, of his day
The Pratt, was officed to explain
And make the basis of her reign:
Peace, crown'd with olive, to her breast
Two smiling twin-born infants prest;

223 Lord Camden, in his charge to the Jury on occasion of the action brought by Mr. Wilkes against Mr. Wood, the Under Secretary of State, for illegally entering his house, and seizing and carrying away his papers, gave his opinion on the warrant in the following words:—"Upon the maturest consideration I am bold to say that this warrant is illegal, but I am far from wishing a matter of this consequence should rest solely on my opinion. I am only one of twelve whose opinions I am desirous should be taken in this matter, and I am very willing to allow myself the meanest of the twelve. There is also a higher court before which this matter may be canvassed, and whose determination is final; and here I cannot help observing the happiness of our constitution in admitting these appeals; in consequence of which, material points are determined on the most mature consideration, and with the greatest solemnity. To this admirable delay of the law (for in this case the law's delay may be styled admirable) I believe it is chiefly owing that we possess the best digested and most excellent body of laws which any nation on the face of the earth, whether ancient or modern, could ever boast of. If these higher jurisdictions should declare my opinion erroneous, I submit, as will become me, and kiss the rod; but I must say I shall always consider it as a rod of iron for the chastisement of the people of Great Britain."

The Jury gave Mr. Wilkes £1,000 damages.

At her feet couching War was laid,
And with a brindled lion play'd:
Justice and Mercy, hand in hand,
Joint guardians of the happy land,
Together held their mighty charge,
And truth walk'd all about at large;
Health for the royal troop the feast
Prepared, and Virtue was high priest.
  Such was the fame our goddess bore,
Her temple such in days of yore.
What changes ruthless Time presents!
Behold her ruin'd battlements,
Her walls decay'd, her nodding spires,
Her altars broke, her dying fires,
Her name despised, her priests destroy'd,
Her friends disgraced, her foes employ'd,
Herself (by ministerial arts
Deprived e'en of the people's hearts,
Whilst they, to work her surer woe,
Feign her to monarchy a foe)
Exiled by grief, self doom'd to dwell
With some poor hermit in a cell;
Or, that retirement tedious grown,
If she walks forth, she walks unknown,
Hooted, and pointed at with scorn
As one in some strange country born.
  Behold a rude and ruffian race,

253 Carrington and his band of King's messengers; a silver greyhound, the emblem of despatch, was then worn by these men as a distinctive badge of office when engaged in the execution of their duty.

A band of spoilers, seize her place:
With looks, which might the heart dis-seat,
And make life sound a quick retreat,
To rapine from the cradle bred,
A staunch old blood-hound at their head,
Who, free from virtue and from awe,
Knew none but the bad part of law.
They roved at large; each on his breast
Mark'd with a greyhound, stood confest;
Controlment waited on their nod
High wielding persecution's rod;
Confusion follow'd at their heels,
And a cast statesman held the seals;

266 The general warrant, so often alluded to by our author, was signed by the Earls of Egremont and Hallifax, joint secretaries of state for the home department, to whom, after being liberated from his confinement in the Tower, Wilkes addressed the following note:

Great George Street, May 6, 1763.

My Lords—On my return here from Westminster Hall, where I have been discharged from my commitment to the Tower under your lordships' warrant, I find that my house has been robbed; and am informed that the stolen goods are in possession of one or both of your lordships, I therefore insist that you forthwith return them to your humble servant,

John Wilkes.

The following answer was returned next day by their lordships.

Sir—In answer to your letter of yesterday, in which you take upon you to make use of the indecent and scurrilous expressions of your having found your house had been robbed; and that the stolen goods are in our possession: we acquaint you that your papers were seized in consequence of the heavy charge brought against you for being the author of an infamous

Those seals, for which he dear shall pay,
When awful Justice takes her day.
The Printers saw—they saw and fled—
Science, declining, hung her head;
Property in despair appear'd,
And for herself destruction fear'd;
Whilst, underfoot, the rude slaves trod
The works of men, and word of God;
Whilst, close behind, on many a book,
In which he never deigns to look,
Which he did not, nay—could not read,
A bold, bad man (by pow'r decreed
For that bad end, who in the dark
Scorn'd to do mischief) set his mark

and seditious libel, tending to inflame the minds, and alienate the affections of the people from his majesty, and excite them to traitorous insurrection against the government; for which libel, notwithstanding your discharge from your commitment to the tower, his majesty has ordered you to be prosecuted by his Attorney-General.

We are at a loss to guess what you mean by stolen goods, but such of your papers as do not lead to a proof of your guilt, shall be restored to you; such as are necessary for that purpose, it was our duty to deliver over to those whose office it is to collect the evidence, and manage the prosecution against you. We are your humble servants,

EGREMONT. DUNK HALLIFAX.

Mr. Wilkes commenced an action against Lord Hallifax, (the earl of Egremont having died soon after this transaction) and obtained a verdict for £4,000 damages. Lord Hallifax, in his defence, availed himself of every subterfuge and evasion to defeat the action by delay and technical objections; he cast essoigns, claimed privilege, resisted the solemn decisions of a court of justice, and finally pleaded the outlawry of Wilkes, although it had been regularly reversed.

In the full day, the mark of Hell,
And on the Gospel stamp'd an L.
Liberty fled, her friends withdrew;
Her friends, a faithful chosen few;
Honour in grief threw up, and Shame,
Clothing herself with Honour's name,
Usurp'd his station; on the throne
Which Liberty once call'd her own,
(Gods! that such mighty ills should spring
Under so great, so good, a king,
So loved, so loving, through the arts
Of statesmen, cursed with wicked hearts!)
For every darker purpose fit,
Behold in triumph State-craft sit.

The following extract from the treasury minute book, produced at the trial, will shew that the expense did not fall on the defendant.

Whitehall, Treasury Chamber, May 31, 1765.

Present, Mr. Grenville, Lord North, Mr. Hunter, and Mr. Harris.

Mr. Chancellor of the Exchequer signifies to my lords his majesty's pleasure, that all expenses incurred, or to be incurred, in consequence of actions brought against the Earl of Hallifax, one of his majesty's principal secretaries of state, the under secretaries and messengers, and the solicitor of this office, for proceedings had by them in executing the business of their respective offices, against the publishers of several scandalous and seditious libels, should be defrayed by the crown; and that a sufficient sum of money should be from time to time issued to the solicitor of the treasury for that purpose.

It was stated by Lord North, in the House of Commons, that the law proceedings against Mr. Wilkes, and in defending the actions, brought by him and the printers had, including the damages, cost government upwards of £100,000.

THE DUELLIST.

BOOK III.

AH me! what mighty perils wait
The man who meddles with a state,
Whether to strengthen, or oppose!
False are his friends, and firm his foes:
How must his soul, once ventured in,
Plunge blindly on from sin to sin!
What toils he suffers, what disgrace,
To get, and then to keep, a place!
How often, whether wrong or right,
Must he in jest or earnest fight,
Risking for those both life and limb
Who would not risk one groat for him!
  Under the temple lay a cave,
Made by some guilty, coward slave,

12 The aspirant to political distinction, who seeks it as here described, by plunging on from sin to sin, deserves that return of ingratitude which is sure to visit every individual who enters into the service of the public; unhappily this visitation attaches in equal if not severer measure to the few, very few real patriots who have been animated in their devoted zeal for their country by no other motive than the public good, and Socrates, Brutus, Simon de Montfort, and John de Witt, sufficiently attest, in characters of blood, this melancholy truth.

Whose actions fear'd rebuke: a maze
Of intricate and winding ways,
Not to be found without a clue;
One passage only, known to few,
In paths direct led to a cell,
Where Fraud in secret loved to dwell,
With all her tools and slaves about her,
Nor fear'd lest Honesty should rout her.
  In a dark corner, shunning sight
Of man, and shrinking from the light,
One dull, dim taper through the cell
Glimmering, to make more horrible
The face of darkness, she prepares,
Working unseen, all kinds of snares,
With curious, but destructive art.
Here, through the eye to catch the heart,
Gay stars their tinsel beams afford,
Neat artifice to trap a lord;
There, fit for all whom Folly bred,
Wave plumes of feathers for the head;
Garters the hag contrives to make,
Which, as it seems, a babe might break,
But which ambitious madmen feel
More firm and sure than chains of steel,
Which, slipp'd just underneath the knee,
Forbid a freeman to be free.
Purses she knew (did ever curse
Travel more sure than in a purse?)
Which, by some strange and magic bands,
Enslave the soul, and tie the hands.

Here Flattery, eldest born of Guile,
Weaves with rare skill the silken smile,
The courtly cringe, the supple bow,
The private squeeze, the levee vow,
With which, no strange or recent case,
Fools in, deceive fools out of place.
Corruption (who in former times,
Through fear or shame conceal'd her crimes,
And what she did, contrived to do it,
So that the public might not view it)
Presumptuous grown, unfit was held
For their dark councils, and expell'd,
Since in the day her business might
Be done as safe as in the night.
Her eye down bending to the ground,
Planning some dark and deadly wound,
Holding a dagger, on which stood,
All fresh and reeking, drops of blood,
Bearing a lanthorn, which of yore,
By Treason borrow'd, Guy Fawkes bore,
By which, since they improved in trade,
Excisemen have their lanthorns made;
Assassination, her whole mind,
Blood-thirsting, on her arm reclined;
Death, grinning at her elbow stood,
And held forth instruments of blood,
Vile instruments, which cowards choose,
But men of honour dare not use;
Around, his Lordship and his Grace,
Both qualified for such a place,

With many a Forbes, and many a Dun,
Each a resolved, and pious son,
Wait her high bidding; each prepared
As she around her orders shared,
Proof 'gainst remorse, to run, to fly,
And bid the destined victim die,
Posting on Villany's black wing,
Whether he patriot is, or king.
  Oppression, willing to appear
An object of our love, not fear,
Or, at the most, a reverend awe
To breed, usurp'd the garb of Law.

[75] One John Forbes, a Scotch Captain in the regiment of Ogilby in the French service, a respectable man of good family, thought proper, while Wilkes was at Paris, very abruptly to challenge him in the public street for being the author of the North Briton; and for having written against Scotland. Wilkes pleaded several pending engagements of the same nature, but expressed his willingness, as soon as they were disposed of, to meet Captain Forbes. The Captain, in a wild manner, insisted upon immediate satisfaction; but not being able to find a second, or any one to vouch for his being a gentleman, Mr. Wilkes declined acceding to his request. This démêlé coming to the knowledge of the French government, the parties were put upon their parole, not to fight within the French dominions. Mr. Wilkes upon this offered to meet him in Flanders, or in any country in Europe, Asia, Africa, or America, except the dominions of France. Soon after the return of Mr. Wilkes to London, Forbes also appeared there, with a view, as it was suspected, of fighting with him; but the ministry, on getting notice of his arrival and intentions, very prudently caused it to be insinuated to him, that his presence on such an errand could not but be very disagreeable; upon which, this doughty champion of Caledonia thought proper to leave the kingdom, and afterwards entered

A book she held, on which her eyes
Were deeply fix'd, whence seem'd to rise
Joy in her breast; a book of might
Most wonderful, which black to white
Could turn, and without help of laws,
Could make the worse the better cause.
She read, by flattering hopes deceived;
She wish'd, and what she wish'd, believed,
To make that book for ever stand
The rule of wrong through all the land;
On the back, fair and worthy note,
At large was Magna Charta wrote,

into the Portuguese service, where he attained the rank of a general.

75 Alexander Dun, a Scotchman, in December, 1763, obtained admittance, by his own appointment, into the house of Mr. Wilkes; but being suspected of a design to assassinate him, was immediately seized by some gentlemen who attended there for the purpose of protecting the demagogue. On being searched, a new penknife was found in his pocket; this circumstance, coupled with a declaration he had been heard to make, that himself and ten more men were determined to cut Mr. Wilkes off, let the event be what it would, afforded materials for a very pathetic account of the danger our pseudo patriot had incurred, of becoming a martyr to the cause of liberty. Administration was of course charged with suborning these attempts; and every effort was ineffectually made to excite the populace to revenge. The papers relating to Dun's attempt were laid before the House of Commons; he was taken into custody by the tipstaff, and an indictment was preferred against him; all these proceedings were dropt upon its appearing, on his first examination, by incontrovertible evidence, that he was altogether deranged, and had given many glaring proofs of insanity. He was delivered over to his friends, who undertook to confine him in a private madhouse.

But turn your eye within and read,
A bitter lesson, Norton's Creed.
Ready, e'en with a look, to run,
Fast as the coursers of the sun,
To worry Virtue, at her hand
Two half-starved greyhounds took their stand.
A curious model, cut in wood,
Of a most ancient castle stood
Full in her view; the gates were barr'd,
And soldiers on the watch kept guard;
In the front openly, in black
Was wrote, The Tower; but on the back,
Mark'd with a Secretary's seal,
In bloody letters, The Bastile.
 Around a table, fully bent
On mischief of most black intent,
Deeply determined, that their reign
Might longer last, to work the bane
Of one firm patriot, whose heart, tied
To honour, all their power defied,
And brought those actions into light
They wish'd to have conceal'd in night,

104 As observed in a former note, the Greyhound was the badge worn by the King's messengers.

112 This was the favourite appellation bestowed by the partisans of Wilkes upon the Tower. His confinement lasted six days, during which time he was debarred the use of pen and ink; and was not permitted to see his friends. To Lord Chief Justice Pratt's active and constitutional interference on this occasion, we are indebted for exemption from similar wanton exertions of power on the part of the servants of the crown.

Begot, born, bred, to infamy,
A privy council sat of three:
Great were their names, of high repute
And favour through the land of Bute.
The first (entitled to the place 125
Of honour both by gown and grace,
Who never let occasion slip
To take right hand of fellowship,

125 This has always been considered as a grossly surcharged caricature of one of the most learned prelates that ever dignified the bench; for, excepting his characteristic haughtiness, we believe every other particular imputed to him by the poet to be utterly destitute of veracity.

William Warburton, D. D., Bishop of Gloucester and dean of Bristol, was the son of an attorney at Newark upon Trent, to which profession he served a regular clerkship; and afterwards practised as an attorney and solicitor two or three years in his native town of Newark; but a very moderate share of business, and a strong bias to literary pursuits, induced him, with the advice of his friends, to take orders, and he was accordingly on the 22d of December, 1723, ordained deacon in the cathedral of York, by Archbishop Dawes. His subsequent rise in the church, he owed principally to the high reputation his solid abilities had so justly gained him in the literary world; but this rise was no doubt accelerated by his marriage, in 1745, with Miss Gertrude Tucker, the favourite niece of Ralph Allen, Esq., of Prior Park, in Somersetshire, the correspondent of Pope, and the Allworthy of Fielding's Tom Jones. Mr. Allen rose to great wealth and consideration by farming the cross posts, which he originated in 1720 and put into admirable order; he died in 1764, and the bulk of his fortune vested in the Bishop, to the prejudice of some nearer relatives. Mr. Allen died worth upwards of £100,000, obtained by cross posts, and from a quarry accidentally discovered on an estate he had purchased near Bath, and from whence the stones for building the most beautiful parts of that city were taken. By Mr. Allen's will he bequeathed Prior

And was so proud, that should he meet
The Twelve Apostles in the street,
He'd turn his nose up at them all,
And shove his Saviour from the wall:
Who was so mean (Meanness and Pride
Still go together side to side)
That he would cringe, and creep, be civil,
And hold a stirrup for the devil;

Park with the lands adjoining, and the Claverton Estate, in all about £3,000 per annum to his widow for life, and at her decease to Mrs. Warburton and to Captain Tucker her brother in succession and their Issue, which failing, to his niece Miss Mary Allen and her Issue. He also left legacies of £5,000 apiece to Dr. and Mrs. Warburton. Mrs. Warburton married again to a clergyman, and on her death the estate devolved to Viscount Hawarden, whose second wife was Miss Mary Allen, by whom he had several children. Warburton, by some contemptuous expressions, had incurred the resentment of Wilkes, and our poet, ever earnest in defence of his friends, made the Bishop an object of his bitterest invective, wherever an opportunity presented; and particularly his last poetical effort, the dedication prefixed to his volume of sermons. It is somewhat singular, that Dr. Hurd, the present Bishop of Worcester, in his "Discourse by way of General Preface to the quarto edition of Bishop Warburton's works, containing some ac count of the life, character, and writings of the author," should not only take no notice of Churchill's repeated attacks; but has studiously omitted any mention of him or Wilkes. Of Dr. Hurd's literary intercourse with Dr. Warburton, Dr. Brown, the author of the "Essay on the Characteristics," made no scruple of talking in very plain terms. Though a friend and admirer of the Bishop of Gloucester, he used frequently to say, "I cannot bring myself to give up the freedom of my mind to Warburton, and therefore we do not agree; *but Dr. Hurd will never quarrel with him.*" The following masterly sketch of the character of Warburton, by

If in a journey to his mind,
He'd let him mount and ride behind;
Who basely fawn'd through all his life,
For patrons first, then for a wife:
Wrote Dedications which must make
The heart of every Christian quake;
Made one man equal to, or more
Than God, then left him, as before
His God he left, and, drawn by pride,

Dr. Johnson, affords at once an antidote and contrast to the envenomed shafts of the Poet.

"About this time (1738) Warburton began to make his appearance in the first ranks of learning. He was a man of vigorous faculties, a mind fervent and vehement, supplied by incessant and unlimited inquiry, with wonderful extent and variety of knowledge, which yet had not oppressed his imagination nor clouded his perspicuity. To every work he brought a memory full fraught, together with a fancy fertile of original combinations: and at once exerted the powers of the scholar, the reasoner, and the wit. But his knowledge was too multifarious to be always exact, and his pursuits were too eager to be always cautious. His abilities gave him a haughty consequence, which he disdained to conceal or mollify; and his impatience of opposition disposed him to treat his adversaries with such contemptuous superiority as made his readers commonly his enemies, and excited against the advocate the wishes of some who favoured the cause. He seems to have adopted the Roman Emperor's determination, "oderint dum metuant;" he used no allurements of gentle language, but wished to compel rather than persuade. His style is copious without selection, and forcible without neatness: he took the words that presented themselves; his diction is coarse and impure, and his sentences are unmeasured. He had in the early part of his life pleased himself with the notice of inferior wits, and corresponded with the enemies of Pope. A letter was produced, when he had perhaps himself forgotten it, in

Shifted about to t'other side;
Was by his sire a parson made,
Merely to give the boy a trade;
But he himself was thereto drawn
By some faint omens of the lawn,
And on the truly Christian plan
To make himself a gentleman,
A title in which form array'd him,
Though fate ne'er thought on't when she made
him.

which he tells Concanen, "Dryden, I observe, borrows for want of leisure, and Pope for want of genius; Milton out of pride, and Addison out of modesty." And when Theobald published Shakspeare in opposition to Pope, the best notes were supplied by Warburton. But the time was now come when Warburton was to change his opinion, and Pope was to find a defender in him, who had contribûted so much to the exaltation of his rival. From this time Pope lived in the closest intimacy with his commentator, and amply rewarded his kindness and his zeal; for he introduced him to Mr. Murray (afterwards Earl of Mansfield) by whose interest he became preacher of Lincoln's Inn, and to Mr. Allen, who gave him his niece and his estate, and by consequence a bishoprick: when he died, Pope left him the property of his works; a legacy which may be reasonably estimated at four thousand pounds."

Something of Dr. Warburton's character may be collected from the following passage in one of his letters to Dr. Lowth, "Whoever injures me, may not, in the long run, have reason to applaud his situation." His style of English composition is of the highest order of purity and power, probably equalled but certainly not excelled by that of Dr. Johnson, nor did he excel only in his vernacular tongue alone, the purity of his Latin being sufficiently evident, from among other specimens his letter to the Bishop of Chichester, prefixed to his emendations of Velleius Paterculus.

The oaths he took, 'tis very true,
But took them as all wise men do,
With an intent, if things should turn,
Rather to temporize, than burn,
Gospel and loyalty were made
To serve the purposes of trade:
Religions are but paper ties,
Which bind the fool, but which the wise,
Such idle notions far above,
Draw on and off, just like a glove:
All gods, all kings, (let his great aim
Be answer'd) were to him the same.
A curate first, he read and read,
And laid in, whilst he should have fed
The souls of his neglected flock,
Of reading such a mighty stock,
That he o'ercharged the weary brain
With more than she could well contain;
More than she was with spirits fraught
To turn and methodize to thought,
And which, like ill-digested food,
To humours turn'd, and not to blood.
Brought up to London, from the plow
And pulpit, how to make a bow
He tried to learn; he grew polite,
And was the poet's parasite.
With wits conversing (and wits then
Were to be found 'mongst noblemen)
He caught, or would have caught, the flame,
And would be nothing, or the same.
He drank with drunkards, lived with sinners,

Herded with infidels for dinners;
With such an emphasis and grace
Blasphemed, that Potter kept not pace:
He, in the highest reign of noon,
Bawl'd bawdy songs to a psalm tune;
Lived with men infamous and vile,
Truck'd his salvation for a smile;
To catch their humour caught their plan,
And laugh'd at God to laugh with man;
Praised them, when living, in each breath,
And damn'd their memories after death.

To prove his faith, which all admit
Is at least equal to his wit,
And make himself a man of note,
He in defence of Scripture wrote:

188 Thomas Potter, Esq. M. P. for Okehampton, was in early life on a very intimate footing with Mr. Allen, of Prior Park, and on the most friendly terms with Warburton; but latterly getting connected with Wilkes and his associates, he was by the bishop suspected of being the author of the notes on the Essay on Woman, and on that account incurred his and Mr. Allen's utmost indignation. Mr. Potter possessed great parliamentary talents and many brilliant accomplishments, but having offended his father, the Archbishop of Canterbury, by an imprudent marriage, and being idolized by his dissolute companions, nothing was too sacred to escape his ridicule; and abilities, which might have done honour to any station, were degraded by him, to obtain the reputation of a wit. He died in June 1759.

200 Warburton was deeply engaged in theological controversy with all the most celebrated divines of the day, and these doughty disputants did not use much courtesy towards each other: the famous Bishop Berkeley said of Warburton, that he wrote neither like a gentleman, a scholar, nor a chris-

So long he wrote, and long about it,
That e'en believers 'gan to doubt it:
He wrote, too, of the inward light,
Though no one knew how he came by't,
And of that influencing grace
Which in his life ne'er found a place:
He wrote, too, of the Holy Ghost,
Of whom no more than doth a post
He knew, nor, should an angel shew him,
Would he or know, or choose to know him.
  Next (for he knew 'twixt every science
There was a natural alliance)
He wrote, to advance his Maker's praise,
Comments on rhymes, and notes on plays,

tian. That there was some foundation for the charge the following epithets, extracted from the Bishop's notes on Shakspeare and on the Dunciad, sufficiently attest: "A mushroom, a gentleman of the last century, a Grub-Street orator, a miserable, lost to shame as a man and as a writer, an idle blunderer, an ass, ridiculously stupid, and intolerably nonsensical."

207 The Bishop was accused of having confounded the office of the Holy Ghost with that of the Redeemer. It was said of him that whenever he attempted to treat any religious subject he was so infatuated by self-sufficiency and so devoted to paradoxical conceits, that he generally played the anti-alchemist and turned gold into lead.

212 The work, by which Warburton first distinguished himself in the literary world, was entitled "The Alliance between Church and State, or the necessity of an established religion and a test law," 1736.

214 Warburton in his notes on Pope lost no opportunity of abusing his former associate Concanen, calling him "a hired scribbler in the Daily Courant, where he poured forth much Billingsgate against Lord Bolingbroke and others, after which this man was surprisingly promoted to administer justice and

And with an all-sufficient air
Placed himself in the critic's chair,
Usurp'd o'er reason full dominion,
And govern'd merely by opinion.

law in Jamaica," and where, he might have added, he administered his high office during seventeen years, with the utmost honour and integrity, to the perfect satisfaction of the inhabitants. Concanen's constitution was so much injured by the climate of the West Indies that he died soon after his return to England in the year 1749, in the 48th year of his age.

How much Theobald considered Warburton jointly implicated with him in Pope's displeasure, appears by the following passage in a letter from him to Warburton, dated Oct. 25, 1729, "A new edition of the Dunciad has been for some weeks threatened, but the sword is yet only kept over our heads."

Warburton soon afterwards having propitiated Pope by an able vindication of the Essay on Man, against the observations of de Crousaz, dropped his intimacy with the enemies of the great Poet, and thus summarily disposed of Concanen in a letter to Dr. Hurd: "I met many years ago with an ingenious Irishman at a coffee-house, near Gray's Inn, where I lodged. He studied the law, and was very poor, I had given him money for many a dinner, and at last I gave him those papers (Enquiry into the causes of Prodigies and Miracles) which he sold to the booksellers for more money than you would think, much more than they were worth. But I must finish the story both of the Irishman and the papers. Soon after he got acquainted with Sir W. Young, wrote for Sir R. Walpole, and was made Attorney-General of Jamaica. He married there an opulent widow, and died very rich a few years ago here in England, but of so scoundrel a temper that he avoided ever coming into my sight, so that the memory of all this intercourse between us has been buried in silence till this moment. And who should this man be but one of the heroes of the Dunciad, Concanen by name." His having been one of the cabal against Pope was however fully established by the discovery of a letter of his to Concanen, highly disrespectful to Pope, which fell into the hands of Dr. Aken-

At length dethroned, and kept in awe
By one plain simple man of law,
He arm'd dead friends, to vengeance true,
To abuse the man they never knew.

side who made it very generally known, after which it was introduced by Malone in his supplement to Shakspeare.

The letter bears date Jan. 2, 1727, at which time Warburton had discontinued practice as an attorney, and was an assistant to a relation at a school at Newark, having taken deacon's orders in 1723. It was found about the year 1750 by Dr. Gawen Knight, first librarian to the British Museum, in fitting up a house which he had taken in Crane Court, Fleet Street, where in all probability Concanen had lodged. It is preserved in Mr. Nichols's Illustrations of the literary history of the 18th century, vol. ii. p. 195, who observes that it affords indisputable evidence that Warburton had been an associate with Theobald and Concanen in the attack made by them on Pope's fame and talents. Warburton concludes his letter with saying, "My thanks are due for all your favours when in town, particularly for introducing me to the knowledge of those worthy and ingenious gentlemen that made up our last night's conversation." Among whom in the notes on the Dunciad are enumerated Theobald, Dennis, Moore, Concanen, and Cooke.

220 Mr. Thomas Edwards, a barrister, and also an accomplished scholar and amiable man, the author of several pleasing sonnets in Dodsley, Pearch, and Nichols's collections, published a very ingenious work, entitled "Canons of Criticism, by a gentleman of Lincoln's Inn," in which Warburton is severely censured; indeed the learned prelate, in his notes on Shakspeare, evinced a want of research in English antiquity, which, accompanied with a dictatorial style, and an offensive contempt for all former and contemporary commentators, justly exposed him to critical reprehension. When Warburton's perverted view of an author, like Shakspeare in the hands of every reader, came to be seen and thus exposed by Edwards, it began to be more than suspected that he might have taken liberties with the sacred writings upon

Examine strictly all mankind,
Most characters are mix'd we find,
And vice and virtue take their turn
In the same breast to beat and burn.
Our priest was an exception here,
Nor did one spark of grace appear,
Not one dull, dim spark in his soul;
Vice, glorious vice possess'd the whole,
And, in her service truly warm,
He was in sin most uniform.
Injurious Satire, own at least
One sniveling virtue in the priest,
One sniveling virtue, which is placed
They say, in or about the waist,

equally slender grounds. This, upon examination, was found to be actually the case, till at length after gradual detections of one reverie after another Dr. Lowth found it as necessary and quite as easy to do the same service for Job as Mr. Edwards had done for Shakspeare.

Warburton took his full revenge by introducing into his next edition of the Dunciad, after Pope's death, a note on the following lines in the fourth book of that poem:

> Next bidding all draw near on bended knees,
> The queen confers her titles and degrees;
> Her children first of more distinguished sort
> Who study Shakspeare at the Inns of Court.

In which note, occasion is taken to state the services done in the cause of Dullness "by one Mr. Thomas Edwards, a gentleman as he is pleased to call himself of Lincoln's Inn, but in reality a gentleman only of the Dunciad; or to speak him better in the plain language of our honest ancestors of such mushrooms, a gentleman of the last edition."

Warburton had another fling at Edwards in a note on v. 463 of the Essay on Criticism, where, illustrative of Black-

Called Chastity; the prudish dame
Knows it at large by Virtue's name.
To this his wife, (and in these days
Wives seldom without reason praise)
Bears evidence—then calls her child,
And swears that Tom was vastly wild.
Ripen'd by a long course of years,
He great and perfect now appears.
In shape scarce of the human kind,
A man, without a manly mind;
No husband, though he's truly wed;
Though on his knees a child is bred,
No father; injured, without end
A foe; and though obliged, no friend;

more and Melbourne, he observes, "these men are of all times, and rise up on all occasions, Sir Walter Raleigh had Alexander Ross, Chillingworth had Cheynel, Milton a first Edwards, and Locke a second, neither of them related to the third Edwards of Lincoln's Inn. They were divines of parts and learning; this a critic without one or the other." All impartial critics, however, as Dr. Warton well observes, allow the remarks of Mr. Edwards to have been decisive and judicious, and his canons of criticism remain unrefuted and unanswerable. Boswell relates, that soon after the Canons of Criticism came out, Johnson was dining with Tonson the Bookseller, Hayman the painter and some others being of the company. Hayman related to Sir Joshua Reynolds, that the conversation having turned upon Edwards's book, the gentlemen praised it much and Johnson allowed its merit. But when they went further and appeared to put the author on a level with Warburton,—no, said Johnson, he has given him some smart hits to be sure, but there is no proportion between the two men; they must not be named together. A fly, Sir, may sting a stately horse and make him wince, but one is but an insect and the other is a horse still.

A heart, which virtue ne'er disgraced;
A head, where learning runs to waste;
A gentleman well-bred, if breeding
Rests in the article of reading;
A man of this world, for the next
Was ne'er included in his text;
A judge of genius, though confess'd
With not one spark of genius bless'd:
Amongst the first of critics placed,
Though free from every taint of taste;
A Christian without faith or works,
As he would be a Turk 'mongst Turks;
A great divine, as lords agree,
Without the least divinity.
To crown all in declining age,
Inflamed with church and party rage,
Behold him, full and perfect quite,
A false saint, and true hypocrite.

268 Had not some of the prominent features of Warburton's character been here so strongly depicted as to render it impossible for it to pass as a general satire or an ideal portrait, we should have been pleased with an opportunity of sparing our author's fame by passing over in silence so personal, false, and calumnious a misrepresentation of worth, talents, and unbounded learning. Such a gross prostitution of satire, is doubly injurious to the cause of virtue; it puts the weapons of ridicule into the hands of weak persons, who are incapable of appreciating the merits of a Johnson, a Warburton, or a Pearce; and impairs, if it cannot destroy, the benefits resulting from their moral and intellectual labours: it also, by imputing vices to men like these, might induce, if corroborating authorities were wanting, doubts of the poetical justice done to the characters of a Sandwich, a Holland, and a Dashwood.

Next sat a lawyer, often tried
In perilous extremes; when Pride
And Power, all wild and trembling, stood,
Nor dared to tempt the raging flood,
This bold, bad man arose to view,
And gave his hand to help them through:
Steel'd 'gainst compassion, as they past
He saw poor Freedom breathe her last;
He saw her struggle, heard her groan;
He saw her helpless and alone,
Whelm'd in that storm, which, fear'd and praised
By slaves less bold, himself had raised.
Bred to the law, he from the first
Of all bad lawyers was the worst.
Perfection (for bad men maintain
In ill we may perfection gain)

The Bishop of Gloucester died in 1779, having attained the great age of 81; he unfortunately survived his relish for society; an habitual melancholy latterly preyed upon his mind, which was aggravated, if not occasioned by the loss of his only child, a very promising young man, who died of a consumption a few years before his father.

269 This character comprises all the qualifications which can render a lawyer truly odious. As regards Sir Fletcher Norton, or Sir Bullface Doublefee, as he was more commonly called, the portrait is so overcharged as to defeat its object, which would have been better attained by conveying the simple fact, that Sir Fletcher was a man of undaunted assurance, stentorian voice and extraordinary fluency, which, combined with little law, very moderate abilities, and no public principle, well qualified him to be at once the organ and the tool of a weak and corrupt administration, under which he was first Attorney-General, then Speaker, and lastly, in 1782, created Lord Grantley.

In others is a work of time,
And they creep on from crime to crime;
He, for a prodigy design'd
To spread amazement o'er mankind,
Started full ripen'd all at once
A perfect knave, and perfect dunce.
Who will for him may boast of sense,
His better guard is impudence;
His front, with tenfold plates of brass
Secured, Shame never yet could pass,
Nor on the surface of his skin
Blush for that guilt which dwelt within.
How often, in contempt of laws,
To sound the bottom of a cause,
To search out every rotten part,
And worm into its very heart,
Hath he ta'en briefs on false pretence,
And undertaken the defence
Of trusting fools, whom in the end
He meant to ruin, not defend?
How often, e'en in open court,
Hath the wretch made his shame his sport,
And laugh'd off, with a villain's ease,
Throwing up briefs, and keeping fees?
Such things, as, though to roguery bred,
Had struck a little villain dead.
Causes, whatever their import,
He undertakes, to serve a court;
For he by art this rule had got,
Power can effect what law cannot.

Fools he forgives, but rogues he fears;
If Genius, yoked with Worth appears,
His weak soul sickens at the sight
And strives to plunge them down in night.
So loud he talks, so very loud,
He is an angel with the crowd,
Whilst he makes Justice hang her head,
And judges turn from pale to red.
Bid all that nature, on a plan
Most intimate, makes dear to man,
All that with grand and general ties
Binds good and bad, the fool and wise,
Knock at his heart; they knock in vain;
No entrance there such suitors gain;
Bid kneeling kings forsake the throne,
Bid at his feet his country groan;
Bid Liberty stretch out her hands,
Religion plead her stronger bands;
Bid parents, children, wife, and friends,
If they come thwart his private ends,
Unmoved he hears the general call
And bravely tramples on them all.
Who will, for him, may cant and whine,
And let weak Conscience with her line
Chalk out their ways; such starving rules
Are only fit for coward fools;
Fellows who credit what priests tell,
And tremble at the thoughts of hell;
His spirit dares contend with Grace,
And meets Damnation face to face.

Such was our lawyer; by his side,
In all bad qualities allied,
In all bad counsels, sat a third,
By birth a lord; O sacred word!
O word most sacred, whence men get
A privilege to run in debt;
Whence they at large exemption claim
From Satire, and her servant Shame;
Whence they, deprived of all her force,
Forbid bold Truth to hold her course.
Consult his person, dress, and air,
He seems, which strangers well might swear,
The master, or, by courtesy,
The captain of a colliery.
Look at his visage, and agree
Half-hang'd he seems, just from the tree
Escaped; a rope may sometimes break,
Or men be cut down by mistake.
He hath not virtue (in the school
Of Vice bred up) to live by rule,
Nor hath he sense (which none can doubt
Who know the man) to live without.
His life is a continued scene
Of all that's infamous and mean;

348 We cannot consent to rake into the annals of a brothel for appropriate anecdotes of this abandoned wretch. Fortunately his capacity did not equal his inclination; for, wallowing in the mire of sensuality, his vicious propensities contributed more to his own detriment than to the ruin of his country:—"*homo post homines natos turpissimus, sceleratissimus contaminatissimus.*"

He knows not change, unless grown nice
And delicate, from vice to vice;
Nature design'd him, in a rage,
To be the Wharton of his age,
But having given all the sin,
Forgot to put the virtues in.
To run a horse, to make a match,
To revel deep, to roar a catch;

372 Philip Duke of Wharton, who was as remarkable for the brilliancy of his genius as for the dissipation of his morals. He was of a higher order of profligacy as well as talent than the fraternity of Medmenham, but with them has obtained the same uneviable distinction of being poetically damned to everlasting fame.

Wharton, the scorn and wonder of our days,
Whose ruling passion was the lust of praise,
Born with whate'er could win it from the wise,
Women and fools must like him, or he dies;
Though wondering senates hung on all he spoke,
The club must hail him master of the joke;
Shall parts so various aim at nothing new,
He'll shine a Tully and a Wilmot too;
Thus with each gift of nature, and of art,
And wanting nothing but an honest heart,
Grown all to all, from no one vice exempt,
And most contemptible to shun contempt,
His passion still to covet general praise,
His life to forfeit it a thousand ways,
A constant bounty, which no friend has made,
An angel tongue which no man can persuade,
A fool with more of wit than half mankind,
Too rash for thought, for action too refined,
A Tyrant to the wife his heart approves,
A Rebel to the very king he loves;

To knock a tottering watchman down,
To sweat a woman of the Town;
By fits to keep the peace, or break it,
In turn to give a pox, or take it;
He is, in faith, most excellent,
And, in the word's most full intent,
A true Choice Spirit we admit;
With wits a fool, with fools a wit.
Hear him but talk, and you would swear
Obscenity herself was there;
And that Profaneness had made a choice,
By way of trump, to use his voice;
That, in all mean and low things great,
He had been bred at Billingsgate;

> He dies sad outcast of each church and state,
> And harder still, flagitious, yet not great;
> Ask you why Wharton broke through every rule;
> 'Twas all for fear that Knaves should call him Fool.
> *Pope's Moral Essays*, Ess. 1.

In 1731 the Duke was seized while at Tarragona, in Spain, with one of those fainting fits to which he had for some time been subject, and being utterly destitute of all the necessaries of life, some charitable fathers of a Bernardine convent there removed him into it and administered all the relief in their power. Under this hospitable roof, after languishing a week, the Duke died, May 31, 1731, without one friend or acquaintance to close his eyes. His funeral was performed in the same manner which the fathers observed to those of their own fraternity. He was no more than 32 years of age, and dying without issue, his title became extinct.

His widow survived until 1777, and lies buried in St. Pancras churchyard. Previous to his death a bill of Attainder for High Treason, in consequence of his joining the Pretender, had passed the House of Lords.

And that, ascending to the earth
Before the season of his birth,
Blasphemy, making way and room,
Had mark'd him in his mother's womb:
Too honest (for the worst of men
In forms are honest now and then)
Not to have, in the usual way,
His bills sent in; too great to pay
Too proud to speak to, if he meets
The honest tradesman whom he cheats;
Too infamous to have a friend;
Too bad for bad men to commend,
Or good to name; beneath whose weight
Earth groans; who hath been spared by Fate
Only to shew, on mercy's plan,
How far and long God bears with man.
 Such were the three who, mocking sleep,
At midnight sat, in counsel deep,
Plotting destruction against a head
Whose wisdom could not be misled;
Plotting destruction 'gainst a heart
Which ne'er from honour would depart.
 "Is he not rank'd amongst our foes?
Hath not his spirit dared oppose
Our dearest measures, made our name
Stand forward on the roll of shame?
Hath he not won the vulgar tribes,
By scorning menaces and bribes,
And proving, that his darling cause
Is of their liberties and laws

To stand the champion? In a word,
Nor need one argument be heard
Beyond this to awake our zeal,
To quicken our resolves, and steel
Our steady souls to bloody bent,
(Sure ruin to each dear intent
Each flattering hope) he, without fear,
Hath dared to make the truth appear."
 They said, and, by resentment taught,
Each on revenge employ'd his thought;
Each, bent on mischief, rack'd his brain
To her full stretch, but rack'd in vain;
Scheme after scheme they brought to view;
All were examined; none would do:
When Fraud, with pleasure in her face,
Forth issued from her hiding place,
And at the table where they meet,
First having blest them, took her seat.
"No trifling cause, my darling Boys!
Your present thoughts and cares employs;
No common snare, no random blow,
Can work the bane of such a foe,
By Nature cautious as he's brave,
To honour only he's a slave;
In that weak part without defence,
We must to honour make pretence;
That lure shall to his ruin draw
The wretch, who stands secure in law:
Nor think that I have idly plann'd
This full-ripe scheme; behold at hand

With three months training on his head,
An instrument, whom I have bred,
Born of these bowels, far from sight
Of virtue's false, but glaring light,
My youngest born, my dearest joy,
Most like myself, my darling boy:
He, never touch'd with vile remorse,
Resolved and crafty in his course,
Shall work our ends, complete our schemes,
Most mine, when most he Honour's seems;
Nor can be found, at home, abroad,
So firm and full a slave of Fraud."
She said, and from each envious son
A discontented murmur run
Around the table; all in place
Thought his full praise their own disgrace,
Wondering what stranger she had got,
Who had one vice that they had not;
When straight the portals open flew,
And, clad in armour, to their view
Martin, the Duellist, came forth;
All knew, and all confess'd his worth;
All justified, with smiles array'd,
The happy choice their dam had made.

SUPPLEMENTAL NOTE.

The share, if not of composition, at all events of revision, taken by Churchill in the conduct of the North Briton, and the historical celebrity attaching to No. XLV. (April 23, 1763) of that periodical, by the parliamentary censure and legal visitations it incurred, and the great constitutional question arising out of it, of the illegality of general warrants, confer an enduring interest on the publication, which will prove our apology for giving at length that once popular number.

The arrest and imprisonment of Wilkes and the printers, and the seizure of the manuscript in their possession, so disturbed the publication as to occasion its discontinuance with its next number only, which followed, at the long interval of upwards of six months, on Nov. 12, 1763.

A new series, commencing with No. XLVII. was, after a period of five years, attempted by some of the subordinate associates of Wilkes in a very inferior style of composition, but in an equally offensive tone of scurrility and abuse: it languished for nearly a twelvemonth, and expired with its hundredth number, April 10, 1769.

It is not easy now to credit the extraordinary popularity which the early numbers of the North Briton acquired, and which, in a particular manner, attached to No. XLV.; a designation which was adopted by patriotic tradesmen to lure equally patriotic customers to the purchase of various kinds of merchandise distinguished by that all-availing number; and, until within a recent period, the favourite article of a snuff shop in Fleet Street was extracted from a canister marked 45, and the mixture known by no other name.

On the other hand, so obnoxious were these numerals to royalty itself, as well as its retainers, that the young Prince of Wales, in 1772, thought he could not exhibit his resentment for some privation or chastisement he had undergone more provokingly towards his Royal father than by roaring out repeatedly, "Wilkes and No. XLV. for ever!"

THE NORTH BRITON.

NO. XLV.* SATURDAY, APRIL 23, 1763.

The following Advertisement appeared in all the Papers on the 13th *of April.*

THE North Briton makes his appeal to the good sense and to the candour of the English nation. In the present unsettled and fluctuating state of the administration, he is really fearful of falling into involuntary errors, and he does not wish to mislead. All his reasonings have been built on the strong foundation of facts; and he is not yet informed of the whole interior state of government with such minute precision as now to venture the submitting his crude ideas of the present political crisis to the discerning and impartial public. The Scottish minister has, indeed, retired. Is his influence at an end? or does he still govern by the † three wretched tools of his power, who, to their indelible infamy, have supported the most odious of his measures, the late ignominious peace, and the wicked extension of the arbitrary mode of excise? The North Briton has been steady in his opposition to a single, insolent, incapable, despotic minister; and is equally ready, in the service of his country, to combat the triple-headed, Cerberean administration, if the Scot is to assume that motley form. By him every arrangement to this hour has been made, and the notification has been as regularly sent by letter under his hand. It therefore seems clear to a demonstration that he intends only to retire into that situation which he held before he first took the seals; I mean the dictating to every part of the king's administration. The North Briton desires to be understood as having pledged himself a firm and intrepid assertor of the rights of his fellow subjects, and of the liberties of Whigs and Englishmen.

---

* The passages included within the inverted commas are the only passages to which any objection is made in the information filed in the King's Bench by the attorney-general against the publisher, Mr. George Kearsly.

† The Earls of Egremont and Halifax, and G. Grenville, Esq.

Genus orationis atrox, et vehemens, cui opponitur lenitatis et mansuetudinis. CICERO.

"THE King's Speech has always been considered by the legislature and by the public at large as the speech of the minister. It has regularly, at the beginning of every session of parliament, been referred by both houses to the consideration of a committee, and has been generally canvassed with the utmost freedom, when the minister of the crown has been obnoxious to the nation. The ministers of this free country, conscious of the undoubted privileges of so spirited a people, and with the terrors of parliament before their eyes, have ever been cautious no less with regard to the matter than to the expressions of speeches which they have advised the Sove-

---

* Anno 14 George II. 1740. *Duke of Argyle:* The king's speech is always in this house considered as the speech of the ministers.—Lords' Debates, vol. vii. p. 413.

Lord Carteret: When we take his majesty's speech into consideration, though we have heard it from his own mouth, yet we do not consider it as his majesty's speech, but as the speech of his ministers, p. 425.

7 George II. 1733. *Mr. Shippen:* I believe it has always been granted that the speeches from the throne are the compositions of ministers of state; upon that supposition we have always thought ourselves at liberty to examine every proposition contained in them; even without doors people are pretty free in their remarks upon them. I believe no gentlemen here is ignorant of the reception the speech from the throne, at the close of the last session, met with from the nation in general.—Commons' Debates, vol. viii. p. 5.

13 George II. 1739. *Mr. Pulteney*, now *Earl of Bath:* His majesty mentions heats and animosities. Sir, I don't know who drew up this speech; but whoever he was, he should have spared that expression. I wish he had drawn a veil over the heats and animosities that must be owned once subsisted upon this head, for I am sure none now subsist. Vol. ii. p. 96,

reign to make from the throne, at the opening of each session. They well knew that an *honest house of parliament, true to their trust, could not fail to detect the fallacious arts, or to remonstrate against the daring acts of violence committed by any minister. The speech at the close of the session has ever been considered as the most secure method of promulgating the favourite court creed among the vulgar; because the parliament, which is the constitutional guardian of the liberties of the people, has in this case no opportunity of remonstrating, or of impeaching any wicked servant of the crown.

"This week has given the public the most abandoned instance of ministerial effrontery ever attempted to be imposed on mankind. The minister's speech of last Tuesday is not to be paralleled in the annals of this country. I am in doubt whether the imposition is greater on the sovereign or on the nation. Every friend of his country must lament that a prince of so many great and amiable qualities, whom England truly reveres, can be brought to give the sanction of his sacred name to the most odious measures, and to the most unjustifiable public declarations, from a throne ever renowned for truth, honour, and unsullied virtue." I am sure all foreigners, especially the King of Prussia, will hold the minister in contempt and abhorrence. He has made our sovereign declare, My expectations have been fully answered by the happy effects which the several allies of my crown have derived from this salutary measure of the Definitive Treaty. The powers at war with my good brother the King of Prussia have been induced to agree to such terms of accommodation as that great prince has approved; and the success which has attended my negociation has necessarily and im-

---

* The House of Commons in 1715 exhibited articles of impeachment of high treason and other high crimes and misdemeanors against Robert, Earl of Oxford and Mortimer. Article 15 is for having corrupted the sacred fountain of truth, and put falsehoods into the mouth of majesty, in several speeches made to parliament.—Vide vol. iii. and Journals of the House of Commons, vol. xviii. p. 214.

mediately diffused the blessings of peace through every part of Europe.—The infamous fallacy of this whole sentence is apparent to all mankind; for it is known that the king of Prussia did not barely approve, but absolutely dictated, as conqueror, every article of the terms of peace. No advantage of any kind has accrued to that magnanimous prince from our negociation; but he was basely deserted by the Scottish prime minister of England. He was known by every court in Europe to be scarcely on better terms of friendship here than at Vienna, and he was betrayed by us in the treaty of peace. What a strain of insolence, therefore, is it in a minister to lay claim to what he is conscious all his efforts tended to prevent, and meanly to arrogate to himself a share in the fame and glory of one of the greatest princes the world has ever seen! The King of Prussia, however, has gloriously kept all his former conquests, and stipulated security for all his allies, even for the Elector of Hanover. I know in what light this great prince is considered in Europe, and in what manner he has been treated here; among other reasons, perhaps, from some contemptuous expressions he may have used of the Scot,—expressions which are every day echoed by the whole body of Englishmen through the southern part of this island.

The preliminary articles of peace were such as have drawn the contempt of mankind on our wretched negociators. All our most valuable conquests were agreed to be restored, and the East India Company would have been infallibly ruined by a single article of this fallacious and baneful negociation. No hireling of the minister has been hardy enough to dispute this; yet the minister himself has made our sovereign declare the satisfaction which he felt at the approaching re-establishment of peace upon conditions so honourable to his crown, and so beneficial to his people. As to the entire approbation of parliament which is so vainly boasted of, the world knows how that was obtained. The large debt on the civil list, already above half a year in arrear, shews pretty clearly the transactions of the winter. It is however remarkable, that the minister's speech dwells on the entire approbation given by parliament to the preliminary articles, which I will venture to say he must by this time be ashamed of; for he has been brought to confess the total want of that knowledge, accuracy, and precision by which such immense advantages both of trade and territory were sacrificed to our inveterate enemies. These gross blunders are, indeed, in some measure set right by the Definitive Treaty; yet the most important articles, relative to cessions, commerce, and the fishery, remain as they were with respect to the French. The proud and feeble Spaniard, too, does not renounce, but only desists from all pretensions which he may have formed to the right of fishing—where? only about the island of Newfoundland—till a favourable opportunity arises of insisting on it, there, as well as elsewhere.

"The minister cannot forbear, even in the king's speech, insulting us with a dull repetition of the word economy. I did not expect so soon to have seen that word again, after it had been so lately exploded, and more than once, by a most numerous audience, hissed off the stage of our English theatres. It is held in derision by the voice of the people, and every tongue loudly proclaims the universal contempt in which these empty professions are held by this nation. Let the public be informed of a single instance of economy, except indeed in the household." Is a regiment which was completed as to its complement of officers on the Tuesday and broke on the Thursday, a proof of economy? Is the pay of a Scottish Master Elliot to be voted by an English Parliament under the head of economy? Is this, among a thousand others, one of the convincing proofs of a firm resolution to form government on a plan of strict economy? Is it not notorious that, in the reduction of the army, not the least attention has been paid to it. Many unnecessary expenses have been incurred, only to increase the power of the crown, that is, to create more lucrative jobs for the creatures of the minister. The staff, indeed, is broke, but the discerning part of mankind immediately comprehended the mean subterfuge, and resented the indignity put upon so brave an officer as Marshal Ligonier. That step was taken to give the whole power of the army to the crown, that is, to the minister. Lord Ligonier is now no longer at the head of the army; but Lord Bute in effect is. I mean that every preferment given by the crown will be found still to be obtained by his enormous influence, and to be bestowed only on the creatures of the Scottish faction. The nation is still in the same deplorable state, while he governs, and can make the tools of his power pursue the same odious measures. Such a retreat as he intends can only mean that personal indemnity which I hope guilt will never find from an injured nation. The negociations of the late inglorious peace and the excise will haunt him wherever he goes, and the terrors of the just resentment which he must be prepared to meet from a brave and insulted people, and which must finally crush him, will be for ever before his eyes.

"In vain will such a minister, or the foul dregs of his power, the tools of corruption and despotism, preach up in the speech that spirit of concord and that obedience to the laws which is essential to good order. They have sent the spirit of discord through the land, and I will prophecy that it will never be extinguished but by the extinction of their power. Is the spirit of concord to go hand in hand with the peace and excise through this nation? Is it to be expected between an insolent exciseman and a peer, gentleman, freeholder, or farmer, whose private houses are now made liable to be entered and searched at pleasure? Gloucestershire, Herefordshire, and in general all the cyder counties are not surely the several counties which are alluded to in the speech. The spirit of concord hath not gone forth among them; but the spirit of liberty has, and a noble opposition has been given to the wicked instruments of oppression. A nation as sensible as the English will see that a spirit of concord when they are oppressed means a tame submission to injury, and that a spirit of liberty ought then to arise, and I am sure ever will, in proportion to the weight of the grievance they feel. Every legal attempt of a contrary tendency to the spirit of concord will be deemed a justifiable resistance, warranted by the spirit of the English constitution.

"A despotic minister will always endeavour to dazzle his prince with high-flown ideas of the prerogative and honour of the crown, which the minister will make a parade of firmly maintaining. I wish as much as any man in the kingdom to see the honour of the crown maintained in a manner truly becoming royalty. I lament to see it sunk even to prostitution. What a shame was it to see the security of this country, in point of military force, complimented away, contrary to the opinion of royalty itself, and sacrificed to the prejudices and to the ignorance of a set of people the most unfit, from every consideration, to be consulted on a matter relative to the security of the House of Hanover!" I wish to see the honour of the crown religiously asserted with regard to our allies, and the dignity of it scrupulously maintained with regard to foreign princes. Is it possible such an indignity can have happened, such a sacrifice of the honour of the crown of England, as that a minister should already have kissed his majesty's hand on being appointed to the most insolent and ungrateful court in the world, without a previous assurance of that reciprocal nomination which the meanest court in Europe would insist upon before she proceeded to an act otherwise so derogatory to her honour? But Electoral policy has ever been obsequious to the court of Vienna, and forgets the insolence with which Count Colloredo left England. Upon a principle of dignity and economy Lord Stormont, a Scottish peer of the loyal house of Murray, kissed his majesty's hand, I think on Wednesday in the Easter week; but this ignominious act has not yet disgraced the nation in the London Gazette. The ministry are not ashamed of doing the thing in private; they are only afraid of the publication. Was it a tender regard for the honour of the late king, or of his present majesty, that invited to court Lord George Sackville in these first days of peace, to share in the general satisfaction which all good courtiers received in the indignity offered to Lord Ligonier, and on the advancement of ——? Was this to shew princely gratitude to the eminent services of the accomplished General of the house of Brunswick, who has had so great a share in rescuing Europe from the yoke of France, and whose nephew we hope soon to see made happy in the possession of the most amiable princess in the world? Or is it meant to assert the honour of the crown only against the united wishes of a loyal and affectionate people, founded in a happy experience of the talents, ability, integrity, and virtue of those who have had the glory of redeeming their country from bondage and ruin, in order to support, by every art of corruption and intimidation, a weak, disjointed, incapable set of—I will call them anything but ministers—by whom the favourite still meditates to rule this kingdom with a rod of iron?

The Stuart line has ever been intoxicated with the slavish doctrines of the absolute, independent, unlimited power of the crown. Some of that line were so weakly advised as to endeavour to reduce them into practice; but the English nation was too spirited to suffer the least encroachment on the ancient liberties of the kingdom. "The King of England is only the first magistrate of this country; * but is invested by law with the whole executive power. He is, however, responsible to his people for the due execution of the royal functions, in the choice of ministers, &c. equally with the meanest of his subjects in his particular duty." The personal character of our present amiable sovereign makes us easy and happy that so great a power is lodged in such hands; but the favourite has given too just cause for him to escape the general odium. The prerogative of the crown is to exert the constitutional powers entrusted to it in a way, not of blind favour and partiality, but of wisdom and judgment. This is the spirit of our constitution. The people too have their prerogative, and I hope the fine words of Dryden will be engraved on our hearts,

"Freedom is the English subject's prerogative."

The public for some time believed that the continued series of the North Briton after No. XLV. proceeded from the old quarter, and for which there was some colour by an increased vituperation of Scotland and Scotchmen. An accident, however, discovered that the original North Briton and its continuation were the work of different (indeed very different) pens; for the successor of Mr. Wilkes having thrown out

* In the first speech of James I. to his English parliament, March 22, 1603, are the following words: "That I am a servant is most true; I will never be ashamed to confess it. My principal honour to be the great servant of the commonwealth."—Journals of the House of Commons, vol. i. p. 145.

some gross reflections * on four Scottish gentlemen lately appointed to governments in North America, one of them, giving too much way to resentment, resolved to have some talk with his anonymous libeller. On inquiry he learnt that the gentleman's name was Brooke. Mr. Johnstone therefore invited Mr. Brooke to an interview, who considered this invitation as a challenge, and only laughed the more in a subsequent paper at Mr. Johnstone; who, thus provoked to still greater lengths of resentment, repaired to the house of the political champion, and inflicted personal chastisement upon him at once summary and severe. A scuffle ensued, and Mr. Brooke's friends coming to the rescue, the enraged Governor reluctantly retired from the conflict.

---

* These reflections were founded on a quotation of the four following appointments, which appeared in the same Gazette:

The King has been pleased to constitute and appoint the Hon. James Murray to be his Majesty's Captain-General and Governor-in-Chief in and over his Majesty's province of Quebec in America.

The King has been pleased to constitute and appoint James Grant, Esq. to be his Majesty's Captain-General and Governor-in-Chief in and over his Majesty's province of East Florida in America.

The King has been pleased to constitute and appoint George Johnstone, Esq. to be his Majesty's Captain-General and Governor-in-Chief in and over his Majesty's province of West Florida in America.

The King has been pleased to constitute and appoint Robert Melvill, Esq. to be his Majesty's Captain-General and Governor-in-Chief in and over his Majesty's islands of Granada, the Grenadines, Dominica, St. Vincent, and Tobago, in America, and of all other islands and territories adjacent thereto, and which now are or heretofore have been dependent thereupon.

GOTHAM.

IN THREE BOOKS.

THE first book of this poem was published in February, 1764, and the whimsical nature of its contents gave scarcely any intimation of the shape it might in its progress assume. The publication of the third book, however, developed the author's plan, by his drawing, in his own person, the portrait of a perfect sovereign; and expatiating on the qualifications requisite for an adequate fulfilment of the functions of that high office. The poem abounds with many exquisite passages, and just delineations of character, and affords the only specimen of our author's powers in the walk of rural imagery; but notwithstanding these and the many other beauties it contains, the plan is in itself so defective, and the vein of egotism that pervades it so disgusting, as, together with its tedious digressions, to have prevented its acquiring that degree of popularity which all Churchill's former productions had obtained.

Gotham contains less personal satire than any other of our author's poems, and probably for that reason, and from the general nature of its subject, may now excite more interest than it did on its first appearance. The name of the author prepared his readers to expect that direct censure of individuals in which he had hitherto indulged, and the consequent disappointment they experienced may have contributed to class this poem in a lower scale of merit than it otherwise deserved.

The first book, as the author acknowledges in the last lines, has but little connection with the real subject. In it he gives ample indulgence to the warmth and luxuriance of his imagination, and represents the animate and inanimate creation as rejoicing at his accession to the throne of Gotham.

In the second book he enters on his subject, and draws the characters of the Stuarts with a discriminating pencil.

The third book inculcates precepts for a monarch to observe in order to render him great, sagacious, and beloved. Whether our poetical Mentor, when he assumed the office of preceptor, had a Telemachus in view, or whether, when he described the characters of the dead in such strong and striking colours, he had any reference to the living, the reader has ample opportunity of determining for himself.

The same apprehension of the Bute influence over the youthful king is alluded to in Canning's Epistle from Lord W. Russell to Lord Cavendish, published the preceding year, 1763.

But should some upstart, train'd in slavery's school,
Learn'd in the maxims of despotic rule,
Full fraught with forms and grave pedantic pride,
(Mysterious cloke! the mind's defects to hide;)
Sordid in small things, prodigal in great,
Saving for minions, squandering for the state,
Should such a miscreant, born for England's bane,
Obscure the glories of a prosperous reign,
Gain by the semblance of each praiseful art,
A pious prince's unsuspecting heart;
Envious of worth and talents not his own,
Clears all experienced merit from the throne,
To guide the helm a motley crew compose,
Servile to him, the king and country's foes,
Meanly descend each paltry place to fill,
With tools of power and pandars to his will,
Brandishing high the scorpion scourge o'er all,
Except such slaves as bow the knee to Baal,
Should Albion's fate decree the baleful hour,
Short be the date of his detested power,
Soon may his sovereign break his iron rod,
And hear his people for their voice is god.

GOTHAM.

BOOK I.

Far off (no matter whether east or west,
A real country, or one made in jest,
Not yet by modern Mandevilles disgraced,
Nor by map-jobbers wretchedly misplaced)
There lies an island, neither great nor small
Which, for distinction sake, I Gotham call.
  The man who finds an unknown country out,
By giving it a name, acquires, no doubt,
A Gospel title, though the people there
The pious Christian thinks not worth his care;
Bar this pretence, and into air is hurl'd
The claim of Europe to the Western world.

3 Sir John Mandeville, a traveller of the 14th century, notorious for the little attention to veracity, observed by him in the narration of his thirty-four years' wanderings. He first discovered the "Anthropophagi, or men whose heads do grow beneath their shoulders;" and in a high northern latitude observed the singular phenomenon of the congelation of words, as they issued from the mouth, and the strange medley of sounds that ensued upon a thaw.

In the 254th number of the Tatler, with the appropriate motto of Splendide mendax, Addison has given a very amusing version of Sir John Mandeville's "Words congealed in Northern Air" in the shape of an extract from a manuscript journal of our English rival of that liar of first rate magnitude Ferdinand Mendez Pinto.

Cast by a tempest on the savage coast,
Some roving buccaneer set up a post;
A beam, in proper form transversely laid,
Of his Redeemer's cross the figure made,
Of that Redeemer, with whose laws his life,
From first to last, had been one scene of strife;
His royal master's name thereon engraved,
Without more process, the whole race enslaved,
Cut off that charter they from Nature drew,
And made them slaves to men they never knew.
Search ancient histories, consult records,
Under this title the most Christian lords
Hold (thanks to conscience) more than half the ball;
O'erthrow this title, they have none at all;
For never yet might any monarch dare,
Who lived to truth, and breathed a Christian air,
Pretend that Christ, (who came, we all agree,
To bless his people, and to set them free)
To make a convert ever one law gave
By which converters made him first a slave.
Spite of the glosses of a canting priest,
Who talks of charity, but means a feast,
Who recommends it (whilst he seems to feel
The holy glowings of a real zeal)
To all his hearers, as a deed of worth,
To give them heaven, whom they have robb'd of earth,
Never shall one, one truly honest man,
Who, bless'd with Liberty, reveres her plan,
Allow one moment, that a savage sire
Could from his wretched race, for childish hire,

By a wild grant, their all, their freedom pass,
And sell his country for a bit of glass.
Or grant this barbarous right, let Spain and France,
In slavery bred, as purchasers advance: 46
Let them, whilst conscience is at distance hurl'd,
With some gay bauble buy a golden world:
An Englishman, in charter'd freedom born, 49
Shall spurn the slavish merchandise, shall scorn
To take from others, through base private views,
What he himself would rather die, than lose.
Happy the savage of those early times,
Ere Europe's sons were known, and Europe's crimes!
Gold, cursed gold! slept in the womb of earth,
Unfelt its mischiefs, as unknown its worth; 56
In full content he found the truest wealth,
In toil he found diversion, food, and health;
Stranger to ease and luxury of courts,
His sports were labours, and his labours sports;
His youth was hardy, and his old age green;
Life's morn was vigorous, and her eve serene;
No rules he held, but what were made for use,
No arts he learn'd, nor ills which arts produce;
False lights he follow'd, but believed them true;
He knew not much, but lived to what he knew.
Happy, thrice happy, now the savage race,
Since Europe took their gold, and gave them grace!
Pastors she sends to help them in their need, 69
Some who can't write; with others who can't read;

And on sure grounds the Gospel pile to rear,
Sends missionary felons every year;
Our vices, with more zeal than holy prayers,
She teaches them, and in return takes theirs:
Her rank oppressions give them cause to rise,
Her want of prudence, means, and arms supplies,
Whilst her brave rage, not satisfied with life,
Rising in blood, adopts the scalping-knife;
Knowledge she gives, enough to make them know
How abject is their state, how deep their woe;
The worth of freedom strongly she explains,
Whilst she bows down, and loads their necks with chains:
  Faith, too, she plants, for her own ends imprest,
To make them bear the worst, and hope the best;
And whilst she teaches, on vile interest's plan,
As laws of God, the wild decrees of man,
Like Pharisees, of whom the Scriptures tell,
She makes them ten times more the sons of Hell.

72 Transportation as a punishment is unknown to the common law of England; it was first inflicted by Statute 39 Elizabeth, and it was warranted by the Habeas Corpus Act 31 Car. II.; from which period, until our colonial war, many capital offences were commuted into transportation to the plantations in America. In 1788, the system was renewed by the foundation of an extensive empire in New Holland, and the interesting prospect afforded of an unlimited diffusion of the blessings of British liberty throughout the Southern Hemisphere, (First edition, 1804.)

The prospect has been realized beyond the most sanguine expectations by the present condition of Australia and its dependencies, while convicts and convict labour, the source of their prosperity, have been necessarily discontinued.

But whither do these grave reflections tend?
Are they design'd for any, or no end?
Briefly but this—to prove, that by no act
Which Nature made, that by no equal pact
'Twixt man and man, which might, if Justice heard,
Stand good; that by no benefits conferr'd,
Or purchase made, Europe in chains can hold
The sons of India, and her mines of gold.
Chance led her there in an accursed hour;
She saw, and made the country hers by power;
Nor drawn by virtue's love from love of fame,
Shall my rash folly controvert the claim,
Or wish in thought that title overthrown
Which coincides with, and involves my own.
Europe discover'd India first; I found
My right to Gotham on the self-same ground;
I first discover'd it, nor shall that plea
To her be granted, and denied to me;
I plead possession, and, till one more bold
Shall drive me out will that possession hold.
With Europe's rights my kindred rights I twine;
Hers be the Western world, be Gotham mine.
Rejoice, ye happy Gothamites, rejoice;
Lift up your voice on high, a mighty voice:
The voice of gladness; and on every tongue,
In strains of gratitude, be praises hung,
The praises of so great and good a king;
Shall Churchill reign, and shall not Gotham sing?
As on a day, a high and holy day,
Let every instrument of music play,

Ancient and modern; those which drew their birth
(Punctilio's laid aside) from Pagan earth,
As well as those by Christian made and Jew,
Those known to many, and those known to few;
Those which in whim and frolic lightly float,
And those which swell the slow and solemn note;
Those which (whilst Reason stands in wonder by)
Make some complexions laugh and others cry;
Those which, by some strange faculty of sound,
Can build walls up, and raze them to the ground;
Those, which can tear up forests by the roots,
And make brutes dance like men, and men like brutes;
Those which, whilst Ridicule leads up the dance,
Make clowns of Monmouth ape the fops of France;
Those which, where Lady Dullness with Lord Mayors
Presides, disdaining light and trifling airs,
Hallow the feast with psalmody, and those
Which, planted in our churches to dispose
And lift the mind to Heaven, are disgraced
With what a foppish organist calls Taste:
All, from the fiddle (on which every fool,
The pert son of dull sire, discharged from school,
Serves an apprenticeship in college ease,
And rises through the gamut to degrees)

132 Our author, in an excursion he made to Wales, took up his residence for a few weeks in Monmouth; the manners of the inhabitants of which town seem to have displeased the irritable bard.

To those which (though less common, not less sweet)
From famed Saint Giles's, and more famed Vine-
street,
(Where Heaven, the utmost wish of Man to grant,
Gave me an old house, and an older aunt)
Thornton, whilst humour pointed out the road
To her arch cub, hath hitch'd into an ode;
All instruments, (attend, ye listening Spheres,
Attend, ye sons of men, and hear with ears)
All instruments, (nor shall they seek one hand
Impress'd from modern Music's coxcomb band)
All instruments, self-acted, at my name
Shall pour forth harmony, and loud proclaim,
Loud but yet sweet, to the according globe,
My praises, whilst gay nature, in a robe,
A coxcomb doctor's robe, to the full sound
Keeps time, like Boyce, and the world dances
round.

147 Alluding to a very humorous burlesque "Ode on St. Cecilia's Day," written by Bonnell Thornton, and adapted to the ancient British music, viz. the salt box, the Jew's harp, the marrow bones and cleavers, the hum-strum, or hurdy-gurdy, &c. as it was performed at Ranelagh, on June 10, 1763. The Ode, with an introduction, giving some account of those truly British Instruments, is preserved in the Annual Register for that year; it is replete with humour, and exhibits strong marks of those powers of wit and pleasantry, which Thornton possessed in a high degree. It would be a piece of injustice to make any extract from so short a poem, which is too good to be mutilated, and will repay the perusal.

158 William Boyce, a celebrated musician, was born in 1710, and bound apprentice to Dr. Green, organist of St. Paul's. He was, whilst a young man, seized with an obsti-

Rejoice, ye happy Gothamites! rejoice;
Lift up your voice on high, a mighty voice,
The voice of gladness; and on every tongue,
In strains of gratitude, be praises hung,
The praises of so great and good a king:
Shall Churchill reign, and shall not Gotham sing?
Infancy, straining backward from the breast,
Tetchy and wayward, what he loveth best
Refusing in his fits, whilst all the while
The mother eyes the wrangler with a smile,
And the fond father sits on t'other side,
Laughs at his moods, and views his spleen with pride,
Shall murmur forth my name, whilst at his hand
Nurse stands interpreter through Gotham's land.
Childhood, who like an April morn, appears
Sunshine and rain, hopes clouded o'er with fears,
Pleased and displeased by starts, in passion warm,
In reason weak; who wrought into a storm,
Like to the fretful billows of the deep,
Soon spends his rage, and cries himself asleep;

nate and incurable deafness; notwithstanding which defect, he continued his professional studies with surprising perseverance, and, in 1749, obtained from the university of Cambridge the degree of Mus. D. In 1757, he was appointed master of the king's band, and organist and composer to his majesty. He died in 1779, and was interred in one of the vaults of St. Paul's cathedral. Only a few of his numerous compositions have been published. His songs are delicate and lively; and his anthems, symphonies, and oratorios are compositions of considerable merit. The prominent feature in his music is an unusual portion of originality.

Who, with a feverish appetite oppress'd,
For trifles sighs, but hates them when possess'd,
His trembling lash suspended in the air,
Half-bent, and stroking back his long, lank hair,
Shall to his mates look up with eager glee,
And let his top go down to prate of me.
Youth, who, fierce, fickle, insolent and vain,
Impatient urges on to Manhood's reign,
Impatient urges on, yet with a cast
Of dear regard, looks back on Childhood past,
In the mid-chase, when the hot blood runs high,
And the quick spirits mount into his eye;
When pleasure, which he deems his greatest wealth,
Beats in his heart, and paints his cheeks with health;
When the chafed steed tugs proudly at the rein,
And, ere he starts hath run o'er half the plain;
When, wing'd with fear, the stag flies full in view,
And in full cry the eager hounds pursue,
Shall shout my praise to hills which shout again,
And e'en the huntsman stop to cry Amen.
Manhood, of form erect, who would not bow
Though worlds should crack around him; on his brow
Wisdom serene, to passion giving law,
Bespeaking love, and yet commanding awe;
Dignity into grace by mildness wrought;
Courage attemper'd, and refined by thought:
Virtue supreme enthroned, within his breast

The image of his Maker deep imprest;
Lord of this earth, which trembles at his nod,
With reason bless'd and only less than God;
Manhood, though weeping Beauty kneels for aid,
Though Honour calls, in Danger's form array'd,
Though clothed with sackcloth, Justice in the gates,
By wicked elders chain'd, Redemption waits,
Manhood shall steal an hour, a little hour,
(Is't not a little one) to hail my power.
Old Age, a second child, by Nature curst
With more and greater evils than the first:
Weak, sickly, full of pains, in every breath
Railing at life and yet afraid of death;
Putting things off, with sage and solemn air,
From day to day, without one day to spare;
Without enjoyment covetous of pelf,
Tiresome to friends, and tiresome to himself;
His faculties impair'd, his temper sour'd,
His memory of recent things devour'd
E'en with the acting, on his shatter'd brain;

214 The many Scripture allusions which occur throughout Churchill's Poems, shew that he had read his Bible with attention, and was not so totally deficient in every branch of his professional duty as his enemies accused him of being. The Monthly Reviewers were very wroth with him for adopting the phrase contained in this line, and are otherwise extremely severe in their strictures on the whole of this book; which they assert to be written in a style very little superior to that of Francis Quarles or George Withers. Of the third book they give a more favourable account, and bestow on it greater praise than on most of the preceding poems.

Though the false registers of youth remain;
From morn to evening babbling forth vain praise
Of those rare men, who lived in those rare days,
When he, the hero of his tale, was young,
Dull repetitions faltering on his tongue;
Praising gray hairs, sure mark of Wisdom's sway,
E'en whilst he curses Time, which made him gray;
Scoffing at youth, e'en whilst he would afford
All but his gold to have his youth restored,
Shall for a moment, from himself set free,
Lean on his crutch, and pipe forth praise to me.
Rejoice, ye happy Gothamites! rejoice;
Lift up your voice on high, a mighty voice,
The voice of gladness; and on every tongue,
In strains of gratitude, be praises hung,
The praises of so great and good a king;
Shall Churchill reign, and shall not Gotham sing?
Things without life shall in this chorus join,
And, dumb to others' praise, be loud in mine.
The snow-drop, who in habit white and plain,
Comes on, the herald of fair Flora's train:
The coxcomb crocus, flower of simple note,
Who, by her side struts in a herald's coat;
The tulip, idly glaring to the view,
Who, though no clown, his birth from Holland drew;

250 The mania that raged in Holland, and particularly among the inhabitants of Haerlem, for the cultivation of tulips in 1634 and the three following years, would scarcely be credited by posterity, was it not authenticated by the incontro-

Who, once full dress'd, fears from his place to stir,
The fop of flowers, the More of a parterre;
The woodbine, who her elm in marriage meets,

vertible testimony of contemporary historians. The commerce of tulips can only be compared to the infatuation which pervaded the French and English nations, during the South Sea and Mississippi bubbles. The price of tulips rose to an extravagant height. Several merchants and tradesmen quitted their counting houses and shops, to devote themselves to the culture of these flowers, and it is related that in the city of Haerlem alone, they had during these three years traded in tulips to the amount of a million sterling. Munting relates the following curious bargain concluded for a single tulip called the Viceroy; the purchaser not possessing the money wherewith to pay for it, exchanged for this rare plant, 36 bushels of wheat, 72 bushels of rice, four fat oxen, a dozen fat sheep, eight fatted hogs, two hogsheads of wine, four barrels of beer, two casks of butter, one thousand pound weight of cheese, a bed, some clothes and a large silver goblet; the whole valued at 2,500 florins, or nearly £300 of our money. About the same period, an individual offered twelve acres of rich land for one tulip bulb, which however the proprietor declined to sell at so low a price. In 1637, one collection of tulips belonging to Wouters Brockholmeister fetched at a public sale above £9,000. In three days the Viceroy was sold for £250, Admiral Tiefkins £440, Admiral Van Eyk £160, Grebber £148, Schilder £100, Semper Augustus £550. One person afterwards sold three Semper Augustuses for £1,000 each. The same gentleman was offered for his flower-garden £1,500 a year for seven years, and every thing to be left as found, only reserving the increase during that time for the money.

An anecdote is related of a Burgomaster that having procured a place of considerable profit for a friend a native of Holland, he generously refused any compensation, and only desired to see his flower garden, which was granted. In about two years afterwards the gentleman came to visit the burgo-

And brings her dowry in surrounding sweets;
The lily, silver mistress of the vale,

master, when perceiving in his garden a scarce tulip of great value, (which the one had clandestinely procured from the garden of the other) he flew into a violent passion, resigned his place of £1,000 per annum, went home, tore up his flower garden, and was never afterwards heard of.

An inhabitant of Brussels possessed a small garden, the soil of which had the singular property of giving to plain tulips the most beautifully variegated colours; this man had roots sent to him from all parts, and received large annual payments for rearing them in his garden. At length the tulipomania rose to such a height as to call for the interference of the States General, who viewing it as attended with serious injury, as well to individuals as to commerce in general, checked the evil by a severe though salutary law for invalidating all contracts respecting these flowers, so that a root was then sold for £5 which a few weeks before would have fetched £500.

The mania must have extended to England, as appears by the following lines in Dr. Young's Love of Fame or Universal Passion.

But Florio's fame, the product of a shower
Grows in his garden an illustrious flower,
Why teems the earth, why melt the vernal skies,
Why shines the sun? to make Paul Diack rise.
From morn to night has Florio gazing stood,
And wondered how the gods could be so good,
What shape, what hue, was ever nymph so fair,
He doats, he dies, he too is *rooted* there.
A friend of mine indulged this noble flame;
A quaker served him, Adam was his name.
To one loved tulip oft the master went,
Hung o'er it, and whole days in rapture spent,
But came and missed it one ill-fated hour;
He raged, he roar'd, " What demon cropp'd my flower,"
Serene, quoth Adam, "lo! 'twas crushed by me,
Fallen is the Baal to which thou bow'dst the knee."

The rose of Sharon, which perfumes the gale;
The jessamine, with which the queen of flowers
To charm her god adorns his favourite bowers,
Which brides, by the plain hand of Neatness drest,
Unenvied rival, wear upon their breast
Sweet as the incense of the morn, and chaste
As the pure zone, which circles Dian's waist;
All flowers of various names, and various forms,
Which the sun into strength and beauty warms,
From the dwarf daisy, which, like infants, clings,
And fears to leave the earth from whence it springs,
To the proud giant of the garden race,
Who, madly rushing to the sun's embrace,
O'ertops her fellows with aspiring aim,
Demands his wedded love, and bears his name;
All, one and all, shall in this chorus join,
And, dumb to others' praise, be loud in mine.
Rejoice, ye happy Gothamites! rejoice;
Lift up your voice on high, a mighty voice,
The voice of gladness; and on every tongue,
In strains of gratitude, be praises hung,
The praises of so great and good a king;
Shall Churchill reign, and shall not Gotham sing?
Forming a gloom, through which, to spleen-struck minds,
Religion, horror stamp'd, a passage finds,
The ivy crawling o'er the hallow'd cell
Where some old hermit's wont his beads to tell
By day, by night; the myrtle ever green,
Beneath whose shade Love holds his rites unseen;

The willow, weeping o'er the fatal wave
Where many a lover finds a watery grave;
The cypress, sacred held, when lovers mourn
Their true love snatch'd away; the laurel worn
By poets in old time, but destined now,
In grief, to wither on a Whitehead's brow;
The fig, which, large as what in India grows,
Itself a grove, gave our first parents clothes;
The vine, which, like a blushing new-made bride,
Clustering, empurples all the mountain's side;
The yew, which in the place of sculptured stone,
Marks out the resting-place of men unknown;
The hedge-row elm, the pine, of mountain race;
The fir, the Scotch fir, never out of place;
The cedar, whose top mates the highest cloud,
Whilst his old father Lebanon grows proud
Of such a child, and his vast body laid
Out many a mile, enjoys the filial shade;
The oak, when living, monarch of the wood;
The English oak, which, dead, commands the flood;
All, one and all, shall in this chorus join,
And dumb to others' praise, be loud in mine.
  Rejoice, ye happy Gothamites! rejoice;
Lift up your voice on high, a mighty voice,
The voice of gladness; and on every tongue,
In strains of gratitude, be praises hung,
The praises of so great and good a king;
Shall Churchill reign, and shall not Gotham sing?
  The showers, which make the young hills, like young lambs,

Bound and rebound; the old hills, like old rams,
Unwieldy, jump for joy; the streams, which glide,
Whilst Plenty marches smiling by their side,
And from their bosom rising Commerce springs,
The winds, which rise with healing on their wings,
Before whose cleansing breath Contagion flies;
The sun, who, travelling in eastern skies,
Fresh, full of strength, just risen from his bed,
Though in Jove's pastures they were born and bred,
With voice and whip, can scarce make his steeds stir,
Step by step, up the perpendicular;
Who, at the hour of eve, panting for rest,
Rolls on amain, and gallops down the west
As fast as Jehu, oil'd for Ahab's sin,
Drove for a crown, or postboys for an inn;
The moon, who holds o'er night her silver reign,
Regent of tides, and mistress of the brain,
Who to her sons, those sons who own her power
And do her homage at the midnight hour,
Gives madness as a blessing, but dispenses
Wisdom to fools, and damns them with their senses;
The stars, who, by I know not what strange right,
Preside o'er mortals in their own despite,
Who, without reason, govern those who most
(How truly, judge from thence!) of reason boast,
And, by some mighty magic yet unknown,
Our actions guide, yet cannot guide their own;
All, one and all, shall in this chorus join,

And, dumb to others' praise, be loud in mine.
  Rejoice, ye happy Gothamites! rejoice;
Lift up your voice on high, a mighty voice,
The voice of gladness; and on every tongue,
In strains of gratitude, be praises hung,
The praises of so great and good a king;
Shall Churchill reign, and shall not Gotham sing?
  The moment, minute, hour, day, week, month, year,
Morning and eve, as they in turn appear;
Moments and minutes, which, without a crime,
Can't be omitted in accounts of time,
Or, if omitted, (proof we might afford)
Worthy by parliaments to be restored;
The hours, which, dress'd by turns in black and white,
Ordain'd as handmaids, wait on day and night;
The day, those hours, I mean, when light presides,
And business in a cart with Prudence rides;
The night, those hours, I mean, with darkness hung,
When Sense speaks free, and Folly holds her tongue,
The morn, when Nature, rousing from her strife
With death-like sleep, awakes to second life;
The eve, when, as unequal to the task,
She mercy from her foe descends to ask;
The week, in which six days are kindly given
To think of earth, and one to think of heaven;
The months, twelve sisters all of different hue,
Though there appears in all a likeness too;

Not such a likeness as, through Hayman's works,
Dull Mannerist! in Christians, Jews, and Turks,
Cloys with a sameness in each female face,
But a strange something, born of Art and Grace,
Which speaks them all, to vary and adorn,
At different times of the same parents born;
All, one and all, shall in this chorus join,
And, dumb to others' praise, be loud in mine.
  Rejoice, ye happy Gothamites! rejoice;
Lift up your voice on high, a mighty voice,
The voice of gladness; and on every tongue,
In strains of gratitude, be praises hung,

369 Francis Hayman, the painter, was a choice spirit, he was a member of the Beef Steak, the Spiller's Head, Old Slaughters, and other clubs of note. A great crony of Jonathan Tyers, for whom he painted the admired historical pictures from Shakspeare's Henry IV. in the Prince's pavilion, Vauxhall, bottle companion moreover of the gay Fleetwood, patentee of Old Drury, and occasionally employed by him as scene painter to the house. He particularly excelled in portraying Falstaff, and in the recruiting scene in Gloucestershire was equally happy in his conception of Justice Shallow.

One of his best paintings was the Archer, at Vauxhall, who appeared, from whatever point of view beheld, to level his arrow at the spectator. The ingenious and unfortunate Christopher Smart alludes to this painting in the following lines:

"Though with prudish airs she starch her,
  Still she longs and still she burns;
Cupid shoots, like Hayman's Archer,
  Wheresoe'er the damsel turns."

He as well as Hogarth attempted to depict Sigismunda, and was equally unsuccessful; it proved a wofully bad picture. Indeed throughout his works there prevailed a tiresome similitude of feature, which precluded his attaining eminence in his art although highly efficient in its secondary departments.

The praises of so great and good a king;
Shall Churchill reign, and shall not Gotham sing?
  Frore January, leader of the year,
Minced-pies in van and calves' heads in the rear;
Dull February, in whose leaden reign
My mother bore a bard without a brain;
March, various, fierce, and wild, with wind-crack'd cheeks,
By wilder Welshmen led, and crown'd with leeks;
April, with fools, and May, with bastards blest;
June, with White Roses on her rebel breast;

384 Alluding to the alleged custom, adopted by the roundheads and their descendants, of celebrating the anniversary of the decapitation of Charles the First, by having a calf's head on table.

In the 6th vol. p. 552, of the first edition of the Harleian Miscellany, is reprinted a very scarce tract called the Secret History of the Calves' Head Club, or the Republican Unmasked, published in 1703, giving an account of the proceedings at their meetings, and their anthems and glees sung on the occasion, the following, as a specimen, being the first stanza of the anniversary anthem sung at the meeting of the Club, held on Jan. 30, 1694.

The storm is blown over, the tempest is past,
The tyrant is fallen, he is conquer'd at last.
Our fathers resolved it, and bravely 'twas done,
To save the whole kingdom, by lopping the crown.
By her looks we discover'd the nation was pleased,
Her fears were all vanish'd, her troubles were eased;
Whilst we yearly commend an attempt so divine,
And applaud the just action, with calves' head and wine.

390 The 10th of June, the birth-day of the old Pretender, whose cognizance, like that of his Yorkish ancestors, was a white rose.

July, to whom the Dog-star in her train,
Saint James gives oysters, and Saint Swithin rain;
August, who banish'd from her Smithfield stand,
To Chelsea flies, with Doggett in her hand;

892 The 25th of July, St. James's day, or the first day of oysters, constituted the subject of one of Hogarth's best paintings, which was presented by him to his friend Brent, by whose executors it was sold to Mr. G. Weller, and was thus described when exhibited a few years ago at Mr. Forest's, in Piccadilly: "The scene lies at the Spiller's Head, in Clare Market. The Duke of Wharton is represented peppering an oyster, served by the well-known Bab Selley, the oyster-wench, a constant attendant at the Spiller's Head. Spiller himself is standing at her back, patting her upon the shoulder humorously. The seated figure smoking is Motley, author of 'Joe Miller;' and the man standing behind is the well-known attendant on the Duke's frolics, Figg, the brother of Figg the boxer. The person drinking at the bar is Corins, the attorney, who generally dressed in the clerical attire. The persons sitting at the table are Dr. Garth and Betterton the actor. The dog, the property of Betterton, is a portrait. He was called Lanthorn, from carrying a lanthorn in his mouth, to light his master home. The two figures in the closet, are Walker, the celebrated Macheath, and Lavinia Fenton, his Polly, afterwards Duchess of Bolton."

893 Alluding to the shortening of Bartholomew fair, and to the annual rowing match for a waterman's coat and silver badge on the 1st of August, being the anniversary of the accession of King George the First to the crown of Great Britain. This ceremony was instituted by Thomas Doggett, an actor, manager, and poet, who flourished in the early part of the last century. He was, to use Sir Richard Steele's expression, a whig up to the head and ears; and shewed his attachment to the house of Hanover, by thus, during his life, celebrating its accession, and at his death bequeathing a certain sum of money, the interest of which was by him directed to be appropriated to the like purpose. The match on the

September, when by custom (right divine)
Geese are ordain'd to bleed at Michael's shrine,
Whilst the priest, not so full of grace as wit,
Falls to unbless'd, nor gives the saint a bit;
October, who the cause of freedom join'd,
And gave a second George to bless mankind;

river is still continued, the claimants setting out on a signal given at that time of the tide when the current is strongest against them, and rowing from the Old Swan near London Bridge to the White Swan at Chelsea.

400 George the Second was born on the 30th of October, 1683. The word Second was printed in Italics in the first edition. Without attributing any greater merit to George the Second than a judicious respect for the judgment of his excellent Queen Caroline, and in deference to that judgment affording his steady support during all the longer and happier portion of his reign to Sir Robert Walpole, we may safely pronounce that England, at no period between the Conquest and the present time, enjoyed in more abundant measure the blessings of internal ease, plenty, and prosperity, than during the thirty years of George the Second's rule.

A few mercantile men had accumulated their plums, and some of the haute noblesse enjoyed large revenues, but the wealth of the country was diffused in almost imperceptible gradations among country gentlemen of from £1000 per annum downwards, merchants, substantial tradesmen, yeomen, and that now extinct class the independent leasehold farmer, these have been mostly absorbed in the vortex of competition, arising from an increasing population and a decreasing demand for it by reason of machinery, and thus the intermediate space abolished between the capitalist and the starving operative, between the wholesale possessor of land, and his dependent tenants at will, and pauper labourers.

Cottages then afforded at once humble and happy homes on the edges of commons which contributed to the support of the small farmer and to the few and scattered parochial poor,

November, who at once to grace our earth,
Saint Andrew boasts, and our Augusta's birth;
December, last of months, but best, who gave
A Christ to man, a Saviour to the slave,
Whilst, falsely grateful, man, at the full feast,
To do God honour makes himself a beast;
All, one and all, shall in this chorus join,
And, dumb to others' praise, be loud in mine.
Rejoice, ye happy Gothamites! rejoice;
Lift up your voice on high, a mighty voice,
The voice of gladness; and on every tongue,
In strains of gratitude, be praises hung,
The praises of so great and good a king;

now immense piles of buildings, under the various designations of unions, county gaols, and lunatic asylums constitute the last resource, and too often witness, if not accelerate, the closing scenes of unavailing industry.

The prosperous condition of the kingdom during the reign of George the Second, is adverted to by Mr. Tooke in his History of Prices, vol. i. p. 60, and who in corroboration of the fact quotes Adam Smith as referring to the "peculiarly happy circumstances of the country during that period," while Mr. Hallam, in his Constitutional History, describes the reign of George II. as the most prosperous period that England had ever experienced.

402 Augusta, daughter of Frederic, Duke of Saxe-Gotha, was born November 30, 1719, and was married April 27, 1736, to Frederic, Prince of Wales, whom she survived, and as Princess Dowager in the early part of the reign of her son George the Third, incurred much popular odium and some scandal on account of the unqualified public support and private friendship vouchsafed by her to the Earl of Bute. Horace Walpole, with wonted malevolence, has given currency to some very injurious reports and inferences on the subject of their intimacy. She died 8th Jan. 1772.

Shall Churchill reign, and shall not Gotham sing?
  The seasons as they roll; Spring by her side
Lechery and Lent, lay-folly and church-pride,
By a rank monk to copulation led,
A tub of sainted salt-fish on her head:
Summer, in light transparent gauze array'd,
Like maids of honour at a masquerade,
In bawdry gauze, for which our daughters leave
The fig, more modest, first brought up by Eve,
Panting for breath, inflamed with lustful fires,
Yet wanting strength to perfect her desires,
Leaning on Sloth, who, fainting with the heat,
Stops at each step, and slumbers on his feet:
Autumn, when Nature, who with sorrow feels
Her dread foe Winter treading on her heels,
Makes up in value what she wants in length,
Exerts her powers, and puts forth all her strength,
Bids corn and fruits in full perfection rise,
Corn fairly tax'd, and fruits without excise:

420 The notorious Duchess of Kingston, when Miss Chudleigh, and a maid of honour to her majesty, appeared at a masquerade in a dress composed entirely of gauze, which was so perfectly transparent as to display, at the same time, the graces of her person and the disposition of her mind. We have already given a characteristic anecdote of this despicable woman in a note upon the Rosciad.

432 The budget of ways and means for the year 1763, consisted, among other articles, of an excise upon cider and perry. This duty being partial and oppressive, and the mode of collecting it vexatious and unconstitutional, met with much opposition, and remonstrances against it were presented by the city of London and the western counties, in which latter partial insurrections were threatened. Notwithstanding the

Winter, benumb'd with cold, no longer known
By robes of fur, since furs became our own;
A hag, who, loathing all, by all is loath'd
With weekly, daily, hourly, libels clothed,
Vile Faction at her heels, who, mighty grown,
Would rule the ruler, and foreclose the throne,
Would turn all state affairs into a trade,
Make laws one day, the next to be unmade,
Beggar at home, a people fear'd abroad,
And, force defeated, make them slaves by fraud;
All, one and all, shall in this chorus join,

clamour it excited, the tax in its full force was persisted in until the year 1766; when it had become so universally obnoxious, as imperiously to call for a repeal.

The excise laws had ever been held in horror by the people of England, especially when less habituated to them than at present. They were arbitrary and contrary to the spirit of the constitution in their origin, and a fruitful source of fraud and oppression in their progress; the system was first imported by James the First from Italy, as a means of satisfying the rapacity of his favourites independent of parliament, by whose subsequent sanction and adoption, under Sir R. Walpole, it became equally efficacious, and as some evidence of its oppressive tendency, until a new arrangement was made some years ago for remunerating the Solicitor (a Barrister) to the Excise Office by a fixed salary, the emoluments of that office arising from prosecutions and compromises conducted in the most rapacious manner, were second only in value to those of the Lord High Chancellor during the most palmy period of the great seal.

434 Probably alluding to the recent acquisition of Canada, and the disappointment experienced by the first adventurers in the fur trade.

436 To which faction Churchill adverts is now immaterial, they were both equally personal and virulent; and the whole winter of 1763-4 teemed with libels of every description.

And, dumb to others' praise, be loud in mine.
  Rejoice, ye happy Gothamites! rejoice;
Lift up your voice on high, a mighty voice,
The voice of gladness; and on every tongue,
In strains of gratitude, be praises hung,
The praises of so great and good a king;
Shall Churchill reign, and shall not Gotham sing?
  The year, grand circle! in whose ample round
The seasons regular and fix'd are bound,
(Who, in his course repeated o'er and o'er,
Sees the same things which he had seen before;)—
The same stars keep their watch, and the same sun
Runs in the track where he from first hath run;
The same moon rules the night; tides ebb and flow,
Man is a puppet and this world a show;
Their old dull follies, old dull fools pursue,
And vice in nothing, but in mode, is new;
He, ——— a lord (now far befall that pride,
He lived a villain, but a lord he died)
Dashwood is pious, Berkeley fix'd as fate,
Sandwich (thank Heaven!) first Minister of State,

461 There would be no difficulty in supplying this blank with one or other of the profligates who then disgraced the peerage, the only difficulty would be that of selection. It is gratifying to add that the succeeding generations of the aristocracy have greatly raised the moral standard of their caste. The few exceptions are objects of public warning and contempt, and not of admiration and imitation, as was too much the case four score years ago.

463 Of Lord le Despencer's abilities as a statesman enough has been said; his piety would afford an inexhaustible theme; the severities exercised by the monks of the order of

And, though by fools despised, by saints unbless'd,
By friends neglected, and by foes oppress'd, 466
Scorning the servile arts of each court elf,
Founded on honour, Wilkes is still himself,
The year, encircled with the various train

St. Francis at Medmenham Abbey, of which he was the founder, are referred to by our author in the poem of the Candidate. We shall here only notice the church erected by his lordship at West Wycombe, near his celebrated seat in Buckinghamshire; and which is built at the *top* of a very steep hill, for the convenience and devotion of the town at the *bottom* of it; some churches have been built from devotion, others from vanity or ostentation; this we believe to be the first church ever erected for a prospect.

463 Colonel Norborne Berkeley, in whose favour the extinct barony of Bottetourt was revived. This mode of giving precedence, which was also adopted in favour of Sir Francis Dashwood, who thus obtained the barony of le Despencer, gave much offence to the antient nobility. The Colonel was second to Lord Talbot in his duel with Mr. Wilkes. The words in the text allude to the expression contained in the following letter addressed by the Colonel to the Freeholders of Gloucestershire.

April 4, 1763.

Gentlemen—Though I am fixed as fate to abide by the determination of the General Meeting of April 13, permit me to declare my wishes that Lord Coleraine may be the object of your choice, as I know him to be a man of honour and principle, and most obnoxious to the late convention of March 28. I have the honour to be, &c. N. Berkeley.

464 At the commencement of the Duke of Bedford's ministry, Lord Sandwich, who had been made First Lord of the Admiralty, through the interest of Lord Holland, was appointed Secretary of State; a situation he held two years, until he was displaced by General Conway, who came in under Lord Rockingham's administration. In 1770, Lord Sandwich was again appointed First Lord of the Admiralty by the influence of his friend Lord North.

Which waits, and fills the glories of his reign,
Shall, taking up this theme, in chorus join,
And, dumb to others' praise, be loud in mine.
  Rejoice, ye happy Gothamites! rejoice;
Lift up your voice on high, a mighty voice,
The voice of gladness; and on every tongue,
In strains of gratitude, be praises hung,
The praises of so great and good a king;
Shall Churchill reign, and shall not Gotham sing?
  Thus far in sport—nor let our critics hence,
Who sell out Monthly trash, and call it Sense,
Too lightly of our present labours deem,
Or judge at random of so high a theme;
High is our theme, and worthy are the men
To feel the sharpest stroke of Satire's pen;
But when kind Time a proper season brings,
In serious mood to treat of serious things,
Then shall they find, disdaining idle play,
That I can be as grave and dull as they.
  Thus far in sport—nor let half patriots, those
Who shrink from every blast of Power which blows,
Who, with tame cowardice familiar grown, [own;
Would hear my thoughts, but fear to speak their
Who, (lest bold truths, to do sage Prudence spite,
Should burst the portals of their lips by night,
Tremble to trust themselves one hour in sleep)
Condemn our course, and hold our caution cheap;
When brave Occasion bids, for some great end,
When Honour calls the poet as a friend,
Then shall they find that, e'en on danger's brink,
He dares to speak what they scarce dare to think.

SUPPLEMENTAL NOTE.

October, who the cause of freedom joined,
And gave a second George to bless mankind.

MR. ALMON, in his Memoirs and Correspondence of Wilkes, gives the following as the remark on this couplet prepared by the latter for his intended edition of Churchill.

This excellent Prince on many occasions ventured his life in the cause of liberty. His distinguished bravery at the battles of Oudenarde and Dettingen was frequently the subject of the unsuspected praise of our inveterate enemies the French. He was always a steady friend to the liberties of mankind, and like the former princes of his house, and of the Nassau line, kept a watchful eye over the Bourbon family, well knowing their rooted enmity to our religion and government, and their long meditated schemes for grasping at universal monarchy. He often checked the restless ambition of France in its mad career, by the most firm, wise, and successful measures. At his death he left us in possession of the capitals of the French in Asia and America, and of many other important conquests there as well as in Europe and Africa, the greatest part of which we lost soon after by a stroke of his grandson's pen, which proved more fatal to England than all the swords of all our enemies. It is justice to the memory of the late king to declare, that he no less endeavoured to make his people free and happy at home, than to carry the glory of the British arms to the highest pitch everywhere abroad. During his reign, the laws were respected and obeyed. Liberty and justice sat with him on the throne. The execution of Earl Ferrers impressed all foreign nations with the greatest idea of the sacredness of our laws, and the protection they afford the meanest subject under a mild and firm sovereign. It was likewise believed, that if the court-martial on Lord George Sackville had given the sentence which all Europe expected, the justice of his late majesty would have ordered it to have been carried into execution.

The poet knew and deeply felt the obligation which a nation has to such a prince. He pays it when he cannot lie under the suspicion of flattery, at a time when it was seen that no man could so effectually make his court as by vilifying the memory of our late sovereign, and tearing the laurels from his tomb. In this task numberless mercenaries were employed, but it is a sufficient answer to a legion of them that in the first address of the House of Lords to the present king, it is observed, that his majesty's predecessor through his whole reign never once suffered the rights of any one of his subjects to be violated. After the demise of the crown, will there be found any lord prostitute enough, will there be a Sandwich to move such a paragraph in the first address to his present majesty's successor?

I hope to be excused, when I add that the praise which the late king now receives, is a tribute of public not of private gratitude. It comes from the meanest of his subjects, who looks back with rapture on the first thirty years of his own life, because they were passed in his native country, in the land of liberty, when the prince on the throne loved and cherished it. The poet is removed from the melancholy scene which has followed. His tears no longer flow for his dear country—his country weeps for him—I will only add in the words of Cicero:—"Nosque malo solatio, sed nonnullo tamen, consolamur, quod ipsius vicem minime dolemus—Immo hercule, quia sic amabat patriam, ut mihi aliquo deorum beneficio videatur ex ejus incendio esse ereptus."

"November, who at once to grace our earth,
Saint Andrew boasts, and our Augusta's birth."

On these lines Wilkes thus remarked, evidently but remotely intending to bring into suspicious juxtaposition the "favourite and the Princess Dowager of Wales." St. Andrew always means the patron of Scotland and Scotsmen. "Augusta is the Princess Dowager of Wales. In the Tale of a Tub, Jack says, "It was ordained some few days before the creation that my *nose* and this very *post* should have a rencounter, and therefore nature thought fit to send us both into the world in the same age and to make us fellow-citizens."

Horace Walpole more unequivocally expressed his view of

the intimacy which subsisted between them, for which see his Memoires of the last ten years of the reign of King George the Second, vol. ii. p. 47 and passim, in which among others this passage occurs: "It now at last appeared that parental tenderness or ambition were not the sole passions that engrossed her thoughts, it had already been whispered that the assiduity ot Lord Bute at Leicester House, and his still more frequent attendance in the gardens at Kew and Carleton House, were less addressed to the Prince of Wales than to his mother. The eagerness of the pages of the back stairs to let her know whenever Lord Bute arrived (and some other symptoms) contributed to dispel the idea that had been conceived of the rigour of her widowhood."

The entire insignificance of Prince Frederic may be collected from Bubb Doddington's Diary, and from an epitaph which had great currency at the time, and is preserved in Walpole's Memoires.

Here lies Fred,
Who was alive and is dead;
Had it been his father
I had much rather;
Had it been his brother,*
Still better than another;
Had it been his sister,
No one would have missed her;
Had it been the whole generation,
Still better for the nation:
But since 'tis only Fred
Who was alive and is dead,
There's no more to be said.

---

* William, Duke of Cumberland, of Culloden memory, and therefore particularly obnoxious to the Jacobites, by one of whom these lines were no doubt penned.

GOTHAM.

BOOK II.

How much mistaken are the men who think
That all who will without restraint may drink;
May largely drink, e'en till their bowels burst,
Pleading no right but merely that of thirst,
At the pure waters of the living well,
Beside whose streams the Muses love to dwell!
Verse is with them a knack, an idle toy,
A rattle gilded o'er, on which a boy
May play untaught, whilst, without art or force,
Make it but jingle, music comes of course.
   Little do such men know the toil, the pains,
The daily, nightly, racking of the brains,
To range the thoughts, the matter to digest,
To cull fit phrases, and reject the rest;
To know the times when Humour on the cheek
Of mirth may hold her sports; when Wit should
         speak,
And when be silent; when to use the powers
Of ornament, and how to place the flowers,
So that they neither give a tawdry glare,
"Nor waste their sweetness in the desert air;"
To form, (which few can do, and scarcely one,
One critic in an age, can find when done)

To form a plan, to strike a grand outline,
To fill it up, and make the picture shine
A full and perfect piece; to make coy Rhyme
Renounce her follies, and with Sense keep time;
To make proud Sense against her nature bend,
And wear the chains of Rhyme, yet call her friend.
Some fops there are, amongst the scribbling tribe,
Who make it all their business to describe,
No matter whether in or out of place;
Studious of finery, and fond of lace,
Alike they trim, as coxcomb fancy brings,
The rags of beggars, and the robes of kings.
Let dull Propriety in state preside
O'er her dull children, Nature is their guide;
Wild Nature, who at random breaks the fence
Of those tame drudges, Judgment, Taste, and Sense,
Nor would forgive herself the mighty crime
Of keeping terms with person, place, and time.
Let liquid gold emblaze the sun at noon,
With borrow'd beams let silver pale the moon;
Let surges hoarse lash the resounding shore,
Let streams meander, and let torrents roar;
Let them breed up the melancholy breeze
To sigh with sighing, sob with sobbing trees;
Let vales embroidery wear; let flowers be tinged
With various tints; let clouds be laced or fringed;
They have their wish; like idle monarch boys,
Neglecting things of weight they sigh for toys;
Give them the crown, the sceptre, and the robe,

Who will may take the power, and rule the globe.
Others there are who, in one solemn pace,
With as much zeal as Quakers rail at lace,
Railing at needful ornament, depend
On sense to bring them to their journey's end;
They would not (Heaven forbid!) their course delay,
Nor for a moment step out of the way,
To make the barren road those graces wear
Which Nature would, if pleased, have planted there.
Vain men! who blindly thwarting Nature's plan,
Ne'er find a passage to the heart of man;
Who, bred 'mongst fogs in academic land,
Scorn every thing they do not understand;
Who, destitute of humour, wit, and taste,
Let all their little knowledge run to waste,
And frustrate each good purpose, whilst they wear
The robes of Learning with a sloven's air.
Though solid reasoning arms each sterling line,
Though Truth declares aloud, "This work is mine,"
Vice, whilst from page to page dull morals creep,
Throws by the book, and Virtue falls asleep.
Sense, mere dull, formal Sense, in this gay town,
Must have some vehicle to pass her down;
Nor can she for an hour insure her reign,
Unless she brings fair Pleasure in her train.
Let her from day to day, from year to year,
In all her grave solemnities appear,

And, with the voice of trumpets, through the streets,
Deal lectures out to every one she meets;
Half who pass by are deaf, and t' other half
Can hear indeed, but only hear to laugh.
Quit then, ye graver sons of letter'd Pride!
Taking for once Experience as a guide;
Quit this grand error, this dull college mode;
Be your pursuits the same, but change the road;
Write, or at least appear to write, with ease,
"And if you mean to profit, learn to please."
In vain for such mistakes they pardon claim,
Because they wield the pen in Virtue's name:
Thrice sacred is that name, thrice bless'd the man
Who thinks, speaks, writes, and lives on such a plan!
This, in himself, himself of course must bless,
But cannot with the world promote success.
He may be strong, but, with effect to speak,
Should recollect his readers may be weak:
Plain rigid truths, which saints with comfort bear,
Will make the sinner tremble and despair.
True Virtue acts from love, and the great end
At which she nobly aims, is to amend;
How then do those mistake, who arm her laws
With rigour not their own, and hurt the cause
They mean to help, whilst with a zealot rage
They make that goddess, whom they'd have engage
Our dearest love, in hideous terror rise!
Such may be honest, but they can't be wise.
In her own full and perfect blaze of light

Virtue breaks forth too strong for human sight;
The dazzled eye, that nice but weaker sense,
Shuts herself up in darkness for defence:
But to make strong conviction deeper sink,
To make the callous feel, the thoughtless think,
Like God, made man, she lays her glory by,
And beams mild comfort on the ravish'd eye:
In earnest most when most she seems in jest,
She worms into, and winds around, the breast;
To conquer vice, of vice appears the friend,
And seems unlike herself to gain her end.
The sons of Sin, to while away the time
Which lingers on their hands, of each black crime
To hush the painful memory, and keep
The tyrant Conscience in delusive sleep,
Read on at random, nor suspect the dart
Until they find it rooted in their heart.
'Gainst vice they give their vote, nor know at first
That cursing that, themselves too they have curst;
They see not till they fall into the snares,
Deluded into virtue unawares.
Thus the shrewd doctor, in the spleen-struck mind,
When pregnant horror sits and broods o'er wind,
Discarding drugs, and striving how to please,
Lures on insensibly, by slow degrees,
The patient to those manly sports which bind
The slacken'd sinews, and relieve the mind;
The patient feels a change as wrought by stealth,
And wonders on demand to find it health.

Some few, whom Fate ordained to deal in rhymes
In other lands, and here, in other times,

Whom, waiting at their birth, the midwife Muse
Sprinkled all over with Castalian dews,
To whom true Genius gave his magic pen,
Whom Art by just degrees led up to men;
Some few, extremes well shunn'd, have steer'd between
These dangerous rocks, and held the golden mean:
Sense in their works maintains her proper state,
But never sleeps, or labours with her weight;
Grace makes the whole look elegant and gay,
But never dares from Sense to run astray:
So nice the master's touch, so great his care,
The colours boldly glow, not idly glare;
Mutually giving, and receiving aid,
They set each other off like light and shade,
And, as by stealth, with so much softness blend,
'Tis hard to say where they begin or end:
Both give us charms, and neither gives offence;
Sense perfects grace, and grace enlivens sense.

Peace to the men who these high honours claim,
Health to their souls, and to their memories fame:
Be it my task, and no mean task, to teach
A reverence for that worth I cannot reach:
Let me at distance, with a steady eye,
Observe and mark their passage to the sky;
From envy free, applaud such rising worth,
And praise their heaven though pinion'd down to earth.

Had I the power I could not have the time,
Whilst spirits flow, and life is in her prime,
Without a sin 'gainst pleasure, to design

A plan, to methodize each thought, each line,
Highly to finish, and make every grace,
In itself charming, take new charms from place.
Nothing of books, and little known of men,
When the mad fit comes on, I seize the pen,
Rough as they run, the rapid thoughts set down,
Rough as they run, discharge them on the town;
Hence rude unfinished brats, before their time,
Are born into this idle world of Rhyme,
And the poor slattern Muse is brought to bed
"With all her imperfections on her head."

171 Notwithstanding this declaration, Churchill's reading was considerable. His knowledge was general and extensive; though not of the most profound or scientific nature. What Prior said of the Duke of Dorset, might with equal propriety be applied to our author; "Contemnebat potius literas quam nesciebat."

173 Churchill wrote with great rapidity, and frequently composed two hundred lines in Hudibrastic measure in the course of a few hours; and no sooner were they composed than the press discharged them on the town.

178 In "The Patriot Poet, a Satire inscribed to the Rev. Mr. Churchill, by a Country Curate," there occurs a happy imitation of the slovenly style too frequently adopted by him.

"O thou sonorous Churchill, teach my line
To flow exuberantly wild like thine,
Teach me to twist a thought a thousand ways,
And string with idle particles my lays,
That one poor sentiment exhausted, when
The weary reader hopes a respite, then
I may spring on with force redoubled, till
I break him panting breathless to my will;
And make him, tired in periods of a mile,
Gape in deep wonder at my *rapid* style."

Some, as no life appears, no pulses play
Through the dull dubious mass, no breath makes way,
Doubt, greatly doubt, till for a glass they call,
Whether the child can be baptized at all;
Others, on other grounds, objections frame,
And, granting that the child may have a name,
Doubt, as the sex might well a midwife pose,
Whether they should baptize it verse or prose.
E'en what my masters please; bards, mild, meek men,
In love to critics stumble now and then.
Something I do myself, and something too,
If they can do it, leave for them to do.
In the small compass of my careless page
Critics may find employment for an age:
Without my blunders they were all undone;
I twenty feed where Mason can feed one.
When Satire stoops, unmindful of her state,
To praise the man I love, curse him I hate;
When sense, in tides of passion borne along,
Sinking to prose, degrades the name of song:
The censor smiles, and whilst my credit bleeds,
With as high relish on the carrion feeds
As the proud Earl fed at a turtle feast,
Who turn'd by gluttony to worse than beast,

181 A common mode of ascertaining whether there are any sparks of life remaining either in an infant or adult person, is by applying a glass to the face of such person to observe whether dew settles on it, formed by the breath of the subject of the experiment.

Ate till his bowels gush'd upon the floor,
Yet still ate on, and dying call'd for more.
When loose Digression, like a colt unbroke,
Spurning connection and her formal yoke,
Bounds through the forest, wanders far astray
From the known path, and loves to lose her way,
'Tis a full feast to all the mongrel pack
To run the rambler down and bring her back.
When gay Description, Fancy's fairy child,
Wild without art, and yet with pleasure wild,
Waking with Nature at the morning hour
To the lark's call, walks o'er the opening flower
Which largely drank all night of heaven's fresh dew,
And, like a mountain nymph of Dian's crew,
So lightly walks she not one mark imprints,
Nor brushes off the dews, nor soils the tints;
When thus description sports, even at the time
That drums should beat and cannons roar in ryhme,
Critics can live on such a fault as that
From one month to the other and grow fat.
Ye mighty Monthly Judges! in a dearth
Of letter'd blockheads, conscious of the worth
Of my materials, which against your will
Oft you've confess'd, and shall confess it still;
Materials rich, though rude, inflamed with thought,
Though more by fancy than by judgment wrought;
Take, use them as your own, a work begin,
Which suits your genius well, and weave them in,
Framed for the critic loom with critic art,
Till thread on thread depending, part on part,

Colour with colour mingling, light with shade,
To your dull taste a formal work is made,
And, having wrought them into one grand piece,
Swear it surpasses Rome, and rivals Greece.
Nor think this much, for at one single word,
Soon as the mighty critic fiat's heard,
Science attends their call; their power is own'd;
Order takes place, and Genius is dethroned!
Letters dance into books, defiance hurl'd
At means, as atoms danced into a world.
Me higher business calls, a greater plan,
Worthy man's whole employ, the good of man,
The good of man committed to my charge;
If idle Fancy rambles forth at large,
Careless of such a trust, these harmless lays
May Friendship envy, and may Folly praise;
The crown of Gotham may some Scot assume,
And vagrant Stuarts reign in Churchill's room.
O my poor People! O thou wretched Earth!
To whose dear love, though not engaged by birth,
My heart is fix'd, my service deeply sworn,
How, (by thy father can that thought be borne,
For monarchs, would they all but think like me,
Are only fathers in the best degree)
How must thy glories fade, in every land
Thy name be laugh'd to scorn, thy mighty hand
Be shorten'd, and thy zeal, by foes confess'd,
Bless'd in thyself, to make thy neighbours bless'd,
Be robb'd of vigour; how must Freedom's pile,
The boast of ages, which adorn the Isle,
And makes it great and glorious, fear'd abroad.

Happy at home, secure from force and fraud;
How must that pile, by ancient Wisdom raised
On a firm rock, by friends admired and praised,
Envied by foes, and wonder'd at by all,
In one short moment into ruins fall,
Should any slip of Stuart's tyrant race,
Or bastard or legitimate, disgrace
Thy royal seat of empire! but what care,
What sorrow, must be mine, what deep despair
And self-reproaches, should that hated line
Admittance gain through any fault of mine!
Cursed be the cause whence Gotham's evils spring,
Though that cursed cause be found in Gotham's king.

Let War, with all his needy ruffian band,
In pomp of horror stalk through Gotham's land
Knee-deep in blood, let all her stately towers
Sink in the dust; that court which now is ours
Become a den, where beasts may, if they can,
A lodging find, nor fear rebuke from man;
Where yellow harvests rise be brambles found;
Where vines now creep let thistles curse the ground;
Dry in her thousand valleys be the rills;
Barren the cattle on her thousand hills:
Where Power is placed let tigers prowl for prey;
Where Justice lodges let wild asses bray;
Let cormorants in churches make their nest,
And on the sails of commerce bitterns rest;
Be all, though princes in the earth before,
Her merchants bankrupts, and her marts no more;

Much rather would I, might the will of Fate
Give me to choose, see Gotham's ruin'd state
By ills on ills, thus to the earth weigh'd down,
Than live to see a Stuart wear a crown.

Let Heaven in vengeance arm all Nature's host,
Those servants who their Maker know, who boast
Obedience as their glory, and fulfil,
Unquestion'd, their great Master's sacred will;
Let raging winds root up the boiling deep,
And with destruction big o'er Gotham sweep;
Let rains rush down, till Faith, with doubtful eye,
Looks for the sign of mercy in the sky;
Let Pestilence in all her horrors rise;
Where'er I turn, let Famine blast my eyes;
Let the earth yawn, and, ere they've time to think,
In the deep gulf let all my subjects sink
Before my eyes, whilst on the verge I reel;
Feeling, but as a monarch ought to feel,
Not for myself, but them, I'll kiss the rod,
And, having own'd the justice of my God,
Myself with firmness to the ruin give,
And die with those for whom I wish to live.

This, (but may Heaven's more merciful decrees
Ne'er tempt his servant with such ills as these)
This, or my soul deceives me, I could bear,
But that the Stuart race my crown should wear;
That crown, where, highly cherish'd, Freedom shone
Bright as the glories of the mid-day sun;

Born and bred slaves, that they, with proud mis-rule,
Should make brave freeborn men, like boys at school,
To the whip crouch and tremble—O, that thought!
The labouring brain is e'en to madness brought
By the dread vision; at the mere surmise
The thronging spirits, as in tumult, rise;
My heart as for a passage, loudly beats,
And turn me where I will, distraction meets.
O, my brave fellows! great in arts and arms,
The wonder of the earth, whom glory warms
To high achievements; can your spirits bend,
Through base control (ye never can descend
So low by choice) to wear a tyrant's chain,
Or let in Freedom's seat a Stuart reign?
If Fame, who hath for ages, far and wide,
Spread in all realms the cowardice, the pride,
The tyranny and falsehood of those lords,
Contents you not, search England's fair records;
England, where first the breath of life I drew,
Where next to Gotham, my best love is due;
There once they ruled, though crush'd by William's hand,
They ruled no more to curse that happy land.
The first, who, from his native soil removed,

348 To confirm this faithful character of James the First, we must refer our readers not to Hume, whose national and political prejudices concurred in prompting him to palliate the vices of all the Stuarts; but to his countryman, Bishop

Held England's sceptre, a tame tyrant proved:
Virtue he lack'd, cursed with those thoughts which
spring
In souls of vulgar stamp to be a king:
Spirit he had not, though he laugh'd at laws,
To play the bold-face tyrant with applause;
On practices most mean he raised his pride,
And Craft oft gave what Wisdom oft denied.
Ne'er could he feel how truly man is blest
In blessing those around him; in his breast,
Crowded with follies, Honour found no room;
Mark'd for a coward in his mother's womb,
He was too proud without affronts to live,
Too timorous to punish or forgive.
  To gain a crown, which had in course of time,
By fair descent, been his without a crime,
He bore a mother's exile; to secure
A greater crown, he basely could endure
The spilling of her blood by foreign knife,
Nor dared revenge her death, who gave him life:

Burnet, who honestly avows his prejudices, but wants the art and ingenuity of a Hume to gloss them over, and deceive the unwary reader with a shew of impartiality. Hume's character of James the First is an insult to every man of understanding, who has made that disgraceful reign an object of his research; facts are distorted, omitted, doubted, or contradicted, as they tend to the dishonour of that monarch; whilst the praises of sagacity, learning and humanity are with no sparing hand bestowed upon the most contemptible of sovereigns. Burnet sums up the habitual character of James in these few words, "His reign in England was one continued course of mean practices."

Nay, by fond Fear, and fond Ambition led,
Struck hands with those by whom her blood was shed.
Call'd up to power, scarce warm on England's throne,
He fill'd her court with beggars from his own:
Turn where you would the eye with Scots was caught,
Or English knaves, who would be Scotsmen thought,
To vain expense unbounded loose he gave,
The dupe of minions, and of slaves the slave;
On false pretences mighty sums he raised,
And damn'd those senates rich, whom poor he praised:
From empire thrown, and doom'd to beg her bread,
On foreign bounty whilst a daughter fed,
He lavish'd sums, for her received, on men
Whose names would fix dishonour on my pen.
  Lies were his playthings, parliaments his sport;

364 Secretary Cecil, who had been a principal agent in the cruel and vindictive proceedings, as well against Mary Queen of Scots, as against her gallant admirer, the Duke of Norfolk, was continued in his employments by her son, and enjoyed his confidence on his accession to the throne of England.

375 The sums of money liberally voted by parliament for the support of the Elector Palatine, titular king of Bohemia, the son-in-law of James, were shamelessly squandered among his Scotch minions.

377 King James was early initiated into that species of king-craft which consists in denying, or suffering to be imputed to the servants of the crown, conduct which might too palpably disgrace the wearer of it.

Book-worms and catamites engross'd the court:
Vain of the scholar, like all Scotsmen since,
The pedant scholar, he forgot the prince;
And having with some trifles stored his brain,
Ne'er learned, nor wish'd to learn, the arts to reign,
Enough he knew, to make him vain and proud,
Mock'd by the wise, the wonder of the crowd;
False friend, false son, false father, and false king,
False wit, false statesman, and false everything:
When he should act he idly chose to prate,
And pamphlets wrote when he should save the state.
  Religious, if religion holds in whim,
To talk with all, he let all talk with him;
Not on God's honour, but his own intent,
Not for religion's sake, but argument;
More vain if some sly, artful High-Dutch slave,
Or, from the Jesuit school, some precious knave
Conviction feign'd, than if, to peace restored
By his full soldiership, worlds hail'd him Lord.
  Power was his wish, unbounded as his will,
The power, without control, of doing ill;
But what he wish'd, what he made bishops preach,
And statesmen warrant, hung within his reach,
He dared not seize; fear gave, to gall his pride,

385 Alluding to the sudden death of Henry, Prince of Wales, whom contemporary writers agree in representing as having, by his superior abilities, incurred the fear, envy, and hatred of his father. Hume observes, that "the bold and criminal malignity of men's tongues spared not even the king on the occasion."

That freedom to the realm his will denied.
Of treaties fond, o'erweening of his parts,
In every treaty, of his own mean arts
He fell the dupe: peace was his coward care,
E'en at a time when justice call'd for war:
His pen he'd draw to prove his lack of wit,
But rather than unsheath the sword, submit.
Truth fairly must record; and, pleased to live
In league with mercy, justice may forgive
Kingdoms betray'd, and worlds resigned to Spain,
But never can forgive a Raleigh slain.
At length, (with white let Freedom mark that year,)

403 The following anecdote has been often related of the ridicule which attached to the timid foreign policy of James the First. In a farce, acted at Brussels, a courier was introduced bringing the doleful news that the Palatinate would soon be wrested from the house of Austria, so powerful were the succours which from all quarters were hastening to the relief of the despoiled elector. The King of Denmark had agreed to contribute to his assistance one hundred thousand pickled herrings; the Dutch one hundred thousand butter-firkins; and the King of England one hundred ambassadors. On other occasions he was painted with a scabbard, but without a sword; or with a sword which nobody could draw, though several were pulling at it.

408 Sir Kenelm Digby says that when James, who had an antipathy to a sword, dubbed him a knight, had not the Duke of Buckingham guided his hand aright, in lieu of touching his shoulder he had certainly run the point of it into his eye.

412 The mean sacrifice of Raleigh to the fears and resentment of the Spanish court is too generally known and execrated to require any further illustration here.

Hume passes no direct censure on this act of atrocious murder, but only observes that it incurred public dissatisfaction.

Nor fear'd by those whom most he wish'd to fear,
Not loved by those whom most he wish'd to love,
He went to answer for his faults above,
To answer to that God from whom alone
He claim'd to hold and to abuse the throne,
Leaving behind, a curse to all his line,
The bloody legacy of Right Divine.
With many virtues which a radiance fling
Round private men, with few which grace a king,
And speak the monarch, at that time of life
When passion holds with reason doubtful strife,
Succeeded Charles, by a mean sire undone,

" Sir Walter Raleigh was tried as an accomplice in the pretended conspiracy of Arabella Stuart. No sufficient evidence appeared against him, nevertheless he was convicted of high treason and suffered an imprisonment of thirteen years in the tower; at length he was released and commissioned to proceed in search of the gold mine in Guiana, but could not obtain a pardon. Upon the return of that great man, James, to satisfy the court of Spain for the depredations he had committed in the Indies, used the power he had reserved in his hands, and signed the warrant for his execution upon his former sentence. No measure of James's reign was attended with more public dissatisfaction than the execution of Sir Walter Raleigh. To execute a sentence which was originally too severe, which had been so long suspended, and which seemed to be tacitly pardoned by conferring on him a new trust and commission, was deemed an instance of cruelty and oppression."

420 The prerogative of the crown was represented by lawyers as something real and durable like those eternal essences of the schools which no time or force could alter. The sanction of religion was by divines called in aid, and the monarch of heaven was supposed to be interested in supporting the authority of his earthly vicegerent. *Hume.*

Who envied virtue even in a son.
His youth was froward, turbulent, and wild;
He took the man up ere he left the child;
His soul was eager for imperial sway
Ere he had learn'd the lesson to obey.
Surrounded by a fawning, flattering throng,
Judgment each day grew weak, and humour strong;
Wisdom was treated as a noisome weed,
And all his follies let to run to seed.
What ills from such beginnings needs must spring?
What ills to such a land from such a king!
What could she hope! what had she not to fear!
Base Buckingham possess'd his youthful ear;
Strafford and Laud, when mounted on the throne
Engross'd his love, and made him all their own;
Strafford and Laud, who boldly dared avow
The traitorous doctrine taught by Tories now;
Each strove t' undo him in his turn and hour,
The first with pleasure and the last with power.
Thinking (vain thought, disgraceful to the throne!)

438 George Villiers, Duke of Buckingham, raised to that exalted rank from the condition of a page, by the infatuated and perverted affection of James, succeeded to an uncontrolled influence over the more amiable Charles, and was a principal cause of the early unpopularity of his young master. "Buckingham was in no wise entitled by his birth, age, services, or merit, to the unlimited confidence reposed in him. To be sacrificed to the interest, policy, and ambition of the great, is so much the common lot of the people, that they may appear unreasonable who pretend to complain of it: but

That all mankind were made for kings alone,
That subjects were but slaves, and what was whim,
Or worse, in common men, was law in him;
Drunk with Prerogative, which Fate decreed
To guard good kings, and tyrants to mislead;
Which in a fair proportion to deny
Allegiance dares not, which to hold too high
No good can wish, no coward king can dare,
And held too high no English subject bear;
Besieged by men of deep and subtle arts,
Men void of principle, and damn'd with parts,
Who saw his weakness, made their king their tool,
Then most a slave when most he seem'd to rule:
Taking all public steps for private ends,
Deceived by favourites, whom he call'd friends.
He had not strength enough of soul to find
That monarchs, meant as blessings to mankind,
Sink their great state, and stamp their fame undone,
When what was meant for all, they give to one.

to be the victim of the frivolous gallantry of a favourite, and of his boyish caprices, seemed the object of peculiar indignation." *Hume.*

The following lines, written by our author, were engraved on a cup of £500 value, presented by a Mr. Stephenson, of Ludgate Hill, to Mr. Wilkes:

Proud Buckingham, for law too mighty grown,
A patriot dagger probed, and from the throne
Sever'd its minion. In succeeding times
May all those favourites who adopt his crimes,
Partake his fate, and every Villiers feel
The keen deep searchings of a Felton's steel.

Listening uxorious whilst a woman's prate
Modell'd the church and parcell'd out the state,
Whilst (in the state not more than women read)
High-churchmen preach'd, and turn'd his pious
head.
Tutor'd to see with ministerial eyes,
Forbid to hear a loyal nation's cries;
Made to believe (what can't a favourite do)
He heard a nation, hearing one or two;
Taught by state-quacks himself secure to think,
And out of danger e'en on danger's brink;
Whilst power was daily crumbling from his hand,
Whilst murmurs ran through an insulted land,
As if to sanction tyrants Heaven was bound,
He proudly sought the ruin which he found.

465 The intriguing character and religious prejudices of Henrietta, contributed in no small degree to the melancholy fate of her deluded husband. Her unconquerable spirit sustained her under the most aggravated circumstances of poverty and distress, which she endured for a series of years: but her fortitude was at length recompensed by witnessing the restoration of her son; an event which she survived upwards of nine years, during which period she resumed her influence over the affairs of England, and by her rooted predilection for France and popery, rendered her eldest son odious, and paved the way for the removal of her youngest. Hume thus glosses over her fatal influence and pernicious counsels: "It is allowed that, being of a passionate temper, she precipitated him into hasty and imprudent counsels. Her religion likewise, to which she was much addicted, must be regarded as a great misfortune, since it augmented the jealousy which prevailed against the court, and engaged her to procure for the Catholics some indulgences which were generally distasteful to the nation."

Twelve years, twelve tedious and inglorious years,
Did England, crush'd by power, and awed by fears,
Whilst proud Oppression struck at Freedom's root,
Lament her senates lost, her Hampden mute:
Illegal taxes and oppressive loans,
In spite of all her pride, call'd forth her groans;
Patience was heard her griefs aloud to tell,
And Loyalty was tempted to rebel.
  Each day new acts of outrage shook the state,
New courts were raised to give new doctrines
      weight;
State-Inquisitions kept the realm in awe,
And cursed Star-Chambers made or ruled the law,
Juries were pack'd, and judges were unsound;

479 From 1628 to 1640 no parliament was summoned, and every endeavour was in that interval used to obtain money from the people by the most vexatious and oppressive exactions, without their consent, by their representatives. Arbitrary courts were erected, and the power of others enlarged; such were the high commission court, the star-chamber, the court of honour, the court of wards, the court of requests, &c. Patents and monopolies of almost every article were sold to individuals to the great injury of the public; knighthood, coat and conduct money, forced loans, benevolences, arbitrary imprisonments, billeting of soldiers, martial law, and many other illegal methods were revived or invented to extort money from the people, in order to support the profusion of the court.

491 Lord Keeper Finch invented the famous expedient of ship money, and by his solicitation and importunities prevailed upon the major part of the judges of Westminster Hall, to declare as law in Hampden's case: that "for the supply of shipping to defend the nation, the king might impose a tax upon the people; that he was to be the judge of the necessity

Through the whole kingdom not one Pratt was found.
From the first moments of his giddy youth
He hated senates, for they told him truth:
At length against his will compell'd to treat,
Those whom he could not fright he strove to cheat,
With base dissembling every grievance heard,
And often giving, often broke his word.
Oh where shall hapless Truth for refuge fly,
If kings, who should protect her, dare to lie?
Those who, the general good their real aim,
Sought in their country's good their monarch's fame;
Those who were anxious for his safety; those
Who were induced by duty to oppose,
Their truth suspected and their worth unknown,
He held as foes and traitors to his throne,
Nor found his fatal error till the hour
Of saving him was gone and past; till power
Had shifted hands, to blast his hapless reign,

of such supply, and of the quantity to be imposed for it: and that he might imprison as well as distrain in case of refusal. Croke and Hutton were the only judges who ventured to dissent from this doctrine.

500 John, King of France, being dissuaded by his council from his intended journey to England, where he had formerly been captive, under an apprehension that advantage might be taken by Edward, in the treaty then negotiating, of the circumstance of his enemy being in his power, made this noble reply: "That though good faith were banished from the rest of the earth, she ought still to retain her habitation in the breast of princes."

Making their faith and his repentance vain.
Hence (be that curse confined to Gotham's foes)
War, dread to mention, Civil War, arose;
All acts of outrage and all acts of shame
Stalk'd forth at large, disguised with honour's name;
Rebellion, raising high her bloody hand,
Spread universal havoc through the land;
With zeal for party, and with passion drunk,
In public rage all private love was sunk;
Friend against friend, brother 'gainst brother stood,
And the son's weapon drank the father's blood;
Nature, aghast, and fearful lest her reign
Should last no longer, bled in every vein.
Unhappy Stuart! harshly though that name
Grates on my ear, I should have died with shame
To see my king before his subjects stand,
And at their bar hold up his royal hand;
At their commands to hear the monarch plead,
By their decrees to see that monarch bleed!

523-528 Wilkes left the following remark on these lines:—
Sydney and Milton considered the death of Charles the First in a different light. In the Memoirs of Algernon Sydney is a letter of the Earl of Leicester to his son, in which is the following passage: " It is said that a minister who hath married a Lady Lawrence here at Chelsea, but now dwelling at Copenhagen, being there in company with you, said, 'I think you were none of the late king's judges nor guilty of his death.' 'Guilty!' said you, 'do you call that guilt? why it was the justest and bravest action that ever was done in England, or any where else; with other words to the same effect."

What though thy faults were many and were great?
What though they shook the basis of the state?
In royalty secure thy person stood,
And sacred was the fountain of thy blood.
Vile ministers, who dared abuse their trust,
Who dared seduce a king to be unjust, [strong,
Vengeance, with justice leagued, with power made

There is scarcely any thing in the Roman classics superior to the following passage of Milton, conveying his sentiments of the transaction. "Eam animi magnitudinem vobis, ô Cives, injecit Deus ut devictum armis vestris et dedititium regem *judicio inclyto* judicare et condemnatum punire primi mortalium non dubitaretis. Post hoc facinus *tam illustre*, nihil humile aut augustum, nihil non magnum atque excelsum et cogitare et facere debetis—amore libertatis, religionis, justitiæ, honestatis, patriæ denique charitate accensos, *tyrannum punisse.*"

Johannis Miltoni, Angli,
pro populo Anglicano defensio.

Cicero's words relative to the death of Cæsar may in a good measure be applied to the second of the Stuarts, Charles I. Milton, in another place, says that he "was *Ipso Nerone Neronior.*" Istius gloriosissimi facti conscientiâ, omnes boni, quantum in ipsis fuit, Cæsarem occiderunt. Aliis consilium, aliis animus, aliis occasio, defuit; voluntas nemini.

It was the favourite maxim of Brutus, that those who live in defiance of the laws, and cannot be brought to a trial, ought to be taken off without a trial. He therefore first planned, executed and justified the death of Cæsar. The conduct of the English nation, with regard to Charles I. is still clearer. His death can never be pretended to be an assassination. Our genius shudders at a practice, too frequent among our polite neighbours. The king had a legal solemn trial; attended with all the fairness, and even candour, which the circumstances of a people, still in arms for their liberties, could permit.—*Wilkes.*

Had nobly crush'd "The king could do no wrong."
Yet grieve not, Charles! nor thy hard fortunes blame;
They took thy life, but they secured thy fame.
Their greater crimes made thine like specks appear,
From which the sun in glory is not clear.
Hadst thou in peace and years resign'd thy breath;
At Nature's call hadst thou laid down in death,
As in a sleep, thy name by Justice borne
On the four winds, had been in pieces torn.
Pity, the virtue of a generous soul,
Sometimes the vice, hath made thy memory whole.
Misfortunes gave what virtue could not give,
And bade, the tyrant slain, the martyr live.

548 Warburton, in a sermon he preached before the House of Lords, on the 30th January, thus ably delineates the character of Charles.

" The king had many virtues, but all of so unsociable a turn as to do him neither service nor credit.

"His religion, in which he was sincerely zealous, was overrun with scruples; and the simplicity if not the purity of his morals was debased by casuistry.

" His natural affections (a rare virtue in that high situation) were so excessive, as to render him a slave to all his kin; and his social, so moderate, as only to enable him to lament, not to preserve, his friends and servants.

" His knowledge was extensive though not exact, and his courage clear though not keen; yet his modesty far surpassing his magnanimity, his knowledge only made him obnoxious to the doubts of his more ignorant ministers; and his courage to the irresolutions of his less adventurous generals.

" In a word, his princely qualities were neither great enough nor bad enough to succeed in that most difficult of all attempts, the enslaving a free and jealous people."

Ye Princes of the earth! ye mighty few!
Who worlds subduing, can't yourselves subdue;
Who, goodness scorn'd, wish only to be great,
Whose breath is blasting, and whose voice is fate;
Who own no law, no reason, but your will,
And scorn restraint, though 'tis from doing ill;
Who of all passions groan beneath the worst,
Then only bless'd when they make others curst;
Think not, for wrongs like these, unscourged to live;
Long may ye sin, and long may Heaven forgive;
But when ye least expect, in sorrow's day,
Vengeance shall fall more heavy for delay:
Nor think, that vengeance heap'd on you alone
Shall (poor amends) for injured worlds atone;
No, like some base distemper, which remains,
Transmitted from the tainted father's veins
In the son's blood, such broad and general crimes
Shall call down vengeance e'en to latest times,
Call vengeance down on all who bear your name,
And make their portion bitterness and shame.
From land to land for years compell'd to roam,
Whilst Usurpation lorded it at home,
Of majesty unmindful, forced to fly,
Not daring, like a king, to reign or die,
Recall'd to repossess his lawful throne
More at his people's seeking than his own,
Another Charles succeeded. In the school
Of travel he had learn'd to play the fool,
And like pert pupils with dull tutors sent
To shame their country on the Continent,

From love of England by long absence wean'd,
From every court he every folly glean'd,
And was, so close do evil habits cling,
Till crown'd a beggar, and when crown'd, no king.
Those grand and general powers which Heaven design'd
An instance of his mercy to mankind
Were lost, in storms of dissipation hurl'd,
Nor would he give one hour to bless a world;
Lighter than levity which strides the blast,
And of the present fond, forgets the past,
He changed and changed, but every hope to curse,
Changed only from one folly to a worse:
State he resign'd to those whom state could please;
Careless of majesty, his wish was ease;
Pleasure, and pleasure only, was his aim;
Kings of less wit might hunt the bubble fame;
Dignity through his reign was made a sport,
Nor dared Decorum shew her face at court:
Morality, was held a standing jest,
And faith, a necessary fraud at best:
Courtiers, their monarch ever in their view,
Possess'd great talents, and abused them too:
Whate'er was light, impertinent, and vain,
Whate'er was loose, indecent, and profane,
(So ripe was folly, folly to acquit)
Stood all absolved in that poor bauble, wit.
In gratitude, alas! but little read,
He let his father's servants beg their bread

His father's faithful servants and his own,
To place the foes of both around his throne.
Bad counsels he embraced through indolence,
Through love of ease, and not through want of sense;
He saw them wrong, but rather let them go
As right, than take the pains to make them so.
Women ruled all, and ministers of state
Were for commands at toilets forced to wait:
Women, who have as monarchs graced the land,
But never govern'd well at second hand.
To make all other errors slight appear,
In memory fix'd stand Dunkirk and Tangier;

606 The Cavaliers were much disappointed at the neglect their claims experienced at the restoration, and expressed great dissatisfaction at the preferments bestowed upon the Presbyterians, whose adherence to royalty was thus conciliated and confirmed. They said of the "act of oblivion and of indemnity," that the King had passed an act of oblivion for his friends, and of indemnity for his enemies.

The celebrated Dr. Isaac Barrow, in a neat distich conveyed his sense of the inattention he experienced—

Te magis optavit rediturum, Carole, nemo,
Et nemo sensit te rediisse minus.

Oh how my breast did ever burn
To see my lawful king return;
Yet, whilst his happy fate I bless,
No one has felt his influence less.

618 Dunkirk, which was delivered to Cromwell in 1658, was, in 1662, sold by Charles II. to the French for £400,000, which sum was immediately squandered away upon his mis-

In memory fix'd so deep, that time in vain 619
Shall strive to wipe those records from the brain,
Amboyna stands—Gods! that a king could hold
In such high estimate vile paltry gold,
And of his duty be so careless found, 623
That when the blood of subjects from the ground
For vengeance call'd, he should reject their cry,
And, bribed from honour, lay his thunders by,
Give Holland peace, whilst English victims groan'd,
And butcher'd subjects wander'd unatoned!

tresses and their creatures. Hume artfully endeavours to exculpate Charles II. from this measure by imputing it to the advice of Clarendon and the parsimony of Parliament.

618 Tangier, in Africa, formed a part of the dowry brought by Catherine of Portugal to Charles II. Vast sums of money were expended on the fortifications during the space of twenty years, after which, to save the necessity of calling a Parliament for the purpose of obtaining farther supplies for its support, Lord Dartmouth was sent with a fleet to destroy the works, and to bring home all the men, which was effected in 1684.

621 The poet is guilty of an anachronism in imputing to Charles II. a tame submission to insult, of which no one but a James could have been guilty. The dreadful cruelties inflicted by the Dutch upon the English at Amboyna, in 1622, were never surpassed under the Roman Emperors, nor in the cells of the Inquisition. A detailed account of the transaction may be found in the first volume of Harris's Collection of Voyages. As characteristic of the commercial jealousy of the Dutch it is worthy of perusal, but too shocking to admit of an extract; but the steady apologist for all the crimes of the Stuarts endeavours to invent a plausible excuse for the infamous apathy of James.

O dear, deep injury to England's fame,
To them, to us, to all! to him deep shame!
Of all the passions which from frailty spring,
Avarice is that which least becomes a king.
  To crown the whole, scorning the public good,
Which through his reign he little understood,
Or little heeded, with too narrow aim
He reassumed a bigot brother's claim,
And having made time-serving senates bow,
Suddenly died, that brother best knew how.
  No matter how—he slept amongst the dead,
And James his brother reigned in his stead:
But such a reign—so glaring an offence
In every step 'gainst freedom, law, and sense,
'Gainst all the rights of Nature's general plan,
'Gainst all which constitutes an Englishman,
That the relation would mere fiction seem,
The mock creation of a poet's dream;
And the poor bard's would, in this sceptic age,
Appear as false as *their* historian's page.

638 This line appears to imply that Charles was poisoned by his brother; his death was certainly sudden, attended with some suspicious appearances, and happened at a critical period; but Burnet, who cannot be accused of partiality to James, admits that he never heard any one suspect him of being accessory to his brother's death.

648 Mr. Hume, in his History of the House of Stuart, which he published before that of the House of Tudor, has omitted no opportunity that offered for defending or palliating the arbitrary proceedings under the Scottish dynasty, and very ingeniously endeavours to prove that the cruelties exercised by the Dutch on the English factors, at Amboyna, could not be resented as they ought.

Ambitious folly seized the seat of wit,
Christians were forced by bigots to submit;
Pride without sense, without religion zeal,
Made daring inroads on the commonweal;
Stern Persecution raised her iron rod,
And call'd the pride of kings the power of God;
Conscience and fame were sacrificed to Rome,
And England wept at Freedom's sacred tomb.

Her laws despised, her constitution wrench'd
From its due natural frame, her rights retrench'd
Beyond a coward's sufferance, conscience forced,
And healing justice from the crown divorced,
Each moment pregnant with vile acts of power,
Her patriot Bishops sentenced to the Tower,
Her Oxford (who yet loves the Stuart name)
Branded with arbitrary marks of shame,
She wept—but wept not long; to arms she flew,
At Honour's call the avenging sword she drew,

662 Alluding to the circumstances attending the committal to the Tower, and acquittal in 1688 of Dr. Sancroft, Archbishop of Canterbury, Dr. Lloyd, Bishop of St. Asaph, Dr. Ken, Bishop of Bath and Wells, Dr. Turner, Bishop of Ely, Dr. Lake, Bishop of Chichester, Dr. White, Bishop of Peterborough, and Sir Jonathan Trelawney, Bishop of Bristol, who were, to prevent disturbances, carried to the Tower by water, the banks of the Thames being crowded with people imploring their blessing and expressing their indignation at the conduct of the court. Allusion is also made by the Poet to the illegal and violent proceedings adopted by James the Second against the fellows of Magdalen College, Oxford, to compel them to elect a Roman Catholic for their President.

Turn'd all her terrors on the tyrant's head,
And sent him in despair to beg his bread;
Whilst she, (may every state in such distress
Dare with such zeal, and meet with such success)
Whilst she, (may Gotham, should my abject mind
Choose to enslave rather than free mankind,
Pursue her steps, tear the proud tyrant down,
Nor let me wear if I abuse the crown)
Whilst she, (through every age in every land,
Written in gold, let Revolution stand)
Whilst she, secured in liberty and law,
Found what she sought, a saviour in Nassau.

678 The illustrious house of Nassau, by a succession of heroes, established its claim to the gratitude of Europe no less than to that of Holland and of England. As statesmen and as warriors, they, with unequal means but undaunted resolution, extended and confirmed the civil and religious liberties of mankind against the sanguinary and gloomy bigotry of Philip II. and the insatiable ambition of Louis XIV.

A departure in this country from the protestant policy of William III. and an indifference on the part of the modern whigs to the protestant principles of their uncompromising ancestors, has paved the way for a restoration of Popish ascendency and its attendant train of idolatry, ignorance, and superstition, tyranny, and persecution. The whigs were relieved from the odium of being the immediate authors of the fatal measure, which was perpetrated, however, at their instance, by their political opponents, who thus basely sacrificed at once their professed principles and the palladium of British freedom, the best safeguard, under Providence, of the British constitution, on the coward plea of expediency, and in weak and credulous reliance on the proverbial moderation and good faith of Popish priests and jesuits.

SUPPLEMENTAL NOTE.

To complete Churchill's poetical sketch of a portion of the history of England, we subjoin a very ingenious chronological summary of its sovereigns from the Conquest, giving one line only to each reign, and that comprising its most distinguishing event. It was written as a memoriter exercise by Daniel Wray, Esq., F.R.S. in the reign of George the Second; the lines therefore relating to whose successors have been added on the present occasion.

WIL. I. *William* the Norman conquers England's state.
WIL. II. In his own forest, *Rufus* meets his fate.
HEN. I. Though elder Robert lives, *Henry* succeeds.
STEPHEN. For *Stephen's* dubious title Albion bleeds.
HEN. II. Victorious *Henry* bows to Becket's shade.
RICH. I. And *Richard* lion's heart a prisoner's made.
JOHN. Deserted *John* to Rome submits his throne.
HEN. III. Now slave, now tyrant, see his long-lived *Son*.
EDW. I. From *Edward's* hand, Scotland her king receives.
EDW. II. His *Heir* his power to wretched minions gives.
EDW. III. Two captive monarchs grace third *Edward's* train.
RICH. II. *Richard* scarce claims a tear, deposed and slain.
HEN. IV. Domestic foes fourth *Henry's* arms engage.
HEN. V. France feels at Agincourt fifth *Henry's* rage.
HEN. VI. The *Sixth*, France, England, Son, life—all must quit.
EDW. IV. Gay, gallant *Edward*, Love and Conquest greet.
EDW. V. O'er his *boy's* head the crown uncertain hangs.
RICH. III. With royal blood fell *Richard* stains his fangs.
HEN. VII. *Tudor* the roses joins, and faction quells.
HEN. VIII. *Harry's* fierce hah! monks, nuns, and pope expels.
EDW. VI. Religion *Edward's* short-lived bloom deplores.
MARY. *Mary* her Rome with ten-fold rage restores.
ELIZA. *Eliza.* forms the church and humbles Spain.
JAMES I. No kingly virtues mark weak *James's* reign.
CHAS. I. *Charles*, by the axe, before his palace dies.
CROMW. Stern *Cromwell* views the crown with eager eyes.

CHAS. II. False power, false pleasures, flatter *Charles* restored.
JAMES II. 'Gainst *James* law, conscience, freedom draw the sword.
WILL. III. The sword consigned to *William's* patriot hand,
MARY. And *Mary's* virtues save the sinking land.
ANNE. In peace inglorious *Anna's* laurels fade.
GEO. I. See *George* the Brunswick line majestic lead.
GEO. II. Wealth, glory, peace, our second *George* attend.
GEO. III. His grandson three score years his people's friend.
Colonial loss and Gallia's rage sustain'd.
GEO. IV. *George* four, the arts and London's pride maintain'd.
WILL. IV. Reform—the boon from sailor *William* gained.
VICTORIA In prime of youth *Victoria* mounts the throne,
And makes her subjects' willing hearts her own.
In her loved Albert and their blooming race,
Their high descent and higher worth we trace.

Thirty-five sovereigns from the Conqueror to William IV. both inclusive, 1066—1837, give an average of 22 years to each reign.

During the same period thirty-three sovereigns reigned in France, from Philip I. to Charles X. 1061—1830, which increases the average duration of their reigns to upwards of 23 years, but such average is materially affected by the extraordinary fact of the united reigns of Louis XIV. and XV. amounting to 131 years, and which, had it been recorded of some ancient dynasty, would scarcely have obtained credit.

The three longest reigns are those of Henry III. (56) Edward III. (50) and George III. (59) each being the third of his name.

George III. is the only English monarch who was upwards of 80 years of age when he died, and his grandfather George II. and his son William IV. are the only others who attained the age of 70.

GOTHAM.

BOOK III.

Can the fond mother from herself depart?
Can she forget the darling of her heart,
The little darling whom she bore and bred,
Nursed on her knees, and at her bosom fed,
To whom she seem'd her every thought to give,
And in whose life alone she seem'd to live?
Yes, from herself the mother may depart,
She may forget the darling of her heart,
The little darling whom she bore and bred,
Nursed on her knees, and at her bosom fed,
To whom she seem'd her every thought to give,
And in whose life alone she seem'd to live;
But I cannot forget, whilst life remains, [veins,
And pours her current through these swelling
Whilst memory offers up at Reason's shrine;
But I cannot forget that Gotham's mine. [wild,
 Can the stern mother, than the brutes more
From her disnatured breast tear her young child,
Flesh of her flesh, and of her bone the bone,
And dash the smiling babe against a stone?
Yes, the stern mother, than the brutes more wild,
From her disnatured breast may tear her child,
Flesh of her flesh, and of her bone the bone,

1 Isaiah, chap. xlix. v. 15.

And dash the smiling babe against a stone;
But I, (forbid it, Heaven!) but I can ne'er
The love of Gotham from this bosom tear;
Can ne'er so far true royalty pervert
From its fair course, to do my people hurt.
With how much ease, with how much confidence,
As if, superior to each grosser sense
Reason had only, in full power array'd,
To manifest her will, and be obey'd,
Men make resolves, and pass into decrees
The motions of the mind; with how much ease,
In such resolves, doth passion make a flaw,
And bring to nothing what was raised to law!
In empire young, scarce warm on Gotham's throne,
The dangers and the sweets of power unknown,
Pleased, though I scarce know why, like some young child,
Whose little senses each new toy turns wild,
How do I hold sweet dalliance with my crown,
And wanton with dominion, how lay down,
Without the sanction of a precedent,
Rules of most large and absolute extent;
Rules, which from sense of public virtue spring,
And all at once commence a patriot king!
But, for the day of trial is at hand,
And the whole fortunes of a mighty land
Are staked on me, and all their weal or woe
Must from my good or evil conduct flow,

Will I, or can I, on a fair review,
As I assume that name, deserve it too?
Have I well weigh'd the great, the noble, part
I'm now to play? have I explored my heart,
That labyrinth of fraud, that deep, dark cell,
Where, unsuspected e'en by me, may dwell
Ten thousand follies? have I found out there
What I am fit to do, and what to bear?
Have I traced every passion to its rise,
Nor spared one lurking seed of treach'rous vice?
Have I familiar with my nature grown?
And am I fairly to myself made known?
  A patriot king—why, 'tis a name which bears
The more immediate stamp of Heaven; which wears
The nearest, best resemblance we can shew
Of God above, through all his works below.
To still the voice of discord in the land,
To make weak Faction's discontented band,
Detected, weak, and crumbling to decay,
With hunger pinched, on their own vitals prey;
Like brethren, in the selfsame interests warm'd,
Like different bodies with one soul informed;
To make a nation, nobly raised above
All meaner thought, grow up in common love;
To give the laws due vigour, and to hold
That secret balance, temperate, yet bold,
With such an equal hand, that those who fear
May yet approve, and own my justice clear;
To be a common father, to secure

The weak from violence, from pride the poor;
Vice and her sons to banish in disgrace,
To make Corruption dread to shew her face;
To bid afflicted Virtue take new state,
And be at last acquainted with the great;
Of all religions to elect the best,
Nor let her priests be made a standing jest;
Rewards for worth with liberal hand to carve,
To love the arts, nor let the artists starve;
To make fair plenty through the realm increase,
Give fame in war, and happiness in peace;
To see my people virtuous, great and free,
And know that all those blessings flow from me;
O! 'tis a joy too exquisite, a thought
Which flatters Nature more than flattery ought;
'Tis a great, glorious task, for man too hard,
But no less great, less glorious, the reward;
The best reward which here to man is given,
'Tis more than earth, and little short of heaven;
A task (if such comparison may be)
The same in nature, differing in degree,
Like that which God, on whom for aid I call,
Performs with ease, and yet performs to all.
How much do they mistake, how little know
Of kings, of kingdoms, and the pains which flow
From royalty, who fancy that a crown
Because it glistens, must be lined with down!
With outside shew, and vain appearance caught,
They look no farther, and, by Folly taught,
Prize high the toys of thrones, but never find

One of the many cares which lurk behind.
The gem they worship which a crown adorns,
Nor once suspect that crown is lined with thorns.
Oh, might reflection folly's place supply!
Would we one moment use her piercing eye,
Then should we find what woe from grandeur springs,
And learn to pity, not to envy kings.
The villager, born humbly and bred hard,
Content his wealth, and Poverty his guard,
In action simply just, in conscience clear,
By guilt untainted, undisturb'd by fear,
His means but scanty, and his wants but few,
Labour his business, and his pleasure too,
Enjoys more comforts in a single hour
Than ages give the wretch condemn'd to power.
Call'd up by health he rises with the day,
And goes to work, as if he went to play,
Whistling off toil, one half of which might make
The stoutest Atlas of a palace quake:
'Gainst heat and cold, which makes us cowards faint,
Harden'd by constant use, without complaint
He bears what we should think it death to bear:
Short are his meals, and homely is his fare;
His thirst he slakes at some pure neighbouring brook,
Nor asks for sauce where Appetite stands cook.
When the dews fall, and when the sun retires
Behind the mountains, when the village fires,
Which, waken'd all at once, speak supper nigh,

At distance catch, and fix his longing eye,
Homeward he hies, and with his manly brood
Of raw-boned cubs enjoys that clean coarse food
Which, season'd with good humour, his fond
bride
'Gainst his return is happy to provide; [creeps
Then, free from care, and free from thought, he
Into his straw, and till the morning sleeps.
Not so the king—with anxious cares opprest
His bosom labours, and admits not rest:
A glorious wretch; he sweats beneath the weight
Of majesty, and gives up ease for state:
E'en when his smiles, which by the fools of pride
Are treasured and preserved from side to side,
Fly round the court, even when compell'd by
form;
He seems most calm, his soul is in a storm;
Care, like a spectre, seen by him alone,
With all her nest of vipers, round his throne
By day crawls full in view; when night bids
sleep,
Sweet nurse of Nature, o'er the senses creep;
When Misery herself no more complains,
And slaves, if possible, forget their chains; [dim,
Though his sense weakens, though his eyes grow
That rest, which comes to all, comes not to him.
E'en at that hour, Care, tyrant Care, forbids
The dew of sleep to fall upon his lids;
From night to night she watches at his bed;
Now, as one moped, sits brooding o'er his head;

Anon she starts, and, borne on raven's wings,
Croaks forth aloud—Sleep was not made for kings.
  Thrice hath the moon, who governs this vast ball,
Who rules most absolute o'er me and all;
To whom, by full conviction taught to bow,
At new, at full, I pay the duteous vow;
Thrice hath the moon her wonted course pursued,
Thrice hath she lost her form, and thrice renew'd,
Since, (blessed be that season, for before
I was a mere, mere mortal, and no more,

166 "Why rather, sleep, liest thou in smoky cribs,
Upon uneasy pallets stretching thee,
And hush'd with buzzing night-flies to thy slumber;
Than in the perfumed chambers of the great,
Under the canopies of costly state,
And lulled with sounds of sweetest melody?
O thou dull god why liest thou with the vile,
In loathsome beds; and leavest the kingly couch,
A watch-case, or a common larum bell?
Wilt thou upon the high and giddy mast
Seal up the ship-boy's eyes, and rock his brains
In cradle of the rude imperious surge;
And in the visitation of the winds,
Who take the ruffian billows by the top,
Curling their monstrous heads, and hanging them
With deafening clamours in the slippery clouds,
That with the hurly death itself awakes?
Can'st thou, O partial sleep! give thy repose
To the wet sea-boy in an hour so rude,
And, in the calmest and most stilled night,
With all appliances and means to boot,
Deny it to a king?"

Shakspeare, Henry IV. Part II.

One of the herd, a lump of common clay,
Inform'd with life, to die and pass away)
Since I became a king, and Gotham's throne,
With full and ample power became my own;
Thrice hath the moon her wonted course pursued,
Thrice hath she lost her form, and thrice renew'd,
Since sleep, kind sleep! who like a friend supplies
New vigour for new toil, hath closed these eyes:
Nor, if my toils are answered with success,
And I am made an instrument to bless
The people whom I love, shall I repine;
Theirs be the benefit, the labour mine.
  Mindful of that high rank in which I stand,
Of millions lord, sole ruler in the land,
Let me, and Reason shall her aid afford,
Rule my own spirit, of myself be lord.
With an ill grace that monarch wears his crown,
Who, stern and hard of nature, wears a frown
'Gainst faults in other men, yet all the while
Meets his own vices with a partial smile.
How can a king (yet on record we find
Such kings have been, such curses of mankind)
Enforce that law 'gainst some poor subject elf
Which Conscience tells him he hath broke himself?
Can he some petty rogue to justice call
For robbing one, when he himself robs all?
Must not, unless extinguish'd, conscience fly
Into his cheek, and blast his fading eye,
To scourge the oppressor, when the state, distress'd
And sunk to ruin, is by him oppress'd?

Against himself doth he not sentence give;
If one must die, t' other's not fit to live.
  Weak is that throne, and in itself unsound,
Which takes not solid virtue for its ground.
All envy power in others, and complain
Of that which they would perish to obtain.
Nor can those spirits, turbulent and bold,
Not to be awed by threats, nor bought with gold,
Be hush'd to peace, but when fair legal sway
Makes it their real interest to obey,
When kings, and none but fools can then rebel,
Not less in virtue, than in power excel.
  Be that my object, that my constant care,
And may my soul's best wishes centre there;
Be it my task to seek, nor seek in vain,
Not only how to live, but how to reign,
And to those virtues which from reason spring,
And grace the man, join those which grace the king.
  First, (for strict duty bids my care extend
And reach to all, who on that care depend,
Bids me with servants keep a steady hand,
And watch o'er all my proxies in the land)
First, (and that method reason shall support)
Before I look into and purge my court,
Before I cleanse the stable of the state
Let me fix things which to myself relate:
That done, and all accounts well settled here,
In resolution firm, in honour clear,
Tremble, ye slaves! who dare abuse your trust,
Who dare be villains when your king is just.

Are there, amongst those officers of state,
To whom our sacred power we delegate,
Who hold our place and office in the realm,
Who, in our name commissioned, guide the helm;
Are there who, trusting to our love of ease,
Oppress our subjects, wrest our just decrees,
And make the laws, warped from their fair intent,
To speak a language which they never meant;
Are there such men, and can the fools depend
On holding out in safety to their end?
Can they so much, from thoughts of danger free,
Deceive themselves, so much misdeem of me,
To think that I will prove a statesman's tool,
And live a stranger where I ought to rule?
What! to myself and to my state unjust,
Shall I from ministers take things on trust,
And, sinking low the credit of my throne,
Depend upon dependants of my own?
Shall I, most certain source of future cares,
Not use my judgment, but depend on theirs?
Shall I, true puppet-like, be mocked with state,
Have nothing but the name of being great;
Attend at councils which I must not weigh,
Do what they bid, and what they dictate, say,
Enrobed, and hoisted up into my chair,
Only to be a royal cipher there?
Perish the thought—'tis treason to my throne—
And who but thinks it, could his thoughts be known,

Insults me more than he, who leagued with Hell,
Shall rise in arms, and 'gainst my crown rebel.
The wicked statesman, whose false heart pursues
A train of guilt, who acts with double views,
And wears a double face; whose base designs
Strike at his monarch's throne; who undermines
E'en whilst he seems his wishes to support;
Who seizes all departments; packs a court;
Maintains an agent on the judgment-seat
To screen his crimes, and make his frauds complete;
New-models armies, and around the throne
Will suffer none but creatures of his own;
Conscious of such his baseness, well may try,
Against the light to shut his master's eye,
To keep him coop'd, and far removed from those
Who, brave and honest, dare his crimes disclose,
Nor ever let him in one place appear,
Where truth, unwelcome truth, may wound his ear.
Attempts like these, well weigh'd, themselves proclaim,
And, whilst they publish, baulk their author's aim,
Kings must be blind into such snares to run,
Or, worse, with open eyes must be undone.
The minister of honesty and worth
Demands the day to bring his actions forth;
Calls on the sun to shine with fiercer rays,
And braves that trial which must end in praise.

None fly the day, and seek the shades of night,
But those whose actions cannot bear the light;
None wish their king in ignorance to hold
But those who feel that knowledge must unfold
Their hidden guilt; and, that dark mist dispell'd
By which their places and their lives are held,
Confusion wait them, and, by justice led,
In vengeance fall on every traitor's head.
Aware of this, and caution'd 'gainst the pit
Where kings have oft been lost, shall I submit,
And rust in chains like these? shall I give way,
And whilst my helpless subjects fall a prey
To power abused, in ignorance sit down,
Nor dare assert the honour of my crown?
When stern rebellion, (if that odious name
Justly belongs to those whose only aim,
Is to preserve their country; who oppose,
In honour leagued, none but their country's foes;
Who only seek their own, and found their cause
In due regard for violated laws)
When stern rebellion, who no longer feels
Nor fears rebuke, a nation at her heels,
A nation up in arms, though strong not proud,
Knocks at the palace gate, and, calling loud
For due redress, presents, from truth's fair pen,
A list of wrongs, not to be borne by men:
How must that king be humbled, how disgrace
All that is royal in his name and place,
Who, thus call'd forth to answer, can advance
No other plea but that of ignorance!
A vile defence, which, was his all at stake,

The meanest subject well might blush to make;
A filthy source from whence shame ever springs;
A stain to all, but most a stain to kings.
The soul, with great and manly feelings warm'd,
Panting for knowledge, rests not till inform'd;
And shall not I, fired with the glorious zeal,
Feel those brave passions which my subjects feel?
Or can a just excuse from ignorance flow
To me, whose first great duty is—to know?
  Hence, ignorance:—thy settled, dull, blank eye,
Would hurt me, though I knew no reason why—
Hence, Ignorance!—thy slavish shackles bind
The free-born soul, and lethargise the mind—
Of thee, begot by Pride, who look'd with scorn
On every meaner match, of thee was born
That grave inflexibility of soul
Which Reason can't convince, nor fear control;
Which neither arguments, nor prayers can reach,
And nothing less than utter ruin teach—
Hence, Ignorance!—hence to that depth of night
Where thou wast born, where not one gleam of light
May wound thine eye—hence to some dreary cell
Where monks with superstition love to dwell;
Or in some college soothe thy lazy pride,
And with the heads of colleges reside;
Fit mate for Royalty thou canst not be,
And if not mate for kings, no mate for me.
  Come, Study! like a torrent swell'd with rains,
Which rushing down the mountains, o'er the plains,

Spreads horror wide, and yet, in horror kind,
Leaves seeds of future fruitfulness behind;
Come, Study!—painful though thy course, and slow,
Thy real worth by thy effects we know—
Parent of Knowledge, come—not thee I call
Who, grave and dull, in college or in hall
Dost sit, all solemn sad, and moping, weigh
Things which, when found, thy labours can't repay—
Nor in one hand, fit emblem of thy trade,
A rod; in t' other, gaudily array'd,
A hornbook, gilt and letter'd, call I thee,
Who dost in form preside o'er A, B, C—
Nor (Siren though thou art, and thy strange charms,
As 'twere by magic, lure men to thine arms)
Do I call thee, who, through a winding maze,
A labyrinth of puzzling pleasing ways,
Dost lead us at the last to those rich plains,
Where, in full glory, real Science reigns;
Fair though thou art, and lovely to mine eye,
Though full rewards in thy possession lie
To crown man's wish, and do thy favourites grace,
Though, (was I station'd in an humbler place)
I could be ever happy in thy sight,
Toil with thee all the day, and through the night,
Toil on from watch to watch, bidding my eye,
Fast riveted on science, sleep defy,
Yet (such the hardships which from empire flow)
Must I thy sweet society forego,

And to some happy rival's arms resign
Those charms which can, alas! no more be mine.
No more from hour to hour, from day to day,
Shall I pursue thy steps, and urge my way
Where eager love of science calls; no more
Attempt those paths which man ne'er trod before;
No more the mountain scaled, the desert cross'd
Losing myself, nor knowing I was lost,
Travel through woods, through wilds, from morn to night,
From night to morn, yet travel with delight,
And having found thee, lay me down content,
Own all my toil well paid, my time well spent.
Farewell, ye Muses too,—for such mean things
Must not presume to dwell with mighty kings—
Farewell, ye Muses! though it cuts my heart,
E'en to the quick, we must forever part.
When the fresh morn bade lusty Nature wake;
When the birds, sweetly twittering through the brake,
Tune their soft pipes; when from the neighbouring bloom
Sipping the dew, each zephyr stole perfume;
When all things with new vigour were inspired,
And seem'd to say they never could be tired,
How often have we stray'd, whilst sportive rhyme
Deceived the way, and clipp'd the wings of Time,
O'er hill, o'er dale, how often laugh'd to see
Yourselves made visible to none but me,
The clown, his works suspended, gape and stare,
And seem'd to think that I conversed with air.

When the sun, beating on the parched soil,
Seem'd to proclaim an interval of toil;
When a faint languor crept through every breast,
And things most used to labour wish'd for rest,
How often, underneath a reverend oak,
Where safe and fearless of the impious stroke,
Some sacred Dryad lived: or in some grove
Where, with capricious fingers, Fancy wove
Her fairy bower, whilst Nature all the while
Look'd on, and view'd her mockeries with a smile,
Have we held converse sweet! how often laid,
Fast by the Thames, in Ham's inspiring shade,
Amongst those poets which make up your train,
And, after death, pour forth the sacred strain,
Have I, at your command, in verse grown grey,
But not impair'd, heard Dryden tune that lay
Which might have drawn an angel from his sphere,
And kept him from his office listening here.

422 The two following lines were intended to close this sentence, but Churchill did not think proper to print them:

Whilst Pope with envy stung, inflamed with pride,
Piped to the vacant air on t' other side.

We have before remarked the preference Churchill entertained for Dryden as an original poet when compared with Pope: but while the poems of the latter, the most correct, elegant, and highly finished in our language, breathe the purest morality, the most perfect humanity and benevolence; the author in the commerce of life shewed himself not scrupulously moral, and was a selfish, splenetic, malevolent being. The friends, whom most he loved, Atterbury, Oxford, and Bolingbroke, were the sworn enemies of the liberties of his country, and on them he lavished the sweet incense of a

When dreary Night, with Morpheus in her train,
Led on by Silence to resume her reign,
With darkness covering, as with a robe.
The scene of levity, blank'd half the globe,
How oft, enchanted with your heavenly strains,
Which stole me from myself; which in soft chains
Of music bound my soul; how oft have I,
Sounds more than human floating through the sky,
Attentive sat, whilst Night, against her will,
Transported with the harmony, stood still!
How oft in raptures, which man scarce could bear,
Have I, when gone, still thought the Muses there,
Still heard their music, and, as mute as death,
Sat all attention, drew in every breath,
Lest, breathing all too rudely, I should wound
And mar that magic excellence of sound;
Then, Sense returning with return of day,
Have chid the night, which fled so fast away.

delicate, exquisite praise, which ought only to have been the meed of virtue. That Bolingbroke *thought* for him is generally admitted; and therefore Pope might very well say, speaking of his grotto at Twickenham,

Here, nobly pensive, St. John sate and thought.

St. John continued in his exile, the guide, philosopher and friend of Pope, sent him from France the plan of the Essay on Man, and even sketched out the ornaments. The reasoning part of it the poet did not at first comprehend. Bolingbroke's posthumous works, and the *first* edition of the Essay, fully prove this. Instead of

Let us (since life can little more supply
Than just to look about us and to die)

Such my pursuits, and such my joys of yore,
Such were my mates, but now my mates no more.
Placed out of Envy's walk, (for Envy, sure,
Would never haunt the cottage of the poor, 444
Would never stoop to wound my homespun lays)

> Expatiate free o'er all this scene of man;
> A mighty maze! but not without a plan—

It was at first published,

> A mighty maze! of walks without a plan.

In the fourth epistle likewise these lines of the first edition,

> God sends no ill, 'tis nature lets it fall,
> Or chance escape, and man improves it all.

were in the later editions altered to the four following:

> God sends not ill; if rightly understood,
> Or partial ill is universal good,
> Or change admits, or nature lets it fall,
> Short, and but rare, till man improved it all.

Crousaz wrote against the first impression of the Essay, Warburton ingeniously defended the poem from one of the subsequent editions.

Time has now fixed the standard of public opinion respecting Pope, to whom may be applied the observation of a celebrated foreign writer on the literary character of Fontenelle, "*Il a eté sans contredit au dessus de tous les sçavans (poetes) qui n'ont pas eu le don de l'invention.*"

There were not wanting some whose admiration for Churchill induced them to rate him higher than either Dryden or Pope, as appears from the following extract from a contemporary poetical epistle.

> You'll own the great Churchill possesses, I hope,
> More fancy than Cowley, more numbers than Pope,
> More strength too than Dryden, for think on what's past,
> He has not only rivall'd but beat him at last.

With some few friends, and some small share of praise,
Beneath oppression, undisturb'd by strife,
In peace I trod the humble vale of life.
Farewell, these scenes of ease, this tranquil state;
Welcome the troubles which an empire wait:
Light toys from this day forth I disavow;
They pleased me once, but cannot suit me now:
To common men all common things are free,
What honours them might fix disgrace on me.
Call'd to a throne, and o'er a mighty land
Ordain'd to rule, my head, my heart, my hand,
Are all engross'd; each private view withstood;
And task'd to labour for the public good:
Be this my study; to this one great end
May every thought, may every action tend.
  Let me the page of history turn o'er,
The instructive page, and heedfully explore
What faithful pens of former times have wrote
Of former kings; what they did worthy note
What worthy blame; and from the sacred tomb
Where righteous monarchs sleep, where laurels bloom
Unhurt by time, let me a garland twine
Which, robbing not their fame, may add to mine.
  Nor let me with a vain and idle eye
Glance o'er those scenes, and in a hurry fly
Quick as a post which travels day and night;
Nor let me dwell there, lured by false delight;
And, into barren theory betray'd
Forget that monarchs are for action made.

When amorous Spring, repairing all his charms,
Calls Nature forth from hoary Winter's arms,
Where, like a virgin to some lecher sold,
Three wretched months, she lay benumb'd, and cold;
When the weak flower, which, shrinking from the breath
Of the rude North, and timorous of death,
To its kind mother earth for shelter fled,
And on her bosom hid its tender head,
Peeps forth afresh, and, cheer'd by milder skies,
Bids in full splendour all her beauties rise,
The hive is up in arms—expert to teach,
Nor, proudly, to be taught unwilling, each
Seems from her fellow a new zeal to catch;
Strength in her limbs, and on her wings dispatch,
The bee goes forth; from herb to herb she flies,
From flower to flower, and loads her labouring thighs
With treasured sweets, robbing those flowers, which, left,
Find not themselves made poorer by the theft,
Their scents as lively, and their looks as fair,
As if the pillager had not been there.
Ne'er doth she flit on Pleasure's silken wing;
Ne'er doth she, loitering, let the bloom of Spring
Unrifled pass, and on the downy breast
Of some fair flower indulge untimely rest:
Ne'er doth she, drinking deep of those rich dews
Which chemist Night prepared, that faith abuse
Due to the hive, and, selfish in her toils,

To her own private use convert the spoils:
Love of the stock first call'd her forth to roam,
And to the stock she brings her booty home.
Be this my pattern—as becomes a king,
Let me fly all abroad on Reason's wing:
Let mine eye, like the lightning, through the earth
Run to and fro, nor let one deed of worth,
In any place and time, nor let one man,
Whose actions may enrich dominion's plan,
Escape my note: be all, from the first day
Of Nature to this hour, be all my prey.
From those whom Time, at the desire of Fame,
Hath spared, let Virtue catch an equal flame:
From those who, not in mercy, but in rage,
Time hath reprieved to damn from age to age,
Let me take warning, lesson'd to distil,
And, imitating Heaven, draw good from ill:
Nor let these great researches in my breast
A monument of useless labour rest;
No—let them spread—the effects let Gotham share,
And reap the harvest of their monarch's care:
Be other times, and other countries known,
Only to give fresh blessings to my own.
Let me, (and may that God to whom I fly,
On whom for needful succour I rely
In this great hour, that glorious God of truth,
Through whom I reign, in mercy to my youth,
Assist my weakness, and direct me right;
From every speck which hangs upon the sight
Purge my mind's eye, nor let one cloud remain

To spread the shades of error o'er my brain,)
Let me, impartial, with unwearied thought,
Try men and things; let me, as monarchs ought,
Examine well on what my power depends;
What are the general principles, and ends
Of government; how empire first began;
And wherefore man was raised to reign o'er man.
  Let me consider; as from one great source
We see a thousand rivers take their course,
Dispersed, and into different channels led,
Yet by their parent still supplied and fed,
That government, (though branched out far and wide,
In various modes to various lands applied)
Howe'er it differs in its outward frame,
In the main ground works every where the same;
The same her view, though different her plan,
Her grand and general view—the good of man.
Let me find out, by reason's sacred beams,
What system in itself most perfect seems,
Most worthy man, most likely to conduce
To all the purposes of general use;
Let me find, too, where, by fair reason tried,
It fails, when to particulars applied;
Why in that mode all nations do not join,
And, chiefly, why it cannot suit with mine.
  Let me the gradual rise of empires trace,
Till they seem founded on perfection's base;
Then (for when human things have made their way
To excellence, they hasten to decay)
Let me, whilst observation lends her clue,
Step after step to their decline pursue,

Enabled by a chain of facts to tell
Not only how they rose, but why they fell.
  Let me not only the distempers know
Which in all states from common causes grow,
But likewise those, which, by the will of Fate,
On each peculiar mode of empire wait;
Which in its very constitution lurk,
Too sure at last to do its destined work:
Let me, forewarn'd, each sign, each system learn,
That I my people's danger may discern,
Ere 'tis too late wish'd health to re-assure,
And, if it can be found, find out a cure.
  Let me, (though great, grave brethren of the gown
Preach all faith up, and preach all reason down,
Making those jar, whom reason meant to join,
And vesting in themselves a right divine)
Let me, through reason's glass, with searching eye,
Into the depth of that religion pry
Which law hath sanction'd: let me find out there
What's form, what's essence; what, like vagrant air,
We well may change; and what, without a crime,
Cannot be changed to the last hour of time;
Nor let me suffer that outrageous zeal
Which, without knowledge, furious bigots feel,
Fair in pretence, though at the heart unsound,
These separate points at random to confound.
  The times have been, when priests have dared to tread,
Proud and insulting, on their monarch's head;
When, whilst they made religion a pretence,

Out of the world they banish'd common sense;
When some soft king, too open to deceit,
Easy and unsuspecting join'd the cheat,
Duped by mock piety, and gave his name
To serve the vilest purposes of shame.
Fear not, my People, where no cause of fear
Can justly rise—your king secures you here;
Your king, who scorns the haughty prelate's nod,
Nor deems the voice of priests, the voice of God.
Let me, (though lawyers may perhaps forbid
Their monarch to behold what they wish hid,
And, for the purposes of knavish gain,
Would have their trade a mystery remain)
Let me, disdaining all such slavish awe,
Dive to the very bottom of the law;
Let me (the weak, dead letter left behind)
Search out the principles, the spirit find,
Till, from the parts, made master of the whole,
I see the Constitution's very soul.
Let me, (though statesmen will no doubt resist,
And to my eyes present a fearful list
Of men, whose wills are opposite to mine,
Of men, great men, determined to resign)
Let me, (with firmness, which becomes a king,
Conscious from what a source my actions spring,
Determined not by worlds to be withstood,
When my grand object is my country's good)
Unravel all low ministerial scenes,
Destroy their jobs, lay bare their ways and means,
And trap them step by step; let me well know
How places, pensions, and preferments, go;

Why Guilt's provided for, when Worth is not,
And why one man of merit is forgot;
Let me in peace, in war, supreme preside,
And dare to know my way without a guide.
  Let me, (though Dignity, by nature proud,
Retires from view, and swells behind a cloud,
As if the sun shone with less powerful ray,
Less grace, less glory, shining every day,
Though when she comes forth into public sight,
Unbending as a ghost, she stalks upright,
With such an air as we have often seen,
And often laugh'd at in a tragic queen,
Nor, at her presence, though base myriads crook
The supple knee, vouchsafes a single look)
Let me, (all vain parade, all empty pride,
All terrors of dominion laid aside,
All ornament, and needless helps of art,
All those big looks, which speak a little heart)
Know (which few kings, alas! have ever known)
How affability becomes a throne,
Destroys all fear, bids love with reverence live,
And gives those graces pride can never give.
Let the stern tyrant keep a distant state,
And, hating all men, fear return of hate,
Conscious of guilt, retreat behind his throne,
Secure from all upbraidings but his own:
Let all my subjects have access to me,
Be my ears open as my heart is free;
In full fair tide let information flow;
That evil is half cured, whose cause we know.

And thou, where'er thou art, thou wretched thing,
Who art afraid to look up to a king,
Lay by thy fears—make but thy grievance plain,
And, if I not redress thee, may my reign
Close up that very moment.—To prevent,
The course of Justice, from her fair intent,
In vain my nearest, dearest, friend shall plead,
In vain my mother kneel—my soul may bleed,
But must not change—when Justice draws the dart,
Though it is doom'd to pierce a favourite's heart,
'Tis mine to give it force, to give it aim—
I know it duty, and I feel it fame.

662 The invariable burthen of all that was said or sung by Wilkes and his adherents was the influence of Lord Bute as a favourite, which, although of short duration and rather nominal than real, laid the foundation for that inner cabinet, that power behind the throne, but greater than the throne itself, which existed during much of George the Third's reign, and tended occasionally to counteract the plans of his ostensible and responsible ministers.

THE AUTHOR.

This Poem was published in December 1763, and for it and the Duellist, Churchill obtained from Mr. Flexney and Mr. Kearsley the sum of £450.

The sale was very extensive, and the price of half a crown required for so short a poem rendered it a profitable concern to the booksellers. The Rosciad, a production of nearly four times the length, had been published by Churchill at the moderate price of one shilling, but at that period his name had not risen to that degree of celebrity which afterwards enabled his majesty of Gotham to impose a monthly poll-tax of half a crown upon his liege subjects.

The poem having been announced and advertised long previous to its actual publication, the following friendly epigram was written by Colman:

But where is this Author was promised so long
From Churchill that giant so tall and so strong?
He's sick, Sir, cries one; he's burnt out, cries another,
And the high flame of genius sinks down into smother:
Like the ghost in Cock Lane he has frighten'd us all,
And knock'd us and scratch'd us the great and the small;
But now of his spirit no more we're afraid,
For Parson and Fanny together are laid.

By contemporary critics, "The Author" was considered as the most agreeable and unexceptionable of Churchill's poems, both as regarded the tendency of the subject and the execution, the interests of genius and learning being cordially espoused and powerfully supported, while the contempt of professed ignorance and the shallowness of pretenders to science were justly exposed and lashed by the blameless rod of general satire.

THE AUTHOR.

ACCURSED the man, whom fate ordains, in spite,
And cruel parents teach, to read and write!
What need of letters? wherefore should we spell?
Why write our names? a mark will do as well.
  Much are the precious hours of youth misspent
In climbing learning's rugged steep ascent;
When to the top the bold adventurer's got,
He reigns vain monarch o'er a barren spot,
Whilst in the vale of ignorance below
Folly and vice to rank luxuriance grow;
Honours and wealth pour in on every side,
And proud preferment rolls her golden tide.
  O'er crabbed authors life's gay prime to waste,
To cramp wild genius in the chains of taste,
To bear the slavish drudgery of schools,
And tamely stoop to every pedant's rules;
For seven long years debarr'd of liberal ease,
To plod in college trammels to degrees;
Beneath the weight of solemn toys to groan,
Sleep over books, and leave mankind unknown;
To praise each senior blockhead's threadbare tale,
And laugh till reason blush, and spirits fail;
Manhood with vile submission to disgrace,
And cap the fool, whose merit is his place;

Vice Chancellors, whose knowledge is but small,
And Chancellors who nothing know at all,
Ill-brook'd the generous spirit in those days
When learning was the certain road to praise,
When nobles, with a love of science bless'd,
Approved in others what themselves possess'd.
  But now, when Dullness rears aloft her throne,
When lordly vassals her wide empire own;
When Wit, seduced by Envy, starts aside,
And basely leagues with Ignorance and Pride;
What, now, should tempt us, by false hopes misled,
Learning's unfashionable paths to tread,
To bear those labours which our fathers bore,
That crown withheld, which they in triumph wore?
  When with much pains this boasted learning's got,
'Tis an affront to those who have it not:
In some it causes hate, in others fear,
Instructs our foes to rail, our friends to sneer.
With prudent haste the worldly-minded fool
Forgets the little which he learnt at school:
The elder brother to vast fortunes born,
Looks on all science with an eye of scorn;
Dependent brethren the same features wear,
And younger sons are stupid as the heir.
In senates, at the bar, in church and state,
Genius is vile, and learning out of date.
  Is this—O death to think! is this the land
Where merit and reward went hand in hand?
Where heroes, parent-like, the poet view'd,
By whom they saw their glorious deeds renew'd?

Where poets, true to honour, tuned their lays,
And by their patrons sanctified their praise?
Is this the land, where, on our Spenser's tongue,
Enamour'd of his voice, Description hung?
Where Jonson rigid Gravity beguiled,
Whilst Reason through her critic fences smiled?
Where Nature listening stood whilst Shakspeare
play'd,
And wonder'd at the work herself had made?
Is this the land, where, mindful of her charge
And office high, fair Freedom walk'd at large?
Where, finding in our laws a sure defence,
She mock'd at all restraints, but those of sense?
Where, Health and Honour trooping by her side,
She spread her sacred empire far and wide;
Pointed the way, Affliction to beguile,
And bade the face of Sorrow wear a smile,
Bade those, who dare obey the generous call
Enjoy her blessings, which God meant for all?
Is this the land, where, in some tyrant's reign
When a weak, wicked, ministerial train,
The tools of power, the slaves of interest, plann'd
Their country's ruin, and with bribes unmann'd
Those wretches, who, ordain'd in Freedom's cause,
Gave up our liberties, and sold our laws;
When Power was taught by Meanness where to go,
Nor dared to love the virtue of a foe;
When, like a leperous plague, from the foul head
To the foul heart her sores Corruption spread,
Her iron arm when stern Oppression rear'd,
And Virtue, from her broad base shaken, fear'd

The scourge of Vice; when, impotent and vain,
Poor freedom bow'd the neck to Slavery's chain;
Is this the land, where, in those worst of times,
The hardy poet raised his honest rhymes
To dread rebuke, and bade Controlment speak
In guilty blushes on the villain's cheek;

88 We feel great pleasure in recording the unsullied name of Andrew Marvell as the character here delineated. His spirited efforts to stem the torrent of corruption, and his noble rejection, in the midst of poverty, of the brilliant offers of a Court, must rank him high in the esteem of every lover of his country. Examples of patriotism so disinterested occur too seldom for us not to wish to dwell upon the merits of Andrew Marvell. His style, whether in prose or verse, was fraught with wit and argument. Of his controversy with Archbishop Parker, Dean Swift said, that the "Rehearsal transprosed" was the only instance of an answer which could be read with pleasure, when the publication which occasioned it was forgotten. His Poems have no high polish, but the circumstance of their being exclusively of a political and personal nature will alone sufficiently account for their being now neglected. He represented his native town of Kingston-upon-Hull, in the several parliaments from the restoration till his death in 1678, and received wages during all that time from his constituents. As a senator he steadily pursued the interests of his country, and his high reputation for integrity gave him a weight in the House which no other member possessed. Charles II. was highly pleased with his conversation, and fruitlessly endeavoured to attach him to the court; and sent to him his old schoolfellow, Lord Treasurer Danby, for that purpose, who accordingly paid a visit to Marvell in his garret. At parting, the Lord Treasurer slipped into his hand an order for £1000 and then stepped away to his chariot. Mr. Marvell looking at the paper called after the Treasurer, "my Lord, I request another moment." Danby mounted again to Mr. Marvell's apartment, and Jack the footboy was called. "Jack,

Bade Power turn pale, kept mighty rogues in awe,
And made them fear the Muse, who fear'd not law?
How do I laugh, when men of narrow souls,
Whom folly guides and prejudice controls;
Who, one dull drowsy track of business trod,
Worship their Mammon, and neglect their God;
Who, breathing by one musty set of rules,

child, what had I for dinner yesterday?" "Don't you remember, Sir, you had the little shoulder of mutton you ordered me to bring from a woman in the market." "Very right, child, what have I for dinner to-day?" "Don't you know, Sir, that you bid me lay by the blade bone to broil." "It is so, child, very right, go away." "My Lord," added Mr. Marvell, addressing himself to the Treasurer, "do you hear that Andrew's dinner is provided, there is your piece of paper, I want it not. I know the sort of kindness intended, I live here to serve my constituents. The ministry may seek men for their purpose, I am not one!"

In 1688 a subscription was raised at Hull for the purpose of erecting a monument with a suitable inscription to his memory, but the rector of that place insisted upon refusing admission into his church of any memorial of so obstinate a whig.

Mason, in one of his Odes, pays the following appropriate and elegant tribute to the distinguished honesty of Andrew Marvell:

Pointed with Satire's keenest steel,
The shafts of wit he darts around;
E'en mitred dullness learns to feel,
And shrinks beneath the wound.
In awful poverty his honest muse
Walks forth vindictive through a venal land,
In vain corruption sheds her golden dews,
In vain oppression lifts her iron hand;
He scorns them both, and arm'd with truth alone,
Bids lust and folly tremble on the throne.

Dote from their birth, and are by system fools;
Who, form'd to dullness from their very youth,
Lies of the day prefer to Gospel-truth;
Pick up their little knowledge from Reviews,
And lay out all their stock of faith in news;
How do I laugh, when creatures, form'd like these,
Whom Reason scorns, and I should blush to please,
Rail at all liberal arts, deem verse a crime,
And hold not truth, as truth, if told in rhyme?
How do I laugh, when Publius, hoary grown
In zeal for Scotland's welfare, and his own,
By slow degrees, and course of office, drawn
In mood and figure at the helm to yawn,
Too mean (the worst of curses Heaven can send)
To have a foe, too proud to have a friend;
Erring by form, which blockheads sacred hold,
Ne'er making new faults, and ne'er mending old,
Rebukes my spirit, bids the daring Muse
Subjects more equal to her weakness choose;
Bids her frequent the haunts of humble swains,
Nor dare to traffic in ambitious strains;
Bids her, indulging the poetic whim
In quaint-wrought ode, or sonnet pertly trim,
Along the church-way path complain with Gray,
Or dance with Mason on the first of May?

107 Dr. Smollett, then editor in chief of the Critical Review.

122 Gray's fame as a poet is invulnerable, and may well defy the off-hand sallies of Churchill, when it has survived the more deliberate but equally impotent attacks of Johnson. Mason comparatively feeble and very affected, laid himself

"All sacred is the name and power of kings;
All states and statesmen are those mighty things
Which, howsoe'er they out of course may roll,
Were never made for poets to control."
Peace, peace, thou Dotard, nor thus vilely deem
Of sacred numbers, and their power blaspheme.
I tell thee, Wretch, search all creation round,
In earth, in heaven, no subject can be found
(Our God alone except) above whose weight
The poet cannot rise, and hold his state.
The blessed saints above, in numbers, speak
The praise of God, though there all praise is weak;
In numbers here below the bard shall teach
Virtue to soar beyond the villain's reach;
Shall tear his labouring lungs, strain his hoarse throat,
And raise his voice beyond the trumpet's note,
Should an afflicted country, awed by men
Of slavish principles, demand his pen,
This is a great, a glorious point of view,
Fit for an English poet to pursue,
Undaunted to pursue, though, in return,

more open to animadversion. Boswell relates that mention having been made in Johnson's company, of Mason's prosecution of Mr. Murray the Bookseller, the father of the late eminent publisher, for an alleged piracy of about fifty lines only of Gray's Poems, in which Mason had an exclusive copyright, Johnson signified his displeasure at Mason's conduct very strongly, but added, by way of shewing that he was not surprised at it, "Mason is a whig." Mrs. Knowles (not hearing distinctly) said, "What, a prig, Sir!" Johnson, "Worse, Madam!—a whig, but he is both."

His writings by the common hangman burn.
  How do I laugh, when men, by fortune placed
Above their betters, and by rank disgraced,
Who found their pride on titles which they stain,
And, mean themselves, are of their fathers vain;
Who would a bill of privilege prefer,
And treat a poet like a creditor,
The generous ardour of the Muse condemn,
And curse the storm they know must break on
        them?
"What, shall a reptile bard, a wretch unknown,
Without one badge of merit but his own,
Great nobles lash, and lords, like common men,
Smart from the vengeance of a scribbler's pen?"
  What's in this name of Lord, that I should fear
To bring their vices to the public ear?
Flows not the honest blood of humble swains
Quick as the tide which swells a monarch's veins?
Monarchs, who wealth and titles can bestow,
Cannot make virtues in succession flow.
Wouldst thou, proud Man, be safely placed above
The censure of the Muse, deserve her love:
Act as thy birth demands, as nobles ought;
Look back, and, by thy worthy father taught,
Who earn'd those honours, thou wert born to wear,
Follow his steps, and be his virtue's heir:
But if, regardless of the road to fame,
You start aside, and tread the paths of shame;
If such thy life, that should thy sire arise,
The sight of such a son would blast his eyes,

Would make him curse the hour which gave thee birth,
Would drive him, shuddering, from the face of earth,
Once more, with shame and sorrow, 'mongst the dead
In endless night to hide his reverend head;
If such thy life, though kings had made thee more
Than ever king a scoundrel made before;
Nay, to allow thy pride a deeper spring,
Though God in vengeance had made thee a king,
Taking on Virtue's wing her daring flight,
The Muse should drag thee trembling to the light,
Probe thy foul wounds, and lay thy bosom bare
To the keen question of the searching air.
Gods! with what pride I see the titled slave,
Who smarts beneath the stroke which Satire gave,
Aiming at ease, and with dishonest art
Striving to hide the feelings of his heart;
How do I laugh, when, with affected air,
(Scarce able through despite to keep his chair,
Whilst on his trembling lip pale anger speaks,
And the chafed blood flies mounting to his cheeks,)
He talks of Conscience, which good men secures
From all those evil moments guilt endures,
And seems to laugh at those who pay regard
To the wild ravings of a frantic bard.
" Satire, whilst envy and ill-humour sway
The mind of man, must always make her way;
Nor to a bosom, with discretion fraught,
Is all her malice worth a single thought.

The wise have not the will, nor fools the power,
To stop her headstrong course; within the hour,
Left to herself she dies; opposing strife
Gives her fresh vigour, and prolongs her life.
All things her prey, and every man her aim,
I can no patent for exemption claim,
Nor would I wish to stop that harmless dart
Which plays around, but cannot wound my heart;
Though pointed at myself, be Satire free;
To her 'tis pleasure, and no pain to me."
   Dissembling Wretch! hence to the Stoic school,
And there amongst thy brethren play the fool;
There unrebuked, these wild, vain doctrines preach:
Lives there a man whom Satire cannot reach?
Lives there a man who calmly can stand by,
And see his conscience ripp'd with steady eye?
When Satire flies abroad on Falsehood's wing,
Short is her life, and impotent her sting;
But when to truth allied, the wound she gives
Sinks deep, and to remotest ages lives.
When in the tomb thy pamper'd flesh shall rot,
And e'en by friends thy memory be forgot,
Still shalt thou live, recorded for thy crimes,

218 There is more poetry than truth in this suggestion of the impotence of falsehood. Voltaire, that emanation from the Father of lies, was wont to assert that "a lie believed for half an hour had done its duty;" his disciples have since continued to carry out the axiom, and many a fair fame has been nipped in the bud, and many an honest heart blighted for life by the baneful influence and effect of one half hour of malignant falsehood.

Live in her page, and stink to after-times.
  Hast thou no feeling yet? Come, throw off pride,
And own those passions which thou shalt not hide.
Sandwich, who from the moment of his birth 227
Made human nature a reproach on earth,
Who never dared, nor wish'd, behind to stay,
When Folly, Vice, and Meanness led the way,
Would blush, should he be told, by Truth and Wit
Those actions, which he blush'd not to commit.
Men the most infamous are fond of fame,
And those who fear not guilt, yet start at shame.
  But whither runs my zeal, whose rapid force,
Turning the brain, bears Reason from her course;
Carries me back to times, when poets, bless'd
With courage, graced the science they profess'd;
When they, in honour rooted, firmly stood
The bad to punish and reward the good;

227 Walpole, in one of his letters to Sir H. Mann, contained in the concluding series of them just published, observes of Churchill, "that many of his characters are obscure even to the (then) present age, and some of the most known were so unknown to *him* that he has missed all resemblance, of which Lord Sandwich is a striking instance." This is one of Walpole's many random inconsistencies; as in several of his letters to George Montagu and others, he repeatedly adverts to Lord Sandwich's profligacies and blasphemies. The satire is no doubt overcharged, but a reduced tone of it would have only rendered it more just, and therefore more severe.

254 The pension bestowed upon Johnson was unaccompanied by any political stipulation, and the triumph it afforded to the enemies of this great man must be attributed to the general tendency of his principles in church and state. The

When, to a flame by public virtue wrought,
The foes of freedom they to justice brought,
And dared expose those slaves who dared support
A tyrant plan, and call'd themselves a Court?
Ah! what are poets now? as slavish those
Who deal in verse, as those who deal in prose.
Is there an Author, search the kingdom round,
In whom true worth and real spirit's found?
The slaves of booksellers, or (doom'd by Fate
To baser chains) vile pensioners of state,
Some, dead to shame, and of those shackles proud
Which Honour scorns, for slavery roar aloud;
Others, half-palsied only, mutes become, [dumb.
And what makes Smollett write makes Johnson
Why turns yon villain pale? why bends his eye
Inward, abash'd when Murphy passes by?
Dost thou sage Murphy for a blockhead take,
Who wages war with vice for virtue's sake?

unfortunate definition he gave of the word pensioner, in his dictionary, whom he describes as one supported by an allowance paid at the will of another, a dependant, a slave of state, hired by a stipend to obey his master, was at once so injudicious and inconsistent with his own subsequent conduct, as to afford a continual source of animadversion to the North Briton, and all other anti-ministerial witlings. For many years he abstained from taking any part as a writer in politics, but at length, irritated by the incessant clamour of the popular party, and impelled by a sense of the rectitude of his opinions, he, in 1770, published "The False Alarm," in which he justly reprobates the seditious conduct of Wilkes, and while he ingeniously vindicates the measures adopted by government, ridicules the alarm attempted to be excited at the occasionally partial decisions of parliament. "We have

No, no, like other worldlings, you will find
He shifts his sails, and catches every wind:
His soul the shock of interest can't endure:
Give him a pension then, and sin secure.
With laurell'd wreaths the flatterer's brows adorn,
Bid Virtue crouch, bid Vice exalt her horn;
Bid cowards thrive, put Honesty to flight,
Murphy shall prove or try to prove it right.
Try, thou state-juggler, every paltry art,
Ransack the inmost closet of my heart,

found," he says, "by experience, that though a squire has given ale and venison in vain, and a borough has been compelled to see its dearest interests in the hands of him whom it did not trust, yet the general state of the nation has continued the same. The sun has risen and the corn has grown, and whatever talk has been of the danger of property, yet he that ploughed the field commonly reaped it, and he that built the house was master of the door."

A very angry pamphlet was written by Wilkes, but without any name, in answer to the "False Alarm," which Dr. Johnson determined not to reply to, but in conversation with Mr. Langton, he mentioned a particular or two which if he had replied might perhaps have been inserted. In the answerer's pamphlet it was asked with solemnity, "Do you consider, Sir, that a House of Commons is to the people as a creature is to its Creator?" To this question, said Johnson, I would have replied, "that in the first place the idea of a Creator must be such as that he has a power to unmake or annihilate his creature. Then it cannot be conceived that a creature can make laws for its Creator."

254 Smollett received pecuniary assistance from government as long as he contributed the Briton to its defence, but no stated pension was ever conferred upon him.

Swear thou'rt my friend; by that base oath make way
Into my breast, and flatter to betray;
Or, if those tricks are vain, if wholesome doubt
Detects the fraud, and points the villain out,
Bribe those who daily at my board are fed,
And make them take my life who eat my bread.
On Authors for defence, for praise depend,
Pay him but well, and Murphy is thy friend:
He, he shall ready stand with venal rhymes,
To varnish guilt, and consecrate thy crimes,
To make corruption in false colours shine,
And damn his own good name, to rescue thine.

But, if thy niggard hands their gifts withhold,
And Vice no longer rains down showers of gold,
Expect no mercy; facts, well grounded, teach:
Murphy, if not rewarded, will impeach.
What though each man of nice and juster thought,
Shunning his steps, decrees, by honour taught,
He ne'er can be a friend, who stoops so low
To be the base betrayer of a foe?
What though, with thine together link'd, his name
Must be with thine transmitted down to shame?
To every manly feeling callous grown,
Rather than not blast thine, he'll blast his own.

To ope the fountain whence sedition springs,
To slander government, and libel kings;
With Freedom's name to serve a present hour,
Though born and bred to arbitrary power;
To talk of William with insidious art,

Whilst a vile Stuart's lurking in his heart,
And, whilst mean Envy rears her loathsome head,
Flattering the living, to abuse the dead,
Where is Shebbeare? Oh let not foul reproach,
Travelling thither in a City-coach,
The pillory dare to name: the whole intent
Of that parade was fame, not punishment;
And that old, staunch Whig, Beardmore, standing by,
Can in full court give that report the lie.

301 Dr. John Shebbeare, a physician and notorious jacobitical writer, after a long course of virulent invectives against the reigning family, was at length, in 1759, prosecuted for writing a seventh letter to the people of England. For this performance he was sentenced to the pillory, and to two years' confinement in prison. The mode of executing the former part of the sentence became the subject of an application to the Court of King's Bench for an attachment against the under-sheriff. The doctor being patronized by the city magistrates, it appeared that he went in one of the city coaches, accompanied by his friend Beardmore (then under-sheriff, and afterwards Wilkes's attorney) to Charing-Cross, where the pillory was erected, and that his progress thither had every appearance of a triumphal procession. Evidence was adduced by the Attorney-General to shew that Shebbeare only stood upon the platform of the pillory unconfined and at his ease, attended by a servant in livery (which servant and livery were hired for the occasion) holding an umbrella over his head all the time: that his head, hands, neck, and arms, were not at all confined, or put into the holes of the pillory; but that he sometimes put his hands upon the holes of the pillory in order to rest himself. It was also proved that Beardmore attended as under-sheriff with his wand, and that he treated the criminal with great complaisance in taking him to and from the pillory. Fourteen or fifteen equivocating affi-

With rude unnatural jargon to support,
Half Scotch, half English, a declining court;
To make most glaring contraries unite,
And prove beyond dispute that black is white;
To make firm Honour tamely league with Shame,
Make Vice and Virtue differ but in name;
To prove that chains and freedom are but one,
That to be saved must mean to be undone, 314
Is there not Guthrie? Who, like him, can call
All opposites to proof, and conquer all?

davits were produced on the part of the under-sheriff, among the rest, one Revie, who had lived near Charing-Cross forty years, swore that he never saw a criminal so publicly exposed upon the pillory before as Shebbeare was; upon this Lord Mansfield observed "to be sure the face of a man who stands upright looking through the pillory is more exposed to view than it would be if his head were bent down in it. So many affidavits so studiously and artfully penned, to be safely sworn in one sense and read in another, are an aggravation." An attachment accordingly issued, and Beardmore was sentenced to pay a fine of *thirty pounds*, and to be committed to custody for two months.

Shebbeare, on the accession of George the Third, had a pension of £200 per annum conferred upon him, and from thenceforth wielded his pen in defence of government; he died in 1788.

315 William Guthrie compiled a peerage on the plan of Sir William Dugdale and Collins, each individual article being first submitted to the immediate inspection of the representative of the noble family treated of. Notwithstanding this degree of care, when published, it was found to contain an unpardonable number of errors in every department, many of them as gross and palpable as those mentioned by the poet. Dates, names, and sexes, were repeatedly mistaken or transposed, and thus almost every article was rendered a medley of

He calls forth living waters from the rock;
He calls forth children from the barren stock:
He, far beyond the springs of Nature led,
Makes women bring forth after they are dead:
He, on a curious, new, and happy plan,
In wedlock's sacred bands joins man to man;
And, to complete the whole, most strange, but true,
By some rare magic, makes them fruitful too,
Whilst from their loins, in the due course of years,
Flows the rich blood of Guthrie's English Peers.
  Dost thou contrive some blacker deed of shame,
Something which Nature shudders but to name,
Something which makes the soul of man retreat,
And the life-blood run backward to her seat?
Dost thou contrive, for some base private end,
Some selfish view, to hang a trusting friend,
To lure him on, e'en to his parting breath,
And promise life to work him surer death?
Grown old in villany, and dead to grace,
Hell in his heart and Tyburn in his face,

absurdities. Guthrie was otherwise not a contemptible writer; he was retained by administration to undertake the defence of government, this he did in various pamphlets now deservedly forgotten, and in a tory History of England, which is by no means destitute of merit; his geographical grammar is a very useful school work, and has not yet been altogether superseded; he died in 1769.

327–340 These lines were originally written by our author with a view to be introduced into his threatened "Elegy, or Ayliffe's Ghost;" from the publication of which he was not to be deterred by the artful promises of a reverend mediator;

Behold, a parson at thy elbow stands,
Lowering damnation, and with open hands
Ripe to betray his Saviour for reward,
The Atheist chaplain of an Atheist lord.
Bred to the church, and for the gown decreed,
Ere it was known that I should learn to read;
Though that was nothing, for my friends, who knew
What mighty Dullness of itself could do,
Never design'd me for a working priest,
But hoped I should have been a Dean at least:
Condemn'd (like many more and worthier men
To whom I pledge the service of my pen) [lawn,
Condemn'd (whilst proud and pamper'd sons of
Cramm'd to the throat, in lazy plenty yawn)
In pomp of reverend beggary to appear,
To pray, and starve on forty pounds a-year.
My friends, who never felt the galling load,
Lament that I forsook the packhorse road,
Whilst Virtue to my conduct witness bears,
In throwing off that gown which Francis wears.

"the atheist chaplain of an atheist lord," for some account of which transaction, see a note on the Epistle to Hogarth.

348 Our author had composed about fifty lines of a poem entitled "The Curate," and, as was generally his custom, repeated them in his family. In all probability he never committed them to writing, as they were not found among his papers. Indeed, his memory being remarkably tenacious, he rarely wrote his poems until they were required by the printer. He had two other poems in contemplation; Woman, a Satire on Man, and a Poem founded on the battle of Culloden.

357 The Rev. Philip Francis, the translator of Horace, chaplain to Lord Holland, at whose recommendation he was

What creature's that, so very pert and prim,
So very full of foppery, and whim,
So gentle, yet so brisk; so wondrous sweet,
So fit to prattle at a lady's feet,
Who looks, as he the Lord's rich vineyard trod,
And by his garb appears a man of God?
Trust not to looks, nor credit outward show;
The villain lurks beneath the cassock'd beau;
That's an informer; what avails the name?
Suffice it that the wretch from Sodom came.
His tongue is deadly—from his presence run,
Unless thy rage would wish to be undone.
No ties can hold him, no affection bind,
And fear alone restrains his coward mind;

promoted to the Rectory of Barrow in Suffolk, and to the chaplainship of Chelsea Hospital. He died in 1773. His Horace still retains its ground. Johnson, on its being on some occasion censured, observed, "The lyrical part of Horace never can be perfectly translated, so much of the excellence is in the numbers and expression. Francis has done it the best: I'll take his five out of six against them all."

Another translation was, in 1793, attempted by Mr. William Boscawen, a Commissioner of the Victualling Office, an amiable man and an elegant scholar, but it is greatly inferior to those either of Francis or of Duncombe.

The late Sir Philip Francis, M. P., was the son of the Rev. Mr. Francis, and according to better evidence than applies to any other individual, was the author of Junius's letters, yet though the circumstantial evidence appears complete, it has failed in carrying conviction to the public or literary mind. Canning said of it, I cannot refute, but I do not believe.

383 John Cleland, the son of Colonel Cleland, who was the friend of Pope, and the Will Honeycomb of the Spectator, was author of an infamously licentious publication, rendered

Free him from that, no monster is so fell,
Nor is so sure a blood-hound found in hell.
His silken smiles, his hypocritic air,
His meek demeanour, plausible and fair,
Are only worn to pave Fraud's easier way,
And make gull'd Virtue fall a surer prey.
Attend his church—his plan of doctrine view—
The preacher is a Christian, dull, but true;
But when the hallow'd hour of preaching's o'er,
That plan of doctrine's never thought of more;
Christ is laid by neglected on the shelf,
And the vile priest is Gospel to himself.
  By Cleland tutor'd, and with Blacow bred,
(Blacow, whom, by a brave resentment led,

the more dangerous and seductive by the elegance of the language and assumed decency of expression, and which he sold for 20 guineas to a bookseller, who cleared above £10,000 by the sale of it. Mr. Cleland having been summoned before the privy council on occasion of his work, pleaded poverty as his excuse, upon which Lord Granville very nobly settled an annuity of £100 per annum upon him, on condition of his refraining from so immoral a style of writing. This annuity he enjoyed until his death in 1789, at the age of 82. He had been educated at Westminster school, where he was contemporary with Lord Mansfield, and was for a short time consul at Smyrna. He there probably imbibed that lax morality which he so licentiously developed in the work alluded to. He adhered to his engagement to the privy council by not offending again, and all his subsequent literary labours were obscure but inoffensive. Among others he published in 1765 an ingenious work, "The Way to Things by Words, and to Words by Things" which was followed by "Specimens of an Etymological Vocabulary, or Essay by means of an analytic method to retrieve the ancient Celtic."

Oxford, if Oxford had not sunk in fame,
Ere this, had damn'd to everlasting shame)
Their steps he follows, and their crimes partakes;
To virtue lost, to vice alone he wakes,
Most lusciously declaims 'gainst luscious themes,
And whilst he rails at blasphemy, blasphemes.
Are these the arts which policy supplies?

388 In the year 1747, a riot happened at Oxford, of which one Mr. Blacow gave information to the Vice-Chancellor. He related that he heard some of the students cry out repeatedly in the public streets, King James for ever! Prince Charles! God bless the great King James the Third! Mr. Blacow complained to the Vice-Chancellor of this misbehaviour, and made the most strenuous exertions against the offenders. The Vice-Chancellor, imputing their misbehaviour to intoxication, for some time endeavoured to waive the inquiry, but at length inflicted some trifling punishment on the delinquents. At last the Duke of Newcastle took cognizance of the offence; a prosecution was commenced in the Court of King's Bench, against Mr. Dawes and Mr. Whitmore, two of the students, who being found guilty, were sentenced to walk through Westminster-hall with a paper on their foreheads denoting their crime, to pay a fine of five nobles each, be imprisoned for two years, and to find security for their good behaviour during seven years more.

396 It is not unusual for Churchill thus ironically to designate the man whom his pen has scarcely ceased from devoting to the execration of the reader. The Rev. Mr. Kidgell, Rector of Horne, in Surrey, and Chaplain to the Earl of March, together with Faden, the publisher of the Public Ledger, contrived to prevail with one Curry, a pressman, employed by Mr. Wilkes, to furnish them with a copy of the Essay on Woman. Having by these surreptitious means obtained their wish, Mr. Kidgell communicated his prize to Lord March, afterwards Duke of Queensbury, who immediately transmitted it to the secretaries of state. A succinct

Are these the steps by which grave churchmen rise?
Forbid it, Heaven; or, should it turn out so,
Let me and mine continue mean and low.
Such be their arts whom interest controls;
Kidgell and I have free and modest souls:
We scorn preferment which is gain'd by sin,
And will, though poor without, have peace within.

narrative of the transaction was published by Kidgell in vindication of himself, in which he seemed to take peculiar delight in quoting and dwelling upon the most objectionable passages of that most atrocious publication. This narrative was very ably answered by Mr. Wilkes as far as related to the pious motives of Mr. Kidgell in procuring the book, and giving information of its contents. It was considered by the public as a singular coincidence that the developement of so infamous a work should be reserved for persons who, in taste and disposition, were not uncongenial with the author of it.

Of Kidgell we can learn no farther particulars, but that he, not finding it convenient to reside in England, emigrated to Flanders, where he died, after having, as it is said, turned Roman Catholic.

Kidgell had been one of the trustees for repairing and amending the turnpike roads in the counties of Surrey and Sussex, and absconded above £100 in debt to the Trust. Upon the election of a successor the following minute was entered in the book, "in the room of the Rev. Mr. Kidgell, who is run away indebted to this Trust."

THE CONFERENCE.

This Poem was published by our Author in November 1763, soon after his elopement with Miss Carr had become a general topic of indignant remark. He in it labours to separate the effects of his private from those of his public conduct, and in the bitterness of his soul contrasts the devious path of the one with the invariable rectitude of the other. At this period of time it is of little importance to inquire into the infirmities of his nature, and, while the precepts of the most rigid virtue, patriotism, and morality are inculcated in his satires, unnecessary to dwell upon the imperfections of their author. To have been deceived in common with Lord Temple and Mr. Pitt, by the assumed patriotism of Wilkes, is scarcely to be imputed to him as a crime, and he did not live to witness the second period of the seditious efforts, and the final tergiversation of that artful demagogue. No exertions were omitted to obtain even the neutrality of Churchill, but pensions and preferments were in vain offered to one whose soul rose superior to all the sordid views of interest, and aspired to the praises of posterity by a steady adherence to the principles of public virtue. Excepting his fatal delusion with regard to Wilkes, Churchill may be instanced as one of the few Poets who have not prostituted their pens by the most fulsome flattery to wealth and power. The adulation which a Young, a Thomson, and a Gray, lavished upon a Walpole, a Doddington, and a Grafton, reflects disgrace upon the Poet, while it can confer no solid fame upon the patron.

At a time when the Bard as well as his adventurous friend becoming more than ordinarily the subject of public attention might expect to suffer more than a due degree of censure for any recent indiscretion, it was not ill-judged in Churchill to submit to bear his portion of the expression of public opinion now loudly directed against the immoralities of himself and Wilkes, and by fairly anticipating greatly to obviate the force of what his enemies might have to urge against him.

THE CONFERENCE.

Grace said in form, which sceptics must agree,
When they are told that grace was said by me;
The servants gone, to break the scurvy jest
On the proud landlord, and his threadbare guest;
The King gone round, my Lady too withdrawn,
My Lord, in usual taste, began to yawn,
And, lolling backward in his elbow-chair,
With an insipid kind of stupid stare,
Picking his teeth, twirling his seals about—
Churchill, you have a poem coming out:
You've my best wishes; but I really fear
Your Muse, in general, is too severe;
Her spirit seems her interest to oppose,
And where she makes one friend makes twenty foes.
C. Your Lordship's fears are just; I feel their force,
But only feel it as a thing of course.
The man whose hardy spirit shall engage
To lash the vices of a guilty age,
At his first setting forward ought to know
That every rogue he meets must be his foe;
That the rude breath of satire will provoke
Many who feel, and more who fear the stroke.

But shall the partial rage of selfish men
From stubborn justice wrench the righteous pen?
Or shall I not my settled course pursue,
Because my foes are foes to virtue too? [schools,
L. What is this boasted Virtue taught in
And idly drawn from antiquated rules?
What is her use? point out one wholesome end:
Will she hurt foes, or can she make a friend?
When from long fasts fierce appetites arise,
Can this same Virtue stifle Nature's cries?
Can she the pittance of a meal afford,
Or bid thee welcome to one great man's board?
When northern winds the rough December arm
With frost and snow, can Virtue keep thee warm?
Canst thou dismiss the hard unfeeling dun
Barely by saying, thou art Virtue's son?
Or by base blundering statesmen sent to jail,
Will Mansfield take this Virtue for thy bail?
Believe it not, the name is in disgrace;
Virtue and Temple now are out of place.
Quit then this meteor, whose delusive ray
From wealth and honour leads thee far astray.
True virtue means, let Reason use her eyes,
Nothing with fools, and interest with the wise.
Wouldst thou be great, her patronage disclaim,
Nor madly triumph in so mean a name:
Let nobler wreaths thy happy brows adorn,
And leave to Virtue poverty and scorn.
Let Prudence be thy guide; who doth not know
How seldom Prudence can with Virtue go?

To be successful try thy utmost force,
And virtue follows as a thing of course.
Hirco, who knows not Hirco? stains the bed
Of that kind master who first gave him bread;
Scatters the seeds of discord through the land,
Breaks every public, every private band;
Beholds with joy a trusting friend undone;
Betrays a brother, and would cheat a son:
What mortal in his senses can endure
The name of Hirco? for the wretch is poor!
"Let him hang, drown, starve, on a dunghill rot,
By all detested live, and die forgot;
Let him, a poor return, in every breath
Feel all death's pains, yet be whole years in death,"
Is now the general cry we all pursue;
Let fortune change, and Prudence changes too;
Supple and pliant, a new system feels,
Throws up her cap, and spaniels at his heels,
Long live great Hirco, cries, by interest taught,
And let his foes, though I prove one, be nought.
C. Peace to such men, if such men can have peace,
Let their possessions, let their state, increase;
Let their base services in courts strike root,
And in the season bring forth golden fruit,
I envy not; let those who have the will,
And, with so little spirit, so much skill,
With such vile instruments their fortunes carve;
Rogues may grow fat, an honest man dares starve.

L. These stale conceits thrown off, let us advance
For once to real life, and quit romance.
Starve! pretty talking! but I fain would view
That man, that honest man, would do it too.
Hence to yon mountain which outbraves the sky,
And dart from pole to pole thy strengthen'd eye,
Through all that space you shall not view one man,
Not one, who dares to act on such a plan.
Cowards in calms will say what in a storm
The brave will tremble at, and not perform.
Thine be the proof, and, spite of all you've said,
You'd give your honour for a crust of bread.

C. What proof might do, what hunger might effect,
What famish'd Nature, looking with neglect
On all she once held dear, what fear, at strife
With fainting virtue for the means of life,
Might make this coward flesh, in love with breath,
Shuddering at pain, and shrinking back from death,
In treason to my soul, descend to bear,
Trusting to fate, I neither know nor care.

Once, at this hour those wounds afresh I feel,
Which nor prosperity nor time can heal,
Those wounds, which, fate severely hath decreed,
Mention'd or thought of, must for ever bleed;
Those wounds, which humbled all that pride of man,
Which brings such mighty aid to virtue's plan;

Once, awed by fortune's most oppressive frown,
By legal rapine to the earth bow'd down,
My credit at last gasp, my state undone,
Trembling to meet the shock I could not shun,
Virtue gave ground, and blank despair prevail'd;
Sinking beneath the storm, my spirits fail'd,
Like Peter's faith, till one, a friend indeed,
May all distress find such in time of need,
One kind good man, in act, in word, in thought,
By virtue guided, and by wisdom taught,
Image of him whom christians should adore,
Stretch'd forth his hand, and brought me safe to shore.
Since, by good fortune into notice raised,
And for some little merit largely praised,
Indulged in swerving from prudential rules,
Hated by rogues, and not beloved by fools;
Placed above want, shall abject thirst of wealth,
So fiercely war 'gainst my soul's dearest health,
That, as a boon, I should base shackles crave,
And, born to freedom, make myself a slave?
That I should in the train of those appear
Whom honour cannot love, nor manhood fear?

118 Churchill, having imprudently involved himself, previous to the publication of the Rosciad, in debts beyond his ability to discharge, was threatened with all the horrors of a jail; from this apprehension he was relieved by the friendly interposition of Dr. Peirson Lloyd, second master of Westminster school, who effected a compromise with our author's creditors, and advanced a part of the sum required for carrying it into effect.

That I no longer skulk from street to street,
Afraid lest duns assail, and bailiffs meet;
That I from place to place this carcase bear;
Walk forth at large, and wander free as air;
That I no longer dread the awkward friend,
Whose very obligations must offend;
Nor, all too froward, with impatience burn
At suffering favours which I can't return.
That from dependance and from pride secure,
I am not placed so high to scorn the poor,
Nor yet so low, that I my Lord should fear,
Or hesitate to give him sneer for sneer;
That, whilst sage Prudence my pursuits confirms,
I can enjoy the world on equal terms;
That, kind to others, to myself most true,
Feeling no want, I comfort those who do,
And with the will have power to aid distress:
These, and what other blessings I possess,
From the indulgence of the public rise,
All private patronage my soul defies.
By candour more inclined to save, than damn,
A generous public made me what I am.
All that I have, they gave; just memory bears

145 The extensive sale of our Author's Poems, and his rapidity of composition, produced him no inconsiderable revenue; and to his credit it should be remembered, that his first earnings were appropriated first to the full discharge of every demand upon him, to which, by the terms of the compromise with his creditors, he was not legally liable, and then to the essential and permanent relief of his friend Robert Lloyd, the son of his benefactor.

The grateful stamp, and what I am, is theirs.
L. To feign a red-hot zeal for freedom's cause,
To mouth aloud for liberties and laws,
For public good to bellow all abroad,
Serves well the purposes of private fraud.
Prudence, by public good intends her own;
If you mean otherwise, you stand alone.
What do we mean by country and by court?
What is it to oppose? what to support?
Mere words of course; and what is more absurd
Than to pay homage to an empty word?
Majors and minors differ but in name;
Patriots and ministers are much the same;
The only difference, after all their rout,
Is, that the one is in, the other out.
Explore the dark recesses of the mind,
In the soul's honest volume read mankind,
And own, in wise and simple, great and small,
The same grand leading principle in all.
Whate'er we talk of wisdom to the wise,
Of goodness to the good, of public ties
Which to our country link, of private bands
Which claim most dear attention at our hands,
For parent and for child, for wife and friend,
Our first great mover, and our last great end
Is one, and, by whatever name we call
The ruling tyrant, self is all in all.
This, which unwilling faction shall admit,
Guided in different ways a Bute and Pitt,
Made tyrants break, made kings observe the law,
And gave the world a Stuart and Nassau.

Hath Nature (strange and wild conceit of pride)
Distinguished thee from all her sons beside?
Doth virtue in thy bosom brighter glow,
Or from a spring more pure doth action flow?
Is not thy soul bound with those very chains
Which shackle us? or is that self, which reigns
O'er kings and beggars, which in all we see
Most strong and sovereign, only weak in thee?
Fond man, believe it not; experience tells
'Tis not thy virtue, but thy pride rebels.
Think, (and for once lay by thy lawless pen)
Think, and confess thyself like other men;
Think but one hour, and, to thy conscience led
By Reason's hand, bow down and hang thy head:
Think on thy private life, recall thy youth,
View thyself now, and own, with strictest truth,
That self hath drawn thee from fair virtue's way
Farther than folly would have dared to stray,
And that the talents liberal Nature gave
To make thee free, have made thee more a slave.
Quit then, in prudence quit, that idle train
Of toys, which have so long abused thy brain,
And captive led thy powers; with boundless will
Let self maintain her state and empire still,
But let her, with more worthy objects caught,
Strain all the faculties and force of thought
To things of higher daring; let her range
Through better pastures, and learn how to change;
Let her, no longer to weak faction tied,
Wisely revolt, and join our stronger side.

C. Ah! what, my Lord, hath private life to do
With things of public nature? why to view
Would you thus cruelly those scenes unfold
Which, without pain and horror to behold,
Must speak me something more, or less than man,
Which friends may pardon, but I never can?
Look back! a thought which borders on despair,
Which human nature must, yet cannot bear.
'Tis not the babbling of a busy world,
Where praise and censure are at random hurl'd,
Which can the meanest of my thoughts control,
Or shake one settled purpose of my soul;
Free and at large might their wild curses roam,
If all, if all alas! were well at home.
No—'tis the tale which angry conscience tells,
When she with more than tragic horror swells
Each circumstance of guilt; when stern, but true,
She brings bad actions forth into review,
And like the dread hand-writing on the wall,
Bids late remorse awake at reason's call;
Arm'd at all points, bids scorpion vengeance pass,
And to the mind holds up reflection's glass,
The mind which, starting, heaves the heart-felt groan,
And hates that form she knows to be her own.

213–236 These lines forcibly allude to the deep sense the Poet entertained of the connexion he had formed with Miss Carr, the particulars of which have been detailed in the memoir of his life. Self-condemnation so just, so public, and severe, if it does not excite compassion, should at least temper justice with mercy.

Enough of this,—let private sorrows rest,—
As to the public, I dare stand the test;
Dare proudly boast, I feel no wish above
The good of England, and my country's love,
Stranger to party-rage, by reason's voice,
Unerring guide, directed in my choice,
Not all the tyrant powers of earth combined,
No, nor of hell, shall make me change my mind.
What! herd with men my honest soul disdains,
Men who, with servile zeal are forging chains
For Freedom's neck, and lend a helping hand
To spread destruction o'er my native land.
What! shall I not, e'en to my latest breath,
In the full face of danger and of death
Exert that little strength which nature gave,
And boldly stem, or perish in the wave?
L. When I look backward for some fifty years,

253 This recapitulation of inconsistencies will apply unfortunately to every period of British history. The peerages conferred on a Wentworth, a Pulteney, a Granville, and a Pitt, the moral declamation of an Earl of Sandwich in the House of Lords, against the Essay on Woman, the religious zeal of a Wharton, and the moderation of a Warburton, would contribute to fill the outline sketched by the satirist. Walpole in a letter to George Montagu writes, "You know I have long had a partiality for your cousin Sandwich, who has out-Sandwiched himself. He has impeached Wilkes for a blasphemous poem, and has been expelled for blasphemy himself by the Beef-steak Club in Covent Garden. Wilkes has been shot by Martin, and instead of being burnt at an auto da fe, as the Bishop of Gloucester intended, is reverenced as a saint by the mob; and if he dies, I suppose the people will squint themselves into convulsions at his tomb in honour of his memory." Wilkes's very portentous squint was no

And see protesting patriots turn'd to peers;
Hear men, most loose, for decency declaim,
And talk of character without a name;
See infidels assert the cause of God,
And meek divines wield persecution's rod;
See men transform'd to brutes, and brutes to men,
See Whitehead take a place, Ralph change his pen,
I mock the zeal, and deem the men in sport,
Who rail at ministers and curse a court.
Thee, haughty as thou art, and proud in rhyme,
Shall some preferment, offered at a time
When virtue sleeps, some sacrifice to pride,
Or some fair victim, move to change thy side.
Thee shall these eyes behold, to health restored,
Using, as Prudence bids, bold Satire's sword,

drawback on his popularity: in one of his triumphal processions, one of his female admirers in the mob observed to another, "It is a pity he squints so." "Squints, do you say, he does not squint more than a gentleman should do," was the reply.

260 Of the exaggerated patriotism of Paul Whitehead, and the price of his apostasy, some notice will be taken in a remark on the third book of the Ghost.

260 Mr. James Ralph, "an author by profession," the claims of which literary class as such, he vindicated in a pamphlet which created some sensation at the time he first appeared as a poet, and was satirized in the Dunciad. He wrote several plays, and among others the Astrologer, borrowed from the old comedy of Albumazar, which was the foundation of Johnson's Alchymist. In the dramatic line he was ever unsuccessful. In the year 1742, the Duchess of Marlborough having published the Memoirs of her own life, Ralph

Galling thy present friends, and praising those
Whom now thy frenzy holds thy greatest foes.
C. May I (can worse disgrace on manhood fall?)
Be born a Whitehead, and baptized a Paul;
May I (though to his service deeply tied
By sacred oaths, and now by will allied)
With false feign'd zeal an injured God defend,
And use his name for some base private end;
May I (that thought bids double horrors roll
O'er my sick spirits, and unmans my soul)
Ruin the virtue which I held most dear,
And still must hold; May I, through abject fear,
Betray my friend; may to succeeding times,

wrote an answer to it called, "The other side of the Question." This performance contributed to raise his reputation in the literary world, and during Sir Robert Walpole's administration he became so formidable as a political writer, as Editor of the Protester and the Remembrancer, that it was thought expedient to engage his services by the payment of an annual stipend, which was continued to him by Mr. Pelham, on condition of his attacking his former patron. Influenced by these motives, he engaged in the defence of government, and laboured so successfully in his vocation, as at the death of George II. to obtain, through the interest of Lord Bute, a settled pension of £600 per annum, which he lived not long to enjoy. He died, in 1762, a martyr to the gout, at the age of 54. He wrote in 1734, a critical review of the public buildings in London, and also a tory history of England commencing with the dynasty of the Stuarts. He was latterly attached to Frederic, Prince of Wales, and his name frequently occurs in Lord Melcombe's Diary, as one of the principal literary agents of the court of Leicester House. Horace Walpole observes of him that his turn seemed to be

Engraved on plates of adamant, my crimes
Stand blazing forth, whilst mark'd with envious blot,
Each little act of virtue is forgot;
Of all those evils which, to stamp men curst,
Hell keeps in store for vengeance, may the worst
Light on my head; and in my day of woe,
To make the cup of bitterness o'erflow,
May I be scorn'd by every man of worth,
Wander, like Cain, a vagabond on earth,
Bearing about a hell in my own mind,
Or be to Scotland for my life confined,
If I am one among the many known
Whom Shelburne fled, and Calcraft blush'd to own.

endeavouring to raise mobs by speculative ideas of government, from which his judgment at least might be calculated, and that he had the good fortune to be bought off from his last journal, the Protester, for the only paper that he did not write in it. Lord Egmont and other distinguished leaders occasionally contributing papers which rose far above the pitch of the avowed Editor.

294 William Petty, Earl of Shelburne, afterwards Marquis of Lansdowne. An account of his Lordship's political career, and of his various intrigues with the ins and the outs from the year 1750 to 1780, may be collected from the numerous political and historical publications of the intervening period. His political sobriquet was Malagrida, (a Jesuit) as that of Lord Sandwich was Jemmy Twitcher, while George Grenville was the Gentle Shepherd. These humorous adaptations were very frequent with our ancestors, but discontinued in our graver age, one only recent instance occurring by the happy application of the significant name of Jem Crow, to a mushroom peer of corresponding character and political growth. Lord Lansdowne died in 1805.

L. Do you reflect what men you make your foes?
C. I do, and that's the reason I oppose.
Friends I have made, whom Envy must commend,
But not one foe whom I would wish a friend.
What if ten thousand Butes and Hollands bawl?
One Wilkes hath made a large amends for all.
'Tis not the title, whether handed down
From age to age, or flowing from the crown
In copious streams on recent men, who came
From stems unknown, and sires without a name:
'Tis not the star which our great Edward gave
To mark the virtuous, and reward the brave,
Blazing without, whilst a base heart within
Is rotten to the core with filth and sin;
'Tis not the tinsel grandeur, taught to wait,
At custom's call, to mark a fool of state
From fools of lesser note, that soul can awe,
Whose pride is reason, whose defence is law.
L. Suppose, (a thing scarce possible in art,
Were it thy cue to play a common part)
Suppose thy writings so well fenced in law,
That Norton cannot find nor make a flaw—
Hast thou not heard, that 'mongst our ancient tribes,
By party warpt, or lull'd asleep by bribes,
Or trembling at the ruffian hand of Force,
Law hath suspended stood, or changed its course?

294 John Calcraft, Esq., M. P. Army Agent and Contractor, of whom some account is given in a note on the Rosciad.

Art thou assured, that, for destruction ripe,
Thou mayest not smart beneath the self-same
        gripe?
What sanction hast thou, frantic in thy rhymes,
Thy life, thy freedom to secure?
  C.   The times.
'Tis not on law, a system great and good,
By wisdom penn'd, and bought by noblest blood,
My faith relies: by wicked men and vain
Law, once abused, may be abused again.—
No; on our great law-giver I depend,
Who knows and guides her to her proper end;
Whose royalty of nature blazes out
So fierce, 'twere sin to entertain a doubt—
Did tyrant Stuarts now the laws dispense,
(Bless'd be the hour and hand which sent them
        hence!)
For something, or for nothing, for a word

328 The poet, with his usual good sense, appears to have been quite aware that of all governments, that carried on according to law, strict unmitigated law, is of all others the most arbitrary, oppressive and vexatious, so as to induce its subjects to fly to the throne for refuge from its vindictive tyranny. It has been well and justly observed, that the highest evidence of the liberty of an Englishman, is the privilege he takes of infringing some law or other every day of his life. This connivance of the law at the breach of its letter, so long as its spirit is not infringed, affords a margin for that latitude of action which it is the tendency of progressive legislation to abridge, until at length a community may be brought to that state of Prussian discipline which converts the greatest blessings of civilized society, religion and education, into a curse, by prescribing them at the point of the bayonet.

Or thought, I might be doom'd to death, unheard.
Life we might all resign to lawless power,
Nor think it worth the purchase of an hour;
But envy ne'er shall fix so foul a stain
On the fair annals of a Brunswick's reign.
If, slave to party, to revenge, or pride;
If, by frail human error drawn aside,
I break the law, strict rigour let her wear;
'Tis hers to punish, and 'tis mine to bear;
Nor, by the voice of Justice doom'd to death,
Would I ask mercy with my latest breath:
But, anxious only for my country's good,
In which my king's of course, is understood;
Form'd on a plan with some few patriot friends,
Whilst by just means I aim at noblest ends,
My spirits cannot sink: though from the tomb
Stern Jefferies should be placed in Mansfield's room:
Though he should bring, his base designs to aid,
Some black attorney, for his purpose made,
And shove, whilst Decency and Law retreat,
The modest Norton from his maiden seat;
Though both in ill, confederates, should agree,
In damned league, to torture law and me,
Whilst George is king, I cannot fear endure;
Not to be guilty, is to be secure.
But when, in after-times, (be far removed
That day!) our monarch, glorious and beloved,
Sleeps with his fathers, should imperious fate,
In vengeance, with fresh Stuarts curse our state;

Should they, o'erleaping every fence of law,
Butcher the brave to keep tame fools in awe;
Should they, by brutal and oppressive force,
Divert sweet Justice from her even course;
Should they, of every other means bereft,
Make my right hand a witness 'gainst my left;
Should they, abroad by inquisitions taught,
Search out my soul, and damn me for a thought;
Still would I keep my course, still speak, still write,
Till death had plunged me in the shades of night.
Thou God of Truth, thou great, all-searching eye,
To whom our thoughts, our spirits, open lie,
Grant me thy strength, and in that needful hour,
(Should it e'er come) when Law submits to Power,
With firm resolve my steady bosom steel,
Bravely to suffer, though I deeply feel.
Let me, as hitherto, still draw my breath
In love with life, but not in fear of death;
And if Oppression brings me to the grave,
And marks me dead, she ne'er shall mark a slave.
Let no unworthy marks of grief be heard,
No wild laments, not one unseemly word;
Let sober triumphs wait upon my bier;
I won't forgive that friend who drops one tear.
Whether he's ravish'd in life's early morn,
Or, in old age drops like an ear of corn,
Full ripe he falls, on nature's noblest plan,
Who lives to reason, and who dies a man.

THE GHOST.

IN FOUR BOOKS.

As a circumstantial account of the mischievous imposture which gave rise to the following poem can alone render it intelligible to the reader, we shall endeavour as succinctly as possible to relate the origin, progress, and termination of the transaction.

Mr. William Kent, who was the postmaster in a considerable market town in Norfolk, had not been married above a twelvemonth to a very respectable woman of that county before she died in childbed; upon this he determined to quit the place, but his engagement with the post-office compelled him to stay there some months longer. During this interval Miss Fanny L. (the Ghost) who was sister to his late wife, and had lived with her as a companion, continued to reside, after her decease, with Mr. Kent, in the character of his housekeeper. The frequent communication attending such a situation soon produced a mutual attachment. Mr. Kent, however, finding that by the strictness of the canon law* he was debarred from legally uniting him self to the object of his affection, resolved to try the effect of absence, with a view of gradual relinquishment of expectations which he considered could not be honourably entertained, and came up to London in the intention of applying for a situation in one of the public offices. This sepa-

---

* Although the canon law discountenances the marriage of a sister of a deceased wife, the law of England held such a marriage as voidable only and not absolutely void: and its issue were considered legitimate if born before the parents' marriage had been declared void; any proceeding towards which could only be taken during their joint lives. This was certainly an unsatisfactory state of the law as affecting so important and not infrequent a connexion,

ration was intolerably irksome to the young woman, who expressed an intention of following him to London on foot, if he did not procure her some other mode of conveyance, as she could not support existence but in his society. By the intervention of a mutual friend she came up to London, and found out the abode of Mr. Kent. The die was now cast, and he determined upon living with her in future as his wife, and as such she was considered by most of his friends and acquaintance. Being called by his name and treated by him with the utmost affection, the contrary would most probably never have transpired had not her relations, who, by all the ties of honour and generosity, were interested in keeping the secret, taken every opportunity of divulging it.

Mr. Kent, in October 1759, took her to his lodging in Cock Lane, Smithfield, the house of Mr. Parsons, the clerk of the parish, from whence, having occasion to go into the country on business, Parsons's daughter, a child of eleven years of age, slept with Miss Fanny, who complained one morning to the family of both having been greatly disturbed by violent noises. Mrs. Parsons, pretending to be at a loss to account for this, bethought herself of a neighbouring industrious shoemaker, whom they concluded to be the cause of this disturbance. Soon after, on a Sunday night, Miss Fanny, getting out of bed, called out to Mrs. Parsons, "Pray does your shoemaker work so hard on Sunday nights too?" to which being answered in the negative, Mrs. Parsons was desired to come into the chamber and herself witness the truth of the assertion. Mr. Kent on his return, being obliged to arrest Parsons for £20 he had lent to him, and which he shewed no disposition to repay, left his house at an hour's warning,

---

and therefore an act was passed 5 and 6 William IV. c. 54, (1836), fully confirming such marriages for the past, but prohibiting them in future. The public opinion was much divided on the occasion, but the better arguments appeared to be in favour of permitting such unions as involving no question of affinity of blood, as between the husband and wife, and giving the benefit of the natural affection of an aunt to the children, if any, of the first marriage.

and took another lodging in the same street, upon which the noises ceased at Parsons's house. At his new lodging Mr. Kent had not remained above a week before Miss Fanny was taken ill. A physician was immediately sent for who had attended her before, and an apothecary was employed; in short, every precaution was taken that tenderness could suggest, as was certified by the following report drawn up, and signed by her medical attendants, men of considerable professional respectability.

"Some time in November 1759, I visited Mr. Kent at his lodgings at Mr. Parsons's in Cock Lane, and was then retained to attend the deceased Fanny L. in her expected labour, she being then in the sixth month of her pregnancy. In the course of the following months I visited her occasionally twice or thrice in the same house. On the 25th of January following I received a message from Mr. Kent about nine in the morning stating that the lady was ill, and wanted my assistance; I found them removed from Mr. Parsons's to an inconvenient apartment in the neighbourhood. I found the lady deceived by an acute pain in the back into an opinion that she was actually in labour; but on my declaring the contrary, not only she but the women about her were extremely uneasy, still suspecting I had formed a wrong judgment. After a few hours Mr. Kent informed me he had taken a house in Bartlet's Court, near Red Lion Street, Clerkenwell, and if I thought there was no danger, would remove her thither; I told him there were no signs of labour, but that from the symptoms, she probably would be ill some time, as I apprehended an eruptive fever, though I had not at that time any suspicion of the smallpox, as I did not know she never had that disorder. In the afternoon I attended the deceased in a coach (having properly secured her from receiving any injury by cold) to the house, Mr. Kent having before sent to prepare the apartment. I had her immediately put to bed, ordered her to be blooded, and prescribed such cordial medicines as I thought were proper to throw out an eruption: a nurse was immediately provided, and all other necessaries for the care of the patient. The next morning I met Mr. Jones, her apothecary, by appointment: the eruption began to appear, and from the violent lumbago of the day before, and other symptoms, we prognosticated confluent small pox of a very virulent nature. Mr. Kent was informed that in her situation the most favourable species of that disorder would be extremely hazardous, and that hers being a bad sort, the danger was very great. We endeavoured to assist nature by early blisterings, and administered medicines of a cordial nature. The symptoms were for the first four or five days rather favourable; but when maturation should have been performed the pulse flagged, the fever sunk, and the whole eruption put on a warty pallid appearance; and as she could not swallow but with difficulty, she could but seldom be prevailed on to take any thing; she was herself sensible of her danger, and Mr. Kent was told she could not survive three or four days. He was advised therefore to procure a minister to visit her, which was accordingly done. For the last two days no persuasion could bring her to taste any thing, so that for nearly fifty hours before she died she hardly swallowed a pint of any fluid whatever, and that only when myself or the apothecary were present to administer it to her. The last morning of her life we found her extremely low, her eyes sunk, her speech failing, and her intellects very imperfect. We told Mr. Kent she could not then live twelve hours. Accordingly a short time after we left her, her speech was wholly taken from her, she became senseless, a little convulsed, and expired in the evening of the 2d of February 1762. T. C.

"The foregoing is a true relation of the case of Fanny L. which we, who attended her in her illness, are ready to attest: as witness our hands,

"Thomas Cooper, M.D. Northumberland Street, Charing-cross.
John Jones, Apothecary, Grafton Street, Soho.
Feb. 8, 1762."

The funeral was as decent as Mr. Kent's circumstances would admit; the corpse was attended by him and a female relation to the vault under St. John's Church, Clerkenwell, where it was deposited, and though there was no name upon the coffin, the registry of her burial was entered in the name of Kent.

Parsons, who had been irritated by Mr. Kent's conduct, contrived a most singular species of revenge; he circulated a report that the spirit which had formerly disturbed the repose of his daughter and Miss Fanny was succeeded by the spirit of the latter, who harassed his house and family with continued visitations, which took place as soon as the child was put to bed. Upon certain knockings, flutterings, or scratchings, which seemed to proceed from under the bedstead, the child appeared to be thrown into violent fits and agitations. While in this state, the father or female attendant put questions to the ghost, and dictated how many knocks should serve for a negative or an affirmative. In this manner long conversations were carried on in public, in the course of which she charged Mr. Kent with having poisoned her by putting arsenic in purl, and administering it to her in her illness. Numbers of persons of rank and character were induced to pay their visits to Cock Lane, and though the floor and wainscoting were ripped up, the fraud remained undetected. The ghost having engaged to follow the girl wherever she might be carried, a plan was devised for developing this dangerous conspiracy by removing the child to the house of some respectable person, and for that purpose the proposal contained in the following advertisement was made to Mr. Parsons:

"We, whose names are underwritten, thought it proper, upon the approbation of the Lord Mayor, received on Saturday last in the afternoon, to see Mr. Parsons yesterday, and to ask him in respect of the time when his child should be brought to Clerkenwell. He replied in these words, 'That he consented to the examination proposed, provided that some persons connected with the girl might be permitted to be there, to divert her in the day-time.' This was refused, being contrary to the plan. He then mentioned a woman whom he affirmed to be unconnected, and not to have been with her. Upon being sent for she came, and was a person well known to us, by having been constantly with her, and very intimate with this Familiar, as she is called. Upon this Mr. Parsons recommended, as he said, an unexceptionable person, the daughter of a relation, who was a gentleman of fortune. After an inquiry into her character, he informed us that this unexceptionable person had disobliged her father, and was out at service. Upon this we answered, "Mr. Parsons, if you can procure any person or persons of strict character and reputation, who are housekeepers, such will be with pleasure admitted." Upon this he required a little time to seek for such a person. Instead of coming himself, as he promised, one William Lloyd by his direction brought us this message:

"Mr. Parsons chooses first to consult with his friends, who are at present not in the way, before he gives a positive answer concerning the removal of his daughter to the Rev. Mr. Aldrich's."

(Signed) WILLIAM LLOYD, Brook Street, Holborn.

Within three hours after we received another message from Mr. Parsons by the same hand, viz.

"If the Lord Mayor will give his approbation the child shall be removed to the Rev. Mr. Aldrich's."

"The plan before mentioned was thus set forth in the public papers: the girl was to be brought to the house of the clergyman, without any person whatever that had, or was supposed to have the least connexion with her. The father was to be there; not suffered to be in the room, but in a parlour, where there could be no sort of communication, attended by a proper person. A bed, without any furniture, was to be set in the middle of a large room, and the chairs to be placed round it. The persons to be present were some of the clergy, a physician, surgeon, apothecary, and a justice of the peace. The child was to be undressed, examined, and put to bed, by a lady of character. Gentlemen, both clergy and laity, (amongst whom was a noble lord, who desired to attend) were to have been present at the examination. We have done, and still are ready to do, every thing in our power to detect an imposture, if any, of the most unhappy tendency both to the public and to individuals."

STEPHEN ALDRICH, Rector of St. John's, Clerkenwell.
JAMES PENN, Lecturer of St. Anne's, Aldersgate.

In pursuance of the above plan, many gentlemen, eminent for their rank and character, by the invitation of the Rev.

Mr. Aldrich, assembled at his house on the 31st of January, and about ten at night met in the chamber in which the girl had, with proper caution, been put to bed by several ladies. They sat rather more than an hour, and hearing nothing went down stairs, where they interrogated the father of the girl, who denied, in the strongest terms, any knowledge or belief of fraud.

As the suppósed spirit had before publicly promised, by an affirmative knock,* that she would attend one of the gentlemen into the vault under the church of St. John's, Clerkenwell, where the body was deposited, and give a token of her presence there by a knock upon her coffin, it was therefore determined to make this trial of the existence or veracity of the spirit.

While they were inquiring and deliberating on this suggestion they were summoned into the girl's chamber by some ladies who were near her bed, and who had heard knocks and scratches. When the gentlemen entered, the girl declared that she felt the 'spirit like a mouse upon her back; and being required to hold her hands out of bed, from that time, though the spirit was very solemnly required to manifest its existence by appearance, by impression on the hand or body of any present, by scratches, knocks, or any other agency, no evidence of any preternatural power was exhibited. The spirit was then seriously advertised, that the person to whom the promise was made of striking the coffin was about to visit the vault, and that the performance of the promise was now claimed. The company, at one in the morning, went into the church, and the gentleman to whom the promise was made entered with one more into the vault: the spirit was solemnly required to perform her promise; but silence alone ensued. The person accused by the ghost then went down, with several others, but no effect was perceived. Upon their return they examined the

---

* The top joke of all, and what pleased me the most,
Some wise ones and I sat up with the Ghost,
With her nails and her knuckles she answer'd so nice,
For yes she knock'd once, and for no she knock'd twice.
Garrick's Farmer's Return.

girl but could draw no confession from her. Between two and three she desired and was permitted to go home with her father. It was therefore the opinion of the whole assembly, " That the child had some art of making or counterfeiting particular noises, and that there was no agency of any higher cause."

To elude the force of this conclusion, it was given out that the coffin in which the body of the supposed ghost had been deposited, or at least the body itself, had been displaced or removed out of the vault. Mr. Kent therefore thought proper to take with him to the vault the undertaker who buried Miss Fanny, and such other unprejudiced persons as, on inspection, might be able to prove the fallacy of such a suggestion.

Accordingly, in the afternoon of 25th of February, Mr. Kent with a clergyman, the undertaker, the clerk, and sexton of the parish, and two or three gentlemen, went into the vault, when the undertaker presently knew the coffin, which was taken from under the others, and easily seen to be the same, as there was no plate or inscription; and, to complete the evidence, the coffin being opened before Mr. Kent the body was found in it.

Other steps were in the meantime taken to find out where the fraud, if any, lay. The girl was removed from house to house, but was still said to be constantly attended with the usual noises, though bound and muffled hand and foot, and that without any motion in her lips, and when she appeared asleep: nay, they were often said to be heard in rooms at a considerable distance from that where she lay.

At last her bed was tied up in the manner of a hammock, about a yard and a half from the ground, and her hands extended as wide as they could without injury, and fastened with fillets, for two nights successively, during which no noises were heard. The next day, being pressed to confess, and being told that if the knockings and scratchings were not heard any more, she, her father and mother would be sent to Newgate, and half an hour being given her to consider, she desired she might be put to bed to try if the noises would come: she lay in bed that night much longer than usual, but no noises ensued. This was on a Saturday. Being told that the approaching night only would be allowed for a trial, she concealed a board about four inches broad and six long under her stays. This board was used to set the kettle upon. Having got into bed she told the gentlemen she would bring Fanny at six the next morning. The master of the house, however, and a friend of his, being informed by the maids that the girl had taken a board to bed with her, impatiently waited for the appointed hour, when she began to knock and scratch upon the board, remarking, however, what they themselves were convinced of, "that these noises were not like those which used to be made." She was then told that she had taken a board to bed, and on her denying it, searched, and caught in a lie.

The two gentlemen, who with the maids were the only persons present at this scene, sent to a third gentleman to acquaint him that the whole affair was detected, and to desire his immediate attendance. Their concurrent opinion was, that the child had been frightened into this attempt by the threats which had been made the two preceding nights; and the master of the house and his friend both declared, "that the noises the girl had made that morning had not the least similitude to the former noises."

Probably the organs with which she performed those strange noises were not always in a proper tone for that purpose, and she imagined she might be able to supply the place of them by a piece of board.

At length Mr. Kent thought proper to vindicate his character in a legal way. On the 10th of July the father and mother of the child, one Mary Frazer, who, it seems, acted as an interpreter between the ghost and those who examined her, the Rev. Mr. Moore, minister of St. Sepulchre, and one James, a reputable tradesman, were tried at Guildhall, before Lord Mansfield and a special jury, and convicted of a conspiracy against the life and character of Mr. Kent. The court being desirous that Mr. Kent, who had been so much injured on this occasion, should receive some pecuniary reparation from the offenders, deferred giving sentence for seven or eight months, in the hope that the parties might in the meantime compromise. Accordingly the clergyman and tradesman agreed to pay Mr. Kent about six hundred pounds to purchase their pardon, and were thereupon dismissed in February, 1763, by Mr. Justice Wilmot, with a severe reprimand and a fine of six shillings and eight pence each. The father was ordered to be set on the pillory three times in one month; once at the end of Cock Lane, and after that to be imprisoned two years, Elizabeth his wife one year, and Mary Frazer six months, in Bridewell, and to be there kept to hard labour. Mr. Brown of Amen Corner, for writing and publishing letters on the subject, was fined £50.

The father appearing to be out of his mind at the time he was first to stand on the pillory, the execution of that part of his sentence was deferred until 16 Feb. 1763, when, as well as on the succeeding days of his standing there, the populace considered him so much an object of compassion, that instead of pelting and otherwise using him ill they made a handsome collection for him.

Several pamphlets were published on the occasion, the most elaborate among which was "The Mystery Revealed," containing a series of transactions and authentic testimonials respecting the supposed Cock Lane Ghost, which have hitherto been concealed from the public.

Boswell mentions of Dr. Johnson that he expressed great indignation at the imposture of the Cock Lane Ghost, and related with much satisfaction how he had assisted in detecting the cheat, and had published an account of it in the newspapers.

There is no doubt now that the deception was carried on by means of ventriloquism, a faculty at that period little known and less understood. The young woman afterwards confessed such to have been the case; she died so recently as 1807, having been twice married; her second husband was a market gardener at Chiswick.

THE GHOST.

BOOK I.*

WITH eager search to dart the soul,
Curiously vain, from pole to pole,
And from the planets' wandering spheres
To extort the number of our years,
And whether all those years shall flow
Serenely smooth, and free from woe,
Or rude misfortune shall deform
Our life with one continual storm;
Or if the scene shall motley be,
Alternate joy and misery,
Is a desire which, more or less,
All men must feel, though few confess.
Hence, every place and every age
Affords subsistence to the sage

* The greater part of the first book of this poem was written when the author was curate of Cadbury, in Somersetshire; and was by him then intended to be published under the title of "The Fortune Teller." It was the least popular of all his productions. The metre is rugged, and, on the whole, inferior to that of the Duellist; and though many fine passages occur, yet the rambling, digressive manner in which the greater part of the poem is written, seldom invites to a re-perusal of it. Colman, under the assumed name of the Cobbler of Cripplegate, in his epistle to Lloyd, after justly condemning the

Who, free from this world and its cares,
Holds an acquaintance with the stars,
From whom he gains intelligence
Of things to come some ages hence,
Which unto friends, at easy rates,
He readily communicates.
At its first rise, which all agree on,
This noble science was Chaldean;

vanity and self-sufficient arrogance of the set (Thornton, &c.), introduces some strictures on the slovenly mode of composition occasionally adopted by our author.

"Say, must the town for ever hear,
And no reviewer dare to sneer,
Of Thornton's humour, Garrick's nature,
And Colman's wit, and Churchill's satire?
Churchill, who,—let it not offend
If I make free, though he's your friend,
And sure we cannot want excuse,
When Churchill's named, for smart abuse—
Churchill, who ever loves to raise
On slander's dung his mushroom bays:
The priest I grant has something clever,
A something that will last for ever.
Let him in part be made your pattern,
Whose muse, now queen and now a slattern,
Trick'd out in Rosciad, rules the roast,
Turns trapes and trollop in the Ghost,
By turns both tickles us and warms,
And, drunk or sober, has her charms."

22 Many circumstances contribute to confirm the probability of the conjecture that astronomy was first studied as a science by the Chaldeans. The serenity of their climate, the advantage they possessed of being the first people united to-

That ancient people, as they fed
Their flocks upon the mountain's head,
Gazed on the stars, observed their motions,
And suck'd in astrologic notions,
Which they so eagerly pursue,
As folks are apt whate'er is new,
That things below at random rove,
Whilst they're consulting things above;
And when they now so poor were grown,
That they'd no houses of their own,

gether in the bands of civil society, and the local situation of Babylon, which was best calculated to assist them in those operations which the study of the heavenly bodies requires, must early have invited them to it. Built on a boundless elevated plain, and open on all sides, no obstacle was presented to the view of the most extensive horizon. The mode of life adopted by the first inhabitants of Chaldea considerably favoured their progress in the science. Pasturage formed one of their chief occupations, passing whole days and nights in the open air; their attention must have been early attracted by the various motions of the celestial bodies. "Principio Assyrii, propter planitiem magnitudinemque regionum quas incolebant, cum cœlum ex omni parte, patens et apertum intuerentur, trajectiones, motusque stellarum observarunt." Cic. de Div. lib. 1.

To no nation could an acquaintance with the stars be more necessary, than to the tribes inhabiting Chaldea, a region principally consisting of immense plains of sand, which, agitated by the wind and leaving no traces of the human footstep, could not admit of the possibility of constructing permanent roads. The stars are, in such a region, the only certain guides to which a traveller can have recourse to direct his steps, especially as the excessive heat of the climate does not admit of his pursuing his journey during the day.

The invention of judicial astrology has also by all antiquity

They made bold with their friends the stars,
And prudently made use of theirs.
To Egypt from Chaldee it travell'd,
And fate at Memphis was unravell'd:
The exotic science soon struck root,
And flourish'd into high repute:
Each learned priest, O strange to tell!
Could circles make, and cast a spell;
Could read and write, and taught the nation
The holy art of divination.

been attributed to the Chaldeans. This vain and ridiculous perversion of the noblest science, soon induced the attempt to ascertain the course of the stars, and their different aspects. Without this knowledge, it would have been impossible to have formed an horoscope. To this frivolous desire of reading in the stars the destinies of mankind, we are therefore principally indebted for the progress and improvements in the study of astronomy. Kepler, with great reason, observed a century ago, that astrology was a weak, foolish daughter of a very wise mother, who, however, would scarcely have been able to subsist without her assistance.

35 The Egyptians improved upon the rudiments of astronomy, as imparted to them by the Chaldeans, and were the first people who gave a determinate period to the year. Herodotus mentions, that owing to their knowledge of the celestial bodies, they had divided it into twelve months. Theirs was the Luni-solar year, consisting of 360 days, before the time of Moses, who adopted it accordingly in his computations. In the reign of Ammon the father of Osiris or Sesac, the Thebans, applying themselves to astronomy and navigation, determined the length of the solar year by the heliacal risings and settings of the stars, and added two days to the old calendar year. In the reign of Amenophis, which was not long after, the use of this year was generally adopted by the Egyptians, who placed the first day of it upon the vernal equinox.

Nobles themselves, for at that time
Knowledge in nobles was no crime,
Could talk as learned as the priest,
And prophesy as much at least:
Hence all the fortune-telling crew,
Whose crafty skill mars nature's hue,
Who, in vile tatters, with smirch'd face,

[52] Bampfylde Moore Carew was the son of a clergyman at Bickley, in Devonshire, and was educated at Tiverton school, with an intention of his taking orders; but falling into the company of sốme gypsies near that town, young Carew, at the age of fifteen, grew so fond of his associates, that he resolved to embrace their vagrant mode of life; and immediately absconded from school. After a short time spent with the fortune-telling fraternity, he returned home, to the great joy of his parents, who had given up all expectation of ever seeing him again. His love for the mendicant life, however, still remained unextinguished, and gradually grew upon him to such a degree, as once more to induce him to quit his father's habitation. His exploits in this course of life were wonderful, and the account of his shifts and impositions still form a part of our popular library. Carew had a peculiar method of enticing away dogs, for which he was twice trans ported from Exeter to North America; but returned before the ship which carried him out. He was a man of retentive memory, and happy address. The fraternity to which he belonged elected him their king; and he remained faithful to his subjects to the last. It is supposed that he died about 1770, aged 77.

[52] Mary Squires, a gypsy, and one of Carew's subjects, was a principal agent in Elizabeth Canning's affair, an account of which transaction will be given in ,a subsequent note.

[54] The origin of this distinct and singular people has hitherto baffled the inquiries of the learned. In the gypsies are united all the vices of savage and civilized society, with-

Run up and down from place to place,
To gratify their friends' desires,
From Bampfield Carew, to Moll Squires,
Are rightly term'd Egyptians all
Whom we, mistaking, Gypsies call.
The Grecian sages borrow'd this,
As they did other sciences,

out the simplicity of the one, or the refinement of the other. They are treacherous and cowardly, indolent and filthy; living upon carrion, and looking upon clothes as an incumbrance. In short, they are a disgrace to every government which tolerates their existence as a body. By Stat. 22 H. viii. and 1 and 2 Philip and Mary, the entrance of outlandish people, calling themselves Egyptians, into this kingdom, is prohibited on pain of death; and they are declared not entitled to the privilege of being tried per medietatem linguæ.

They principally abound in Hungary, and their language appears to be a mixture of the Latin and Sclavonic: a dissertation on the gypsies was published in German, by Grellman, which has been translated into English by Mr. Raper, but the information contained in it is far from satisfactory.

In the prevailing rage for researches into Oriental History, they are supposed to be a branch of the Indian degraded caste of the Parias, who emigrated from, or were expelled their country, in consequence of the invasion of Timour.

55 The Greeks were totally ignorant of the science of astronomy in the time of Herodotus, who, in mentioning an eclipse which took place in the midst of a battle between the Medes and Lydians, and finding no word in the Greek language to describe it, is compelled to resort to a periphrasis for that purpose. He says, that while the two armies were engaged, night suddenly took place of the day. Thales, he adds, predicted this event to the Ionians; and specified the

From fertile Egypt, though the loan
They had not honesty to own.
Dodonna's oaks, inspired by Jove,
A learned and prophetic grove,
Turn'd vegetable necromancers,
And to all comers gave their answers.
At Delphos, to Apollo dear,
All men the voice of Fate might hear;
Each subtle priest on three-legg'd stool,
To take in wise men, play'd the fool;
A mystery, so made for gain,
E'en now in fashion must remain.
Enthusiasts never will let drop
What brings such business to their shop,
And that great saint, we Whitfield call,

year in which this change of day into night would take place. Thales probably had obtained his information from the Egyptian tables.

71 George Whitfield, one of the apostles of methodism, was born in Gloucester, in December, 1714, at the Bell Inn, which was then kept by his mother. At this Inn, until about the 18th year of his age, he was waiter; and in the memoirs of his own life, gives no favourable account of his conduct while in that menial capacity; his life, he says, was passed in a continual course of vicious habits; lying, lewdness, filthy talking, swearing, and foolish jesting; and he concludes his catalogue of offences with observing, that if traced from his cradle up to manhood, he could see nothing in himself but a fitness to be damned. His mother failing in business, he became utterly destitute, until through the interest of a friend, he was admitted a Servitor at Oxford; he here acquired the character on which his future eminence was to be built. In the austerities of his devotion, and in the squalidness of his person, he almost equalled what is related

Keeps up the humbug spiritual.
  Among the Romans, not a bird
Without a prophecy, was heard ;

of the Egyptian anchorites, or Indian faquirs: he describes himself as lying whole days and weeks prostrate on the ground in silent or vocal prayer; leaving off the eating of fruits, choosing the worst sort of food, thinking it unbecoming a penitent to have his hair powdered, and wearing woollen gloves, a patch gown, and dirty shoes, to contract a habit of humility. Struck by the young man's piety and austerity of manner, Benson, then Bishop of Gloucester, made him a voluntary offer of ordination, which Whitfield accepted, and in June 1736 began his spiritual mission, preaching in the streets, in the fields, and in prisons; and his labours proved eminently successful. By his eloquence and his zeal the great body of the poorer and many of the middling and upper classes of society, were roused to a sense of their religious privileges and obligations.

Wesley, also a churchman, at the same period, laid the foundation for his more elaborate and permanent system of religious domination, which occasioned a schism between him and Whitfield, and although diverging too much as one did to Arminianism, and the other to Hyper-Calvinism, England and America are still deeply indebted to both for the awakening impulse given by them to the highest faculties and purposes of our nature.

Whitfield erected two extensive tabernacles, one in Tottenham Court Road, and the other in Moorfields; and was also chaplain to the Countess of Huntingdon, and superintendent of the various chapels erected under her patronage.

The influence of methodism, being extended by his nurturing care over all parts of this kingdom, his attention was engaged by America, whither he repeatedly went and prosecuted his mission with extraordinary success. In the new world which he had conquered, he was doomed to meet his fate; a violent asthma put a period to his life, in 1770, in the 56th year of his age, near Boston in New England, being his seventh visit to America.

Fortunes of empires often hung
On the magician magpie's tongue,
And every crow was to the state
A sure interpreter of fate,
Prophets, embodied in a college
(Time out of mind your seat of knowledge,
For genius never fruit can bear
Unless it first is planted there;
And solid learning never falls

79 The College of Augurs consisted of fifteen persons of the first distinction in Rome: it was a priesthood for life, of a character indelible, which no crime could forfeit or efface. They presided over the auspices as the supreme interpreters of the will of Jove; and determined what signs were propitious, or otherwise. A powerful influence was by these means vested in the aristocracy, who thus were able to repress or check the precipitate measures of the people and their tribunes. Cicero, with the great body of philosophers and men of influence, considered the whole system as politically useful, and therefore gave it their support and countenance; for of the whole College of Augurs, there was but one man, Appius Claudius, who held with the people that the gods out of their goodness to man, had imprinted on the nature of things certain marks or notices of future evénts; as on the entrails of beasts, the flight of birds, thunder, and other celestial signs which, by long observation, and the experience of ages, had been reduced to an art, by which the meaning of each sign might be determined, and applied to the event that was signified by it. This was called artificial divination, by way of distinction from the natural, which was supposed to flow from an instinctive or native power implanted in the soul; which it exerted always with the greatest efficacy, when it was the most free and disengaged from the body, as in dreams and madness. Augustus with his wonted policy combined in his own person, the dignified and important functions of supreme pontiff, censor, and chief civil magistrate.

Without the verge of college walls)
Infallible accounts would keep
When it was best to watch or sleep,
To eat or drink, to go or stay,
And when to fight or run away;
When matters were for actions ripe,
By looking at a double tripe;
When emperors would live or die
They in an ass's skull could spy;
When generals would their station keep,
Or turn their backs, in hearts of sheep,
In matters, whether small or great,
In private families or state
As amongst us, the holy seer
Officiously would interfere;

84 The poet's antipathy to colleges may be dated from his rejection by the university of Oxford, on account of his want of a competent skill in the learned languages. Instead of making proper replies to the questions proposed to him he not only launched out into satirical reflections on the abilities of the gentlemen whose office it was to make trial of his classical proficiency, but presumed to put some questions to the Examiner, which were of course indignantly declined, and the candidate very unceremoniously dismissed.

94 A flam more senseless than the rog'ry
Of old aurispicy and aug'ry,
That out of garbages of cattle
Presag'd th' events of truce, or battle
From flights of birds, or chicken's-pecking
Success of great'st attempts would reckon.
Though cheats, yet more intelligible
Than those that with the stars do fribble.

HUDIBRAS, *part* ii. *canto* 3.

With pious arts and reverend skill
Would bend lay bigots to his will;
Would help or injure foes or friends,
Just as it served his private ends.
Whether, in honest way of trade
Traps for virginity were laid,
Or if, to make their party great,
Designs were form'd against the state,
Regardless of the common weal,
By interest led, which they call zeal,
Into the scale was always thrown
The will of Heaven to back their own.
England, a happy land we know,
Where follies naturally grow,
Where, without culture they arise,
And tower above the common size;
England, a fortune-telling host
As numerous as the stars, could boast;
Matrons, who toss the cup, and see
The grounds of fate in grounds of tea;
Who, versed in every modest lore,
Can a lost maidenhead restore,
Or, if their pupils rather choose it,
Can show the readiest way to lose it.
Gypsies, who every ill can cure
Except the ill of being poor,
Who charms 'gainst love and agues sell,
Who can in hen-roost set a spell,
Prepared by arts, to them best known
To catch all feet except their own,
Who as to fortune, can unlock it

As easily as pick a pocket;
Scotchmen, who, in their country's right,
Possess the gift of second sight,
Who (when their barren heaths they quit,
Sure argument of prudent wit,
Which reputation to maintain,
They never venture back again)
By lies prophetic heap up riches,
And boast the luxury of breeches.
  Amongst the rest, in former years,
Campbell, illustrious name, appears,
Great hero of futurity,
Who blind, could every thing foresee,

132 Dr. Johnson, in his Journey to the Western Islands, fully discusses the superstitious acquiescence of the Highlanders of all ranks, in the claim made by some of their countrymen to second-sight, or the faculty of sensibly perceiving future transactions and events. With an avowed inclination to establish the existence of so extraordinary a privilege, he regrets his having been unable to collect sufficient testimonies for the satisfaction of himself or of the public. He dismisses the question in the state he found it, and concludes with saying, "That there is against it, the seeming analogy of things confusedly seen and little understood; and for it the indistinct cry of national persuasion, which may be perhaps resolved at last into prejudice and tradition. I never could advance my curiosity to conviction; but came away at last, only willing to believe." Mr. Croker observes on this and other dicta of Dr. Johnson on the same subject, that although he generally leaned to the superstitious side of this question, yet that he occasionally took a more rational view of it.

140 Campbell, a deaf and dumb fortune-teller, who for a number of years imposed upon the credulity of the public. So gainful a trade occasioned a succession of impostors, who

Who dumb, could every thing foretell,
Who, fate with equity to sell,
Always dealt out the will of Heaven
According to what price was given.
  Of Scottish race, in Highlands born,
Possess'd with native pride and scorn,
He hither came, by custom led,
To curse the hands that gave him bread.
With want of truth, and want of sense,
Amply made up by impudence.
(A succedaneum, which we find
In common use with all mankind)
Caress'd and favour'd too by those
Whose heart with patriot feelings glows,
Who foolishly, where'er dispersed,
Still place their native country first;
(For Englishmen alone have sense
To give a stranger preference,
Whilst modest merit of their own
Is left in poverty to groan)
Campbell foretold just what he would,
And left the stars to make it good,
On whom he had impress'd such awe,
His dictates current pass'd for law;
Submissive, all his empire own'd;
No star durst smile, when Campbell frown'd.
  This sage deceased, for all must die,

unhappily still, under various forms, but working on the same staple, obtain a golden harvest from the folly, ignorance, and superstition of mankind.

And Campbell's no more safe than I,
No more than I can guard the heart,
When Death shall hurl the fatal dart,
Succeeded, ripe in art and years,
Another favourite of the spheres;
Another and another came,
Of equal skill, and equal fame;
As white each wand, as black each gown,
As long each beard, as wise each frown,
In every thing so like, you'd swear,
Campbell himself was sitting there:
To all the happy art was known,
To tell our fortunes, make their own.
  Seated in garret; for you know
The nearer to the stars we go
The greater we esteem his art,
Fools curious flock'd from every part:
The rich, the poor, the maid, the married,
And those who could not walk, were carried.
  The butler, hanging down his head,
By chambermaid, or cookmaid led,
Inquires, if from his friend the moon
He has advice of pilfer'd spoon?
  The court-bred woman of condition,
(Who to approve her disposition
As much superior, as her birth
To those composed of common earth,
With double spirit must engage
In every folly of the age)
The honourable arts would buy,
To pack the cards, and cog a die.

The hero (who for brawn and face
May claim right honourable place
Amongst the chiefs of Butcher-row,)
Who might some thirty years ago,
If we may be allow'd to guess
At his employment by his dress,
Put medicines off from cart or stage,
The grand Toscano of the age,
Or might about the country go
High steward of a puppet-show,
Steward and stewardship most meet,
For all know *puppets never eat:*
Who would be thought (though, save the mark,
That point is something in the dark)
The man of honour, one like those
Renown'd in story, who loved blows
Better than victuals, and would fight,
Merely for sport, from morn to night:
Who treads like Mavors firm, whose tongue
Is with the triple thunder hung,
Who cries to Fear—stand off—aloof—
And talks as he were cannon proof,

202 At the publication of the first edition of this work Butcher-row, a very narrow timber-built gable-ended street, running along side of St. Clement's church in the Strand, constituted a perfect specimen of old London, as it was when Justice Shallow studied the law in Clement's Inn. It has been since wholly removed, and forms a part of the site of Pickett Street.

212 Alluding to the economical regulations unsuccessfully attempted to be introduced into the royal household by Lord Talbot.

Would be deem'd ready, when you list,
With sword and pistol, stick and fist,
Careless of points, balls, bruises, knocks,
At once to fence, fire, cudgel, box,
But at the same time bears about
Within himself, some touch of doubt,
Of prudent doubt, which hints—that fame
Is nothing but an empty name;
That life is rightly understood
By all to be a real good;
That, even in a hero's heart
Discretion is the better part;
(That this same honour may be won,
And yet no kind of danger run)
Like Drugger comes, that magic powers
May ascertain his lucky hours;
For at some hours the fickle dame,
Whom fortune properly we name,
Who ne'er considers wrong or right,
When wanted most plays least in sight,
And, like a modern court-bred jilt,
Leaves her chief favourites in a tilt:
Some hours there are, when from the heart
Courage into some other part,
No matter, wherefore, makes retreat,
And fear usurps the vacant seat,
Whence, planet-struck, we often find
Stuarts and Sackvilles of mankind.

237 Abel Drugger, in Jonson's Alchymist.

250 James the Second's dastardly conduct at the battle of

Farther, he'd know (and by his art
A conjurer can that impart)
Whether politer it is reckon'd
To have or not to have a second?
To drag the friends in, or alone
To make the danger all their own?

the Boyne, and the consternation with which he retreated to Dublin, and from thence to France, are facts difficult to be accounted for in the man who, as Duke of York, had displayed so much personal courage and magnanimity in the various desperate naval engagements with the Dutch. Instead of being animated with redoubled ardour by the magnitude of the stake for which he contended, his spirits sank under the superior genius of his rival! and his base dereliction of his people proved the conscious sense he entertained of his inability to govern them.

250 Lord George Sackville, commander of the British and of several brigades of German cavalry, by not advancing with them at the battle of Minden, pursuant to the orders of the commander-in-chief, Prince Ferdinand of Brunswick, rendered the success of the day infinitely less brilliant and complete than it would otherwise have been. A few days after the battle, his lordship resigned the command, and returned to London, where, on his arrival, he was deprived of all his military commands, in which he was succeeded by the Marquis of Granby.

Under these circumstances, he applied to be tried by a court-martial for his supposed misconduct at the battle of Minden; his request was complied with, the trial was of considerable length, and the defence was managed with great ingenuity. On the 26th of April, 1760, the following sentence and observation on it were inserted in the London Gazette: "This court, upon due consideration of the whole matter before them, is of opinion that Lord George Sackville is guilty of having disobeyed the orders of Prince Ferdinand of Brunswick, whom he was by his commission and instructions directed to obey, as commander-in-chief, according to the rules

Whether repletion is not bad,
And fighters with full stomachs mad?
Whether, before he seeks the plain,
It were not well to breathe a vein?
Whether a gentle salivation,
Consistently with reputation,
Might not of precious use be found,
Not to prevent indeed a wound,

of war; and it is the further opinion of the court that the said Lord George Sackville is, and he is hereby adjudged, unfit to serve his majesty in any military capacity whatever.

"Which sentence his majesty has been pleased to confirm. It is his Majesty's pleasure that the above sentence be given out in public orders, that officers being convinced that neither high birth nor great employments can shelter offences of such a nature; and that seeing they are subject to censures much worse than death, to a man who has any sense of honour, they may avoid the fatal consequences arising from disobedience of orders.

"At the court of St. James's, the 25th day of April, 1760. Present the King's most excellent majesty in council. His majesty called for the council book, and ordered the name of Lord George Sackville to be struck out of the list of Privy Counsellors."

On the trial, Colonel Sloper deposed, that his lordship appeared confused on receiving the order to advance, whereupon Colonel Sloper said to Colonel Ligonier, who brought the order: "For God's sake repeat your orders to that man, that he may not pretend not to understand them; but you see the condition he is in."

Thus stigmatized, much surprise was excited when Lord Sackville was admitted to the honour of kissing George the Third's hand immediately on his accession, and while his predecessor lay dead in his palace. In 1765, he was restored to his rank of Privy Counsellor and appointed one of the Vice Treasurers of Ireland. In 1775, during Lord North's admi-

But to prevent the consequence
Which oftentimes arises thence,
Those fevers which the patient urge on
To gates of death, by help of surgeon?
Whether a wind at east or west
Is for green wounds accounted best?
Whether (was he to choose) his mouth
Should point towards the north or south?
Whether more safely he might use,
On these occasions, pumps or shoes?

nistration, he was appointed by the name of the Right Honourable Lord George Sackville Germain, to be one of his majesty's principal Secretaries of State, and took the American department, in which situation he displayed considerable ability as a statesman, and was the ablest supporter in parliament of the measures of administration. Soon after his degradation he declared, in the course of a debate in the House of Commons, that he bled for the distresses of his country, arising from the heavy expenses of the German war; upon which Mr. Pitt rose, and in his most energetic manner replied, that in his opinion the honourable gentleman ought to throw himself at his majesty's feet, and there bleed at every pore.

In 1782 he was created a peer by the title of Baron Bolebrooke, Viscount Sackville. On the report of this intended creation, a motion was made in the House of Lords by the Marquis of Carmarthen, "that it is derogatory to the honour of this house, that any person labouring under the censure of a court martial, whose sentence the crown had been pleased to confirm, should be recommended to his majesty to be raised to the dignity of the peerage." Upon this motion the question of adjournment was put and carried by a majority of 75 against 30. Lord Sackville died in August, 1785. He is one of the many persons to whom the authorship of Junius's Let ters has been attributed.

Whether it better is to fight
By sunshine or by candlelight?
Or (lest a candle should appear
Too mean to shine in such a sphere,
For who could of a candle tell
To light a hero into hell,
And lest the sun should partial rise
To dazzle one or t'other's eyes,
Or one or t'other's brains to scorch)
Might not Dame Luna hold a torch?
  These points with dignity discuss'd,
And gravely fixed, a task which must
Require no little time and pains,
To make our hearts friends with our brains,
The man of war would next engage
The kind assistance of the sage,
Some previous method to direct,
Which should make these of none effect.
  Could he not, from the mystic school
Of art, produce some sacred rule,
By which a knowledge might be got
Whether men valiant were, or not;
So he that challenges, might write
Only to those who would not fight?
  Or could he not some way dispense
By help of which (without offence
To Honour, whose nice nature's such
She scarce endures the slightest touch)
When he for want of t'other rule
Mistakes his man, and like a fool,
With some vain fighting blade gets in,

He fairly may get out again?
  Or should some demon lay a scheme
To drive him to the last extreme,
So that he must confess his fears,
In mercy to his nose and ears,
And, like a prudent recreant knight,
Rather do any thing than fight,
Could he not some expedient buy
To keep his shame from public eye?
For well he held, and, men review,
Nine in ten hold the maxim too,
That honour's like a maidenhead,
Which, if in private brought to bed,
Is none the worse, but walks the town,
Ne'er lost, until the loss be known.
  The parson, too, (for now and then
Parsons are just like other men,
And here and there a grave divine
Has passions such as yours and mine)
Burning with holy lust to know
When fate preferment will bestow,
'Fraid of detection, not of sin,
With circumspection sneaking in
To conjurer, as he does to whore,
Through some bye-alley, or back-door,
With the same caution Orthodox
Consults the stars, and gets a pox.
  The citizen in fraud grown old,
Who knows no deity but gold,
Worn out, and gasping now for breath,
A medicine wants to keep off death,

Would know, if that he cannot have,
What coins are current in the grave;
If, when the stocks (which, by his power,
Would rise or fall in half an hour,
For, though unthought of and unseen,
He work'd the springs behind the screen)
By his directions came about,
And rose to par, he should sell out;
Whether he safely might, or no,
Replace it in the funds below?
By all address'd, believed, and paid,
Many pursued the thriving trade,
And, great, in reputation grown,
Successive held the magic throne,
Favour'd by every darling passion,
The love of novelty and fashion,
Ambition, avarice, lust, and pride,
Riches pour'd in on every side;
But when the prudent laws thought fit
To curb this insolence of wit;
When senates wisely had provided,
Decreëd, enacted, and decided,
That no such vile and upstart elves
Should have more knowledge than themselves;
When fines and penalties were laid
To stop the progress of the trade,

358 It was by stat. 17 Geo. 2, c. 5, s. 2, enacted that all persons pretending skill in palmistry, telling fortunes, &c., should be deemed rogues and vagabonds, and punished accordingly.

And stars no longer could dispense,
With honour, farther influence;
And wizards (which must be confest
Was of more force than all the rest)
No certain way to tell had got
Which were informers and which not;
Affrighted sages were, perforce,
Obliged to steer some other course:
By various ways, these sons of Chance
Their fortunes labour'd to advance,
Well knowing, by unerring rules,
Knaves starve not in the land of fools.
  Some, with high titles and degrees,
Which wise men borrow when they please,
Without or trouble or expense,
Physicians instantly commence,
And proudly boast an equal skill
With those who claim the right to kill.
  Others about the country roam
(For not one thought of going home)
With pistol and adopted leg,
Prepared at once to rob or beg.
  Some, the more subtle of their race,
(Who felt some touch of coward grace,
Who Tyburn to avoid had wit,
But never fear'd deserving it)
Came to their brother Smollett's aid,

389 We have before noticed the cause of the enmity borne by Churchill to Smollett, and to the Critical Review carried on under his management.

And carried on the critic trade.
  Attach'd to letters and the Muse,
Some verses wrote, and some wrote news;
Those each revolving month are seen
The heroes of a magazine;
These every morning great appear
In Ledger or in Gazetteer,
Spreading the falsehoods of the day,
By turns, for Faden and for Say;
Like Swiss, their force is always laid
On that side where they best are paid:
Hence mighty prodigies arise,
And daily monsters strike our eyes;
Wonders, to propagate the trade,
More strange than ever Baker made,
Are hawk'd about from street to street,
And fools believe, whilst liars eat.
  Now armies in the air engage,
To fright a superstitious age;

398 The editors of the newspapers mentioned in the preceding couplet. Faden was particularly obnoxious on account of the share he took in procuring, at the instigation of Kidgell, a copy of the Essay on Woman, with a view to the prosecution of Wilkes.

404 Sir Richard Baker, a chronicler of marvellous memory, who flourished towards the conclusion of the sixteenth century: the last and best edition of his celebrated book of wonders was in 1733. Churchill here takes occasion very justly to reprehend that love of the wonderful which pervaded all ranks of people amongst his contemporaries, and which contributed to fill the newspapers and magazines with the most preposterous tales that the human imagination could devise.

Now comets through the ether range,
In governments portending change;
Now rivers to the ocean fly
So quick, they leave their channels dry;
Now monstrous whales on Lambeth shore
Drink the Thames dry, and thirst for more;
And every now and then appears
An Irish savage, numbering years
More than those happy sages could
Who drew their breath before the flood;
Now, to the wonder of all people,
A church is left without a steeple;
A steeple now is left in lurch,
And mourns departure of the church,
Which, borne on wings of mighty wind,
Removed a furlong off we find;

413 One of the periodical wonders of the metropolis; but no whale has yet appeared in the river of such monstrous dimensions as that which, on the 9th of July 1574, shot himself ashore at Broad Stairs; and where, for want of sufficient depth of water, he died next day: his roaring was heard above a mile, his length was 22 yards, his nether jaw opening 12 feet, one of his eyes was more than a cart with six horses could draw. A man stood upright in the place from whence the eye was taken, the thickness from his belly to the top of his back was 14 feet, his tail of the same breadth, the distance between his eyes was 12 feet. Three men stood upright in his mouth, some of his ribs were 16 feet long, his tongue was 15 feet long, his liver was two cart loads, and a man might creep into his nostrils. *Kilburn's Survey of Kent*, p. 215.

This far exceeded the dimensions of the skeleton of a whale exhibited at Charing Cross a few years ago under the designation of the Prince of Whales.

Now, wrath on cattle to discharge,
Hailstones as deadly fall, and large,
As those which were on Egypt sent,
At once their crime and punishment,
Or those which, as the prophet writes,
Fell on the necks of Amorites,
When, struck with wonder and amaze,
The sun suspended, stay'd to gaze,
And, from her duty longer kept,
In Ajalon his sister slept.
But if such things no more engage,
The taste of a politer age,
To help them out in time of need
Another Tofts must rabbits breed:

438 As an instance of the credulity of the public, in addition to the subject of this poem, the singular imposture of Mary Tofts is deserving of notice. The following relation of it by a believer is too singular to be omitted. The author was no less a man than the eminent mathematician and learned translator of Josephus, the Rev. William Whiston, who in the memoirs of his life, Vol. II. p. 108, contends strongly for the fulfilment of a prophecy of Esdras, viz.: *there should be signs in the woman*, in the person of Mrs. Mary Tofts, the rabbit woman of Godalming, in 1727. The account this woman gave of herself was briefly this:—She had been weeding in a field, and seeing a rabbit spring up near her, ran after it, with another woman, but could not catch it. Her companion charged her with longing for the rabbit, but she denied it. Soon after another rabbit sprung up which she also endeavoured to catch. The same night she dreamt she had the two rabbits in her lap, and awakened with a sick fit which lasted till morning. For three months she had a constant and strong desire to eat rabbits; but being in indigent circumstances she could not procure any, till at last she was marvellously brought to bed of them. Mr. Whiston proceeds—"this story

Each pregnant female trembling hears,
And, overcome with spleen and fears,
Consults her faithful glass no more,
But madly bounding o'er the floor,
Feels hairs all o'er her body grow,
By Fancy turn'd into a doe.
Now, to promote their private ends,
Nature her usual course suspends,
And varies from the stated plan
Observed e'er since the world began.
Bodies, (which foolishly we thought,
By Custom's servile maxims taught,

has been so long laughed out of countenance that I must distinctly give my reasons for believing it true, and alleging it here as fulfilling an ancient prophecy. Accordingly, besides the testimony of the woman herself, who moved great compassion and was relieved by charitable persons, Mr. Howard, a man-midwife of great skill, honour, and reputation in his profession, attested it. It was then believed by King George to be real, and was generally believed by sober persons in the neighbourhood, till it was unjustly laughed out of countenance in London, and those who acted in the matter were made sport of by the sceptics of the town; nor did the woman ever confess the fraud till she was herself threatened with a painful operation, and with imprisonment. Nor did the surgeons and men-midwives pretend to any ground of suspicion, till they found they were likely to suffer greatly in their reputation and practice had they supported that story any longer. Of which sort of confessions like those made upon torture I have no opinion at all. So I have all along gone by my original evidence, and have ever since believed the fact to have been true, and an eminent completion of the prophecy before us."

The circumstance excited a lively controversy in the medical world, particularly between Dr. Douglas and Sir Richard Manningham, Knt., F. R. S., the latter of whom, in 1726, pub-

Needed a regular supply,
And without nourishment must die)
With craving appetites, and sense
Of hunger easily dispense,
And, pliant to their wondrous skill,
Are taught, like watches, to stand still,
Uninjured, for a month or more,
Then go on as they did before.
The novel takes, the tale succeeds,
Amply supplies its author's needs,
And Betty Canning is at least,
With Gascoyne's help, a six months' feast.

lished "an exact diary of what was observed during a close attendance upon Mary Toft, the pretended Rabbit breeder of Godalming in Surrey, from Monday, Nov. 28 to Wednesday, Dec. 7 following, together with an account of her confession of the fraud."

Mr. St. André, an eminent surgeon, after having lent himself to the delusion, found it necessary to publish the following recantation.

"Having contributed in some measure to the belief of an imposture in a narrative lately published by me of an extraordinary delivery of rabbits performed by Mr. John Howard, surgeon at Guilford, and having been since instrumental in discovering the same, so that I am now thoroughly convinced it is a most abominable fraud: I think myself obliged, in strict regard to truth, to acquaint the public thereof, and that I intend in a short time to publish a full account of this discovery, with some considerations on the extraordinary circumstances of this case, which misled me in my apprehensions thereof; and which as I hope they will in some measure excuse the mistakes made by myself and others who have vilified the woman concerned therein, will also be acceptable to the world in separating the innocent from those who have been guilty."

461 In the year 1753, an extraordinary affair attracted

Whilst in contempt of all our pains
The tyrant Superstition reigns
Imperious in the heart of man,
And warps his thoughts from Nature's plan;
Whilst fond Credulity, who ne'er
The weight of wholesome doubts could bear,
To reason and herself unjust,
Takes all things blindly upon trust;

the notice and divided the opinion of the public. A girl of eighteen years of age, named Elizabeth Canning, having been missing from her master eighteen days, came home to her mother in a deplorable and emaciated condition, and declared upon oath that on the 1st of January, about nine in the morning, while walking from Rosemary Lane, she was seized by two men in Moorfields, who first robbed and then gagged her, and that in consequence of their ill usage she fell into a fit, and so continued for some hours; on recovering she found herself in a kitchen with an old gypsy woman and two young women, the former took her by the hand and promised to give her some fine clothes, which expression Elizabeth Canning considering as an invitation to be a prostitute, she utterly refused to comply with it; whereupon the old woman almost stript her and pushed her into a back room like a hay-loft, without any furniture in it, and there locked her up, threatening to cut her throat if she made any disturbance. On looking about her in the morning she discovered a large jug filled with water and several pieces of bread, amounting to about a quartern loaf, scattered on the floor together with some hay. In this room she said she continued from that time until 4 o'clock P. M. of 29 January following, being 27 days and upwards, without any other sustenance than the bread and water mentioned and a minced pie she had in her pocket. She likewise said she left some of these provisions behind her when she made her escape by breaking out of the house. She said that during her confinement not a creature had come near her to see or speak to her. Upon her return an investigation was set on foot, and having fixed upon a house at Enfield

Whilst Curiosity, whose rage
No mercy shows to sex or age,
Must be indulged at the expense
Of judgment, truth, and common sense:
Impostures cannot but prevail,
And when old miracles grow stale,
Jugglers will still the art pursue,
And entertain the world with new.
For them, obedient to their will,
And trembling at their mighty skill,

Wash, on the Hertford road, as the place where she had been confined, one Mrs. Wills, who kept it, together with Mary Squires, the gypsy, and Virtue Hall, a young woman who lived with Wills, were taken up and committed for trial. Upon the examination the young woman fully confirmed the statement of Canning. After a full and long trial, Wills and Squires were found guilty, and the latter sentenced to suffer death. Sir Crisp Gascoyne, the Lord Mayor, being dissatisfied with the evidence, took extraordinary pains to unravel the conspiracy, in which he succeeded to his utmost wish. An alibi was clearly made out, and a free pardon granted to Mary Squires. An indictment for perjury was preferred against Elizabeth Canning, who was convicted, on the clearest evidence, of wilful and corrupt perjury, and thereupon sentenced to be transported for seven years.

The Egyptian Hall, in the Mansion House, received that appellation from the circumstance of the examinations of the gypsies in this matter having been taken in it.

Sir Crisp Gascoyne incurred a great deal of unpopularity by the zeal he displayed in detecting the fraud; but at the expiration of his mayoralty the Common Council did justice to his motives by a special vote of thanks for his conduct on the occasion.

Henry Fielding, who as a magistrate took the charge and first examinations in support of it, was apparently piqued by the Lord Mayor's superior tact and perseverance in detecting

Sad spirits, summon'd from the tomb,
Glide glaring, ghastly through the gloom,
In all the usual pomp of storms,
In horrid customary forms,
A wolf, a bear, a horse, an ape,
As fear and fancy give them shape,
Tormented with despair and pain,
They roar, they yell, and clank the chain.
Folly and Guilt (for Guilt, howe'er
The face of Courage it may wear,
Is still a coward at the heart)
At fear-created phantoms start.
The priest, that very word implies
That he's both innocent and wise,
Yet fears to travel in the dark,

the conspiracy, wrote a pamphlet in vindication of Canning, called a clear state of the case; he was conclusively refuted by Dr. Hill, in a tract entitled the story of Elizabeth Canning Considered.

The public were inflamed to an incredible pitch of folly and injustice on the occasion; they not only raised subscriptions for the artful girl's defence, but insulted the Lord Mayor, and threatened the lives of the witnesses called in support of the poor old gypsy woman.

The conspiracy and alibi were however incontrovertibly proved, Moll Squires's innocence clearly established, and no doubt entertained that the girl never was at the house of Mrs. Wills, much less confined and starved there, as was alleged, the whole story being a tissue of falsehood, which Virtue Hall had been suborned or intimidated partially to confirm, but who on being strictly interrogated apart by the Lord Mayor, acknowledged the fabrication, and which was confirmed by Bet Canning's contradictory statements. She, however, was a heroine and a martyr in the estimation of the mob, and was celebrated as such in several popular street ballads.

Unless escorted by his clerk.
But let not every bungler deem
Too lightly of so deep a scheme;
For reputation of the art
Each Ghost must act a proper part,
Observe decorum's needful grace,
And keep the laws of time and place;
Must change, with happy variation,
His manners with his situation;
What in the country might pass down,
Would be impertinent in town.
No spirit of discretion here
Can think of breeding awe and fear,
'Twill serve the purpose more by half
To make the congregation laugh.
We want no ensigns of surprise,
Locks stiff with gore, and saucer eyes;
Give us an entertaining sprite,
Gentle, familiar, and polite,
One who appears in such a form
As might an holy hermit warm,
Or who on former schemes refines,
And only talks by sounds and signs,
Who will not to the eye appear,
But pays her visits to the ear,
And knocks so gently, 'twould not fright
A lady in the darkest night.
Such is our Fanny, whose good will,
Which cannot in the grave lie still,
Brings her on earth to entertain
Her friends and lovers in Cock Lane.

SUPPLEMENTAL NOTES.

Some passages, in the preceding book, bearing no distant allusion to Lord Talbot's duel with Mr. Wilkes, we think the humorous account of it given by the latter, in a letter to Lord Temple, may not be displeasing to the reader.

In No. 12 of the North Briton, for the 21st of August, 1762, the Lord Steward's sumptuary regulations, respecting the royal kitchen, were placed in a ludicrous point of view, and the author of them ironically praised. His lordship naturally displeased with this species of panegyric, applied to Mr. Wilkes by letter to know if he was the author of that paper. Mr. Wilkes replied by questioning his lordship's right to catechise him, and concluded by declining giving any farther answer: a challenge ensued, and the parties, with their seconds, met at Bagshot, from whence the following epistle was written:

My Lord, Red Lion at Bagshot, Tuesday, 10 at night.

I had the honour of transmitting to your lordship copies of seven letters, which passed between Lord Talbot and me. As the affair is now over, I enclose an original letter of Colonel Berkeley, with a copy of mine previous to it, which fixed the particulars of our meeting, and therefore remained a secret, very sacredly kept by the four persons concerned.

I came here at three this afternoon, and about five I was told that Lord Talbot and Colonel Berkeley were in the house. Lord Talbot had been here at one, and was gone again, leaving a message however that he would soon return. I had continued in the room where I was at my first coming, for fear of raising any suspicion. I sent a compliment to Colonel Berkeley, and that I wished to see him. He was so obliging as to come to me directly. I told him that I supposed we were to sup together with Lord Talbot, whom I was ready to attend, as became a private gentleman, and that he and Mr. Harris, as our seconds, would settle the business of the next morning, according to my letter to him from Winchester, and his answer. Berkeley said that his lordship desired to finish the business immediately; I replied, that the appointment was to sup together that evening, and to fight in the morning; that in consequence of such an arrangement, I had, like an idle man of pleasure, put off some business of real importance, which I meant to settle before I went to bed. I added, that I was come from Medmenham Abbey, where the jovial Monks of St. Francis had kept me up till four in the morning, that the world would therefore conclude I was drunk, and form no favourable opinion of his lordship from a duel at such a time; that it more became us both to take a cool hour of the next morning, as early a one as was agreeable to Lord Talbot. Berkeley said, that he had undertaken to bring us together, and as we were now both at Bagshot, he would leave us to settle our own business. He then asked me, if I would go with him to Lord Talbot. I said I would any moment he pleased. We went directly, with my adjutant, Mr. Harris.

I found Lord Talbot in an agony of passion. He said, that I had injured, that I had insulted him, that he was not used to be injured, or insulted: what did I mean? Did I, or did I not, write the North Briton of August the 21st, which affronted his honour? He would know; he insisted on a direct answer: here were his pistols. I replied, that he would soon use them; that I desired to know by what right his lordship catechised me about a paper, which did not bear my name; that I should never resolve him that question, till he made out the right of putting it; and that if I could have entertained any other idea, I was too well bred to have given his Lordship and Colonel Berkeley the trouble of coming to Bagshot. I observed, that I was a private English gentleman, perfectly free and independent, which I held to be a character of the highest dignity; that I obeyed with pleasure a gracious sovereign, but would never submit to the arbitrary dictates of a fellow-subject, a lord steward of his household, my superior indeed in rank, fortune, and abilities, but my equal only in honour, courage, and liberty. Lord Talbot then asked me, if I would fight him that evening. I said, that I preferred the next morning, as it had been settled before, and gave my reasons. His lordship replied, that he insisted on finishing the affair immediately. I told him, that I should very soon be ready; that I did not mean to quit him, but would absolutely first settle some important business relative to the education of an only daughter, whom I tenderly loved; that it would take up a very little time, and I would immediately after decide the affair in any way he chose, for I had brought both sword and pistols. I rung the bell for pen, ink, and paper, desiring his lordship to conceal his pistols, that they might not be seen by the waiter. He soon after became half frantic, and made use of a thousand indecent expressions, that I should be hanged, damned, &c. I said, that I was not to be frighted, nor in the least affected, by such violence; that God had given me a firmness and spirit, equal to his lordship's, or any man's; that cool courage should always mark me, and that it would be seen how well bottomed I was.

After the waiter had brought pen, ink, and paper, I proposed that the door of the room might be locked, and not opened till our business was decided. Lord Talbot on this proposition became quite outrageous, declared that this was mere butchery, and that I was a wretch, who sought his life. I reminded him, that I came there on a point of honour, to give his lordship satisfaction; that I mentioned the circumstance of locking the door only to prevent all possibility of interruption, and that I would in every circumstance be governed, not by the turbulence of the most violent temper I had ever seen, but by the calm determinations of our two seconds, to whom I implicitly submitted. Lord Talbot then asked me, if I would deny the paper. I answered that I neither would own nor deny it: if I survived, I would afterwards declare, not before. Soon after he grew a little cooler, and in a soothing tone of voice, said, I have never, I believe, offended Mr. Wilkes, why has he attacked me? he must be sorry to see me unhappy. I asked upon what grounds his lordship imputed the paper to me; that Mr. Wilkes would justify any paper to which he had put his name, and would equally assert the privilege of not giving any answer whatever about a paper to which he had not; that this was my undoubted right, which I was ready to seal with my blood. He then said he admired me exceedingly, really loved me, but I was an unaccountable animal—such parts! but would I kill him, who had never offended me, &c., &c.

We had, after this, a good deal of conversation about the Buckinghamshire militia, and the day his lordship came to see us on Wycombe Heath, before I was colonel. He soon after flamed out again, and said to me, you are a murderer; you want to kill me, but I am sure that I shall kill you; I know I shall, by God. If you will fight, if you kill me, I hope you will be hanged. I know you will. Berkeley and Harris were shocked. I asked, if I was first to be killed, and afterwards hanged; that I knew his lordship fought me with the king's pardon in his pocket, and I fought him with a halter about my neck; that I would fight him for all that, and if he fell, I should not tarry here a moment for the tender mercies of such a ministry, but would directly proceed to the next stage, where my valet de chambre waited for me, and from thence I would make the best of my way to France, for men of honour were sure of protection in that kingdom. He seemed much affected by this. He then told me, that I was an unbeliever, and wished to be killed. I could not help smiling at this, and observed that we did not meet at Bagshot to settle articles of faith, but points of honour; that indeed I had no fear of dying, but I enjoyed life as much as any man in it; that I was as little subject to be gloomy, or even peevish, as any Englishman whatever; that I valued life, and the fair enjoyments of it so much, I would never quit it by my own consent, except on a call of honour.

I then wrote a letter to your lordship, respecting the education of Miss Wilkes, and gave you my poor thanks for the steady friendship with which you have so many years honoured me. Colonel Berkeley took the care of the letter, and I have since desired him to send it to Stowe; for the sentiments of the heart at such a moment are beyond all politics, and indeed every thing else, but such virtue as Lord Temple's.

When I had sealed my letter, I told Lord Talbot that I was entirely at his service, and I again desired that we might decide the affair in the room, because there could not be a possibility of interruption; but he was quite inexorable. He then asked me, how many times we should fire. I said that I left it to his choice; I had brought a flask of powder and a bag of bullets. Our seconds then charged the pistols, which my lord had brought. They were large horse pistols. It was agreed that we should fire at the word of command, to be given by one of our seconds. They tossed up, and it fell to my adjutant to give the word. We then left the Inn, and walked to a garden at some distance from the house. It was near seven, and the moon shone very bright. We stood about eight yards distant, and agreed not to turn round before we fired, but to continue facing each other. Harris gave the word. Both our fires were in very exact time, but neither took effect. I walked up immediately to Lord Talbot, and told him that I now avowed the paper. His lordship paid me the highest encomiums on my courage, and said he would declare everywhere that I was the noblest fellow God had ever made. He then desired that we might now be good friends, and retire to the Inn to drink a bottle of claret together, which we did with great good humour and much laugh. Lord Talbot afterwards went to Windsor, Berkeley and Harris to Winchester, and I continue here till to-morrow morning, waiting the return of my valet de chambre, to whom I have sent a messenger. Berkeley told me, that he was grieved for Lord Talbot's passion, and admired my courage and coolness beyond his farthest idea: that was his expression.

I have a million of other particulars to relate, but I blush already at the length of this letter. Your lordship will soon see Colonel Berkeley, and I hope in a very few days to pay my devoirs at Stowe. I intend to be at Aylesbury quarter sessions by Thursday dinner.

My most respectful compliments always attend Lady Temple.

I am ever, my dear Lord, your lordship's very devoted and obedient humble servant,

JOHN WILKES.

Directed to Earl Temple.

When the above letter was first published, which was in

Almon's Political Register, Lord Talbot supposed that Lord Temple had furnished the editor of that work with a copy of it; and very abruptly charged Lord Temple with it as a fact in the House of Lords, not publicly but privately. The rude manner in which Lord Talbot spoke prevented Lord Temple giving any answer, upon which Lord Talbot declared that he expected immediate satisfaction. Lord Temple went out of the house and beckoned Lord Gower after him. Lord Talbot followed and brought Lord Pomfret. They were in the Princes Chamber, Lord Temple's sword was out, when Lord Montfort coming through stept into the house and informed it of what was going on, upon which the four Lords were instantly ordered into the house, and obliged to pledge their honours that the affair should go no farther. The fact was, Lord Temple had no concern in the publication of the letter, a copy of which had been furnished to the Editor by Wilkes himself.

438 "Another Tofts must rabbits breed." We should, with greater interest, if not satisfaction, record the gullible propensities of our forefathers in the articles of Toft, Canning, monstrous whales, mermaids, fortune-tellers, and bottle-conjurers, were it not our mortifying duty to admit, that notwithstanding our boasted intellectual advance, by the professed diffusion of useful knowledge,* and of a too ambitious system of education altogether unsuitable to the class for whom intended, the same appetite for the marvellous still exists, and has been and is amply supplied by a succession of delusions, as ludicrous and more mischievous than those we have noticed. In proof of which we need only allude to the Princess Caraboo of Bristol, Miss M'Evoy of Liverpool, metallic tractors, hydropathy, homœopathy, mesmerism, and by way of climax Puseyism.

---

* As specimens of *useful* knowledge provided for the million, it is enough to give the names only of some of the subjects propounded for *popular* instruction. Pneumatics, hydrostatics, dynamics, plane and sphere trigonometry, the integral calculus, the doctrine of probabilities, and algebra in all its phases.

THE GHOST.

BOOK II.

A SACRED standard rule we find,
By poets held time out of mind,
To offer at Apollo's shrine,
And call on one, or all the Nine.
 This custom, through a bigot zeal
Which moderns of fine taste must feel,
For those who wrote in days of yore,
Adopted stands like many more;
Though every cause which then conspired
To make it practised and admired,
Yielding to Time's destructive course,
For ages past hath lost its force.
 With ancient bards, an invocation
Was a true act of adoration,
Of worship an essential part,
And not a formal piece of art,
Of paltry reading a parade,
A dull solemnity in trade,
A pious fever, taught to burn
An hour or two, to serve a turn.
 They talk'd not of Castalian springs,
By way of saying pretty things,
As we dress out our flimsy rhimes;
'Twas the religion of the times,

And they believed that holy stream
With greater force made fancy teem,
Reckon'd by all a true specific
To make the barren brain prolific:
Thus Romish church, (a scheme which bears
Not half so much excuse as theirs)
Since Faith implicitly hath taught her,
Reveres the force of holy water.
The Pagan system, whether true
Or false, its strength, like buildings, drew
From many parts disposed to bear,
In one great whole, their proper share.
Each god of eminent degree
To some vast beam compared might be;
Each godling was a peg, or rather
A cramp, to keep the beams together:
And man as safely might pretend
From Jove the thunderbolt to rend,
As with an impious pride aspire
To rob Apollo of his lyre.
With settled faith and pious awe,
Establish'd by the voice of Law,
Then poets to the Muses came,
And from their altars caught the flame.
Genius, with Phœbus for his guide,
The Muse ascending by his side,
With towering pinions dared to soar,
Where eye could scarcely strain before.
But why should we, who cannot feel
These glowings of a Pagan zeal,

That wild enthusiastic force,
By which, above her common course,
Nature, in extasy upborne,
Look'd down on earthly things with scorn;
Who have no more regard, 'tis known,
For their religion than our own,
And feel not half so fierce a flame
At Clio's as at Fisher's name;
Who know these boasted sacred streams
Were mere romantic idle dreams,
That Thames has waters clear as those
Which on the top of Pindus rose,
And that the fancy to refine,
Water's not half so good as wine;
Who know, if profit strikes our eye,
Should we drink Helicon quite dry,
The whole fountain would not thither lead
So soon as one poor jug from Tweed:
Who, if to raise poetic fire,
The power of Beauty we require,
In any public place can view
More than the Grecians ever knew;
If wit into the scale is thrown,
Can boast a Lennox of our own;

[62] Catherine Fisher, better known by the name of Kitty Fisher, a courtesan of exquisite beauty, and first rate celebrity in the annals of fashionable dissipation.

[78] Mrs. Arabella Lennox, the author of some very pleasing novels, was the daughter of a North American gentleman of the name of Ramsay, and was born at New York. Sir John Hawkins, in his life of Dr. Johnson, tells an amusing anecdote of the celebration of the birth of her first literary child,

Why should we servile customs choose,
And court an antiquated Muse?
No matter why—to ask a reason
In pedant bigotry is treason.
  In the broad beaten turnpike-road
Of hackneyed panegyric ode,
No modern poet dares to ride
Without Apollo by his side,
Nor in a sonnet take the air

as the Doctor called it, entitled "The life of Harriot Stuart." and published in 1751. Johnson in his club proposed devoting to it a whole night spent in festivity, to which proposition all the company acceded. The place appointed was the Devil Tavern, and there, about the hour of eight, Mrs. Lennox and her husband, and a lady of her acquaintance, as also the club and friends to the number of twenty, assembled. The supper was elegant, and Johnson had directed that a magnificent hot apple pie should make a part; and this he insisted upon having stuck with bay leaves, because Mrs. Lennox was an authoress, and had written verses; and further, he had prepared for her a crown of laurel, with which, but not till he had invoked the muses by some ceremonies of his own invention, he encircled her brows. The night passed in pleasant conversation and harmless mirth, intermingled at different periods with the refreshments of tea and coffee. About five Johnson's face shone with meridian splendour, though his drink had been only lemonade. The greater part of the company had deserted the colours of Bacchus, and were with difficulty rallied to partake of a second refreshment of tea and coffee, which was scarcely ended when the day began to dawn. This phenomenon began to put them in mind of their reckoning, but the waiters were all so overcome with sleep, that it was two hours before a bill could be got; and it was not till near eight that the creeking of the street door gave the signal for their departure. She being a Roman Catholic translated into English the Memoirs of Sully a Huguenot.

Unless his lady Muse be there ;
She, from some amaranthine grove,
Where little Loves and Graces rove,
The laurel to my Lord must bear,
Or garlands make for whores to wear ;
She, with soft elegiac verse,
Must grace some mighty villain's hearse,
Or for some infant, doom'd by fate
To wallow in a large estate,
With rhymes the cradle must adorn,
To tell the world a fool is born.
  Since then our critic Lords expect,
No hardy poet should reject
Establish'd maxims, or presume
To place much better in their room,
By nature fearful, I submit,
And in this dearth of sense and wit,
With nothing done, and little said,
(By wild excursive Fancy led
Into a second Book thus far,
Like some unwary traveller,
Whom varied scenes of wood and lawn
With treacherous delight have drawn
Deluded from his purposed way,
Whom every step leads more astray :
Who, gazing round, can no where spy,
Or house or friendly cottage nigh,
And resolution seems to lack
To venture forward or go back)
Invoke some goddess to descend,
And help me to my journey's end ;

Though conscious Arrow all the while
Hears the petition with a smile,
Before the glass her charms unfolds,
And in herself my Muse beholds.
Truth, goddess of celestial birth,
But little loved or known on earth,
Whose power but seldom rules the heart,
Whose name, with hypocritic art,
An arrant stalking-horse is made,
A snug pretence to drive a trade,
An instrument, convenient grown
To plant, more firmly, Falsehood's throne,
As rebels varnish o'er their cause
With specious colouring of laws,
And pious traitors draw the knife
In the king's name against his life;
Whether (from cities far away,
Where Fraud and Falsehood scorn thy sway)
The faithful nymph's and shepherd's pride,
With Love and Virtue by thy side,
Your hours in harmless joys are spent
Amongst the children of Content;
Or, fond of gayety and sport,
You tread the round of England's court,
Howe'er my Lord may frowning go,
And treat the stranger as a foe,
Sure to be found a welcome guest
In George's and in Charlotte's breast;
If, in the giddy hours of youth,
My constant soul adhered to truth;
If, from the time I first wrote Man,

I still pursued thy sacred plan,
Tempted by Interest in vain
To wear mean Falsehood's golden chain;
If, for a season drawn away,
Starting from virtue's path astray,
All low disguise I scorned to try,
And dared to sin, but not to lie;
Hither, O hither! condescend,
Eternal Truth! thy steps to bend,
And favour him, who, every hour,
Confesses and obeys thy power!
  But come not with that easy mien
By which you won the lively Dean,
Nor yet assume that strumpet air
Which Rab'lais taught thee first to wear,
Nor yet that arch ambiguous face
Which, with Cervantes gave thee grace;
But come in sacred vesture clad,
Solemnly dull, and truly sad!
  Far from thy seemly matron train
Be idiot Mirth, and Laughter vain!
For Wit and Humour, which pretend
At once to please us and amend;
They are not for my present turn;
Let them remain in France with Sterne.
  Of noblest City parents born,
Whom wealth and dignities adorn,

156 The offence to which our author here pleads guilty had been before alluded to by him in "The Conference," in which he severely condemned his own conduct, and anticipated the just censure of the public.

Who still one constant tenor keep,
Not quite awake nor quite asleep;
With thee let formal Dullness come,
And deep Attention, ever dumb,
Who on her lips her fingers lays,
Whilst every circumstance she weighs,
Whose downcast eye is often found
Bent without motion to the ground,
Or, to some outward thing confined,
Remits no image to the mind,
No pregnant mark of meaning bears,
But stupid, without vision stares;
Thy steps let Gravity attend,
Wisdom's and Truth's unerring friend;
For one may see with half an eye,
That gravity can never lie,
And his arch brow, pull'd o'er his eyes,
With solemn proof proclaims him wise.
Free from all waggeries and sports,
The produce of luxurious courts,
Where sloth and lust enervate youth,
Come thou, a downright City Truth:
The City, which we ever find
A sober pattern for mankind,
Where man, in equilibrio hung,
Is seldom old, and never young,
And from the cradle to the grave,
Not Virtue's friend nor Vice's slave;
As dancers on the wire we spy,
Hanging between the earth and sky.
She comes—I see her from afar

Bending her course to Temple-Bar;
All sage and silent is her train,
Deportment grave, and garments plain,
Such as may suit a parson's wear,
And fit the headpiece of a mayor.
  By truth inspired, our Bacon's force
Open'd the way to learning's source;
Boyle through the works of nature ran,
And Newton, something more than man,
Dived into nature's hidden springs,
Laid bare the principles of things,
Above the earth our spirits bore,
And gave us worlds unknown before.
By Truth inspired, when Lauder's spite
O'er Milton cast the veil of night.

221 William Lauder was by birth a Scotchman, and taught Latin at the University of Edinburgh, where in 1739 he published an edition of Johnston's psalms. From thence he came to London, where in 1747, he made a memorable attack on Milton in a book entitled "An Essay on Milton's use and imitation of the Moderns in his Paradise Lost." In which he asserted that Milton had borrowed a great part of the two first books of Paradise Lost from a Latin epic poem written on the fall of man, by Masenius, a German Jesuit. He likewise accused Milton of having borrowed from a tragedy written by the celebrated Grotius, entitled Adamus Exul; and from several other Latin and Italian poets of the middle ages. His quotations, consisting of purposely interpolated passages in old and obscure authors, passed as genuine for a time; but at length the forgeries were detected by Dr. Douglas, who had likewise unmasked Archibald Bower, another imposter and renegade, who professed to have escaped from the dungeons of the Inquisition. He wrote a History of the Popes in 2 vols. 4to, and contrived to secure

Douglas arose, and through the maze
Of intricate and winding ways
Came where the subtle traitor lay,
And dragg'd him, trembling, to the day;
Whilst he, (O shame to noblest parts!
Dishonour to the liberal arts!

the steady patronage of Lord Lyttelton, the historian of Henry II. notwithstanding Dr. Douglas's convincing exposure of his frauds and falsehoods. Bower died in 1766, aged 80. Lauder, on being discovered, subscribed a confession of his offence, and went to Barbadoes, where he kept a school, and died in 1771.

223 Dr. Douglas, Canon of Windsor, Bishop of Carlisle in 1788, of Salisbury in 1791, and died in 1807. He assisted Lord Bath, whose chaplain he was, in writing a piece called "A Letter to two great men," (Mr. Pitt and the Duke of Newcastle) which excited more attention than it deserved. His principal merit consists in having detected the literary forgeries of Bower and Lauder.

227 Dr. Johnson, under the influence of strong political prejudice, and of an honest persuasion of Lauder's veracity, was induced to give credence to the charge brought by him against Milton, and so far promoted it as to assist him in writing or revising the preface to his book. Upon the detection of the forgeries by Mr. Douglas in a pamphlet entitled "Milton Vindicated from the charge of Plagiarism brought against him by Mr. Lauder," Dr. Johnson, who was now convinced of the fraud, advised Lauder to subscribe an ample confession of his guilt, which was very ably penned by the Doctor, and published in the form of a letter from Lauder to Mr. Douglas. Notwithstanding this abject humiliation, he shortly after renewed his attacks on Milton, and disclaimed his confession, which he said was written entirely by Dr. Johnson; and to which he had been induced unadvisedly to subscribe his name. This matchless impudence excited no farther notice, and he took refuge in the West Indies from that contempt which overwhelmed him here.

To Traffic in so vile a scheme.)
Whilst he, our letter'd Polypheme,
Who had confederate forces join'd,
Like a base coward skulk'd behind.
By Truth inspired, our critics go
To track Fingal in Highland snow,
To form their own and other's creed
From manuscripts they cannot read.
By Truth inspired, we numbers see
Of each profession and degree,
Gentle and simple, lord and cit,
Wit without wealth, wealth without wit,
When Punch and Sheridan have done,
To Fanny's ghostly lectures run.
By Truth and Fanny now inspired,
I feel my glowing bosom fired;
Desire beats high in every vein
To sing the spirit of Cock Lane;
To tell (just as the measure flows
In halting rhyme, half verse, half prose)
With more than mortal arts endued,
How she united force withstood,
And proudly gave a brave defiance
To Wit and Dullness in alliance.

234 In a note on the Prophecy of Famine, some account has been given of Macpherson and his Ossian, and of the subscription raised to enable him to authenticate the fragments he had already published, and to obtain fresh materials; the latter he of course fabricated to earn the subscription, but the authentication, for the best of all possible reasons, never took place.

This apparition (with relation
To ancient modes of derivation,
This we may properly so call,
Although it ne'er appears at all,
As by the way of innuendo,
Lucus is made *à non lucendo*)
Superior to the vulgar mode,
Nobly disdains that servile road
Which coward Ghosts, as it appears,
Have walk'd in, full five thousand years,
And, for restraint too mighty grown,
Strikes out a method of her own.
Others may meanly start away,
Awed by the herald of the day:
With faculties too weak to bear
The freshness of the morning air,
Nay vanish with the melting gloom,
And glide in silence to the tomb;
She dares the sun's most piercing light,
And knocks by day as well as night:
Others, with mean and partial view,
Their visits pay to one or two;
She, great in reputation grown,
Keeps the best company in Town.
Our active enterprising Ghost,
As large and splendid routs can boast
As those, which, raised by Pride's command,
Block up the passage through the Strand.

279 The parties of the Countess-Duchess of Northumberland at Charing Cross were the rendezvous of all the elegance

Great adepts in the fighting trade,
Who served their time on the parade;
She-saints, who, true to pleasure's plan,
Talk about God, and lust for man;
Wits who believe nor God nor Ghost,
And fools who worship every post;
Cowards, whose lips with war are hung;
Men truly brave, who hold their tongue;
Courtiers, who laugh they know not why,
And cits, who for the same cause cry;
The canting tabernacle brother,
(For one rogue still suspects another)
Ladies, who to a spirit fly,
Rather than with their husbands lie;
Lords, who as chastely pass their lives
With other women as their wives;
Proud of their intellects and clothes,
Physicians, lawyers, parsons, beaus,
And, truant from their desks and shops,
Spruce Temple clerks and 'prentice fops,
To Fanny come, with the same view,
To find her false, or find her true.
Hark! something creeps about the house!
Is it a spirit or a mouse?

and fashion of the town. She was the Lady Elizabeth Seymour, the daughter of Algernon, the proud Duke of Somerset, by her mother, the last of the Percies, whose name and dignities were transferred by her to the Smithsons. Her Grace was fond of seeing literary persons attend them, but was unfortunate in her selection of them. Sir John Hill, Mallet, &c. being of the chosen few.

Hark! something scratches round the room!
A cat, a rat, a stubb'd birch broom.
Hark! on the wainscot now it knocks!
"If thou'rt a Ghost," cried Orthodox,
With that affected solemn air
Which hypocrites delight to wear,
And all those forms of consequence
Which fools adopt instead of sense;
"If thou'rt a Ghost, who from the tomb
Stalk'st sadly silent through this gloom,
In breach of nature's stated laws,
For good, or bad, or for no cause,
Give now nine knocks; like priests of old,
Nine we a sacred number hold."
"Psha," cried Profound, (a man of parts,
Deep read in all the curious arts,
Who to their hidden springs had traced
The force of numbers rightly placed)
"As to the number, you are right;
As to the form mistaken quite.
What's nine?—Your adepts all agree
The virtue lies in three times three."
He said; no need to say it twice,
For thrice she knock'd, and thrice, and thrice.
The crowd, confounded and amazed,
In silence at each other gazed:
From Cælia's hand the snuff-box fell,
Tinsel, who ogled with the belle,
To pick it up attempts in vain,
He stoops, but cannot rise again.

Immane Pomposo was not heard
T' import one crabbed foreign word:
Fear seizes heroes, fools and wits,
And Plausible his prayers forgets.
  At length, as people just awake,
Into wild dissonance they break;
All talk'd at once, but not a word
Was understood or plainly heard.
Such is the noise of chattering geese,
Slow sailing on the summer breeze;
Such is the language Discord speaks
In Welsh women o'er beds of leeks;

335 Dr. Johnson's diction and dictionary afforded to Wilkes and his partisans a never-failing source of ridicule, which occasionally was not misplaced, as the following extracts will evince:

Whig—The name of a faction.

Tory—One who adheres to the ancient constitution of the state, and the apostolical hierarchy of the Church of England,—opposed to a whig.

Network—anything reticulated or decussated at equal distances, with interstices between the intersections.

Cough—A convulsion of the lungs vellicated by some sharp serosity.

Excise—A hateful tax levied upon commodities, and adjudged not by the common judges of property; but wretches hired by those to whom excise is paid.

This definition of the word Excise gave great offence to government, and the opinions of the Attorney and Solicitor General were taken as to the libellous nature of it, and the expediency of prosecuting the author and publishers. These high law officers concurred in opinion that the words were libellous, but dissuaded against the prosecution. In a subsequent edition of his dictionary Johnson was desired to alter

Such the confused and horrid sounds
Of Irish in potatoe grounds.
But tired, for even C——'s tongue
Is not on iron hinges hung,
Fear and Confusion sound retreat,
Reason and Order take their seat.
The fact confirm'd beyond all doubt,
They now would find the causes out.
For this a sacred rule we find
Among the nicest of mankind,
Which never might exception brook
From Hobbes even down to Bolingbroke,

or soften the article, "No, said he, it had done all the mischief, and I owe no complaisance to excisemen or their masters."

Favourite—A mean wretch, whose business is by any means to please; one chosen as a companion by a superior.

Gazetteer—was lately a term of the utmost infamy, being usually applied to wretches who were hired to vindicate the court. (Omitted in the recent editions of the Dictionary.)

Oats—A grain which in England is generally given to horses, but in Scotland supports the people.

Alias—A Latin word often used in the trials of criminals; as Mallett alias Malloch; (in the later editions altered to Smith, alias Baker, thus extracting the sting from the Doctor's just reprehension of McGregor, alias Malloch, alias Mallet, as contemptible a poet as a man.)

Pension—An allowance made to any one without an equivalent. In England it is generally understood to mean pay given to a state hireling for treason to his country.

Pensioner—One who is supported by an allowance paid at the will of another; a dependent.

349 We know not, nor is it now material, to ascertain which of the City magnates or orators was intended by this initial.

To doubt of facts, however true,
Unless they know the causes too.
  Trifle, of whom 'twas hard to tell
When he intended ill or well;
Who, to prevent all farther pother,
Probably meant nor one nor t'other;
Who to be silent always loath,
Would speak on either side, or both;
Who led away by love of fame,
If any new idea came,
What'er it made for, always said it,
Not with an eye to truth, but credit;
For orators profess'd 'tis known,
Talk not for our sake, but their own;
Who always shew'd his talents best
When serious things were turn'd to jest.
And under much impertinence
Possess'd no common share of sense;
Who could deceive the flying hours
With chat on butterflies and flowers;
Could talk of powder, patches, paint,
With the same zeal as of a saint;
Could prove a Sibyl brighter far
Than Venus or the Morning Star;
Whilst something still so gay, so new,
The smile of approbation drew,
And females eyed the charming man,
Whilst their hearts flutter'd with their fan;
Trifle, who would by no means miss
An opportunity like this,
Proceeding on his usual plan,

Smiled, stroked his chin, and thus began.
"With shears or scissors, sword or knife,
When the Fates cut the thread of life,
(For if we to the grave are sent,
No matter with what instrument)
The body in some lonely spot,
On dunghill vile, is laid to rot,
Or sleep among more holy dead
With prayers irreverently read,
The soul is sent where Fate ordains,
To reap rewards, to suffer pains.
The virtuous, to those mansions go,
Where pleasures unembitter'd flow,
Where, leading up a jocund band,
Vigour and Youth dance hand in hand,
Whilst Zephyr, with harmonious gales,
Pipes softest music through the vales,
And Spring and Flora, gaily crown'd
With velvet carpet spread the ground;
With livelier blush where roses bloom,
And every shrub expires perfume,
Where crystal streams meandering glide,
Where warbling flows the amber tide,
Where other suns dart brighter beams,
And light, through purer æther streams.
Far other seats, far different state,
The sons of wickedness await,
Justice, (not that old hag I mean
Who's nightly in the Garden seen,

418 One of the greatest abuses that existed in Churchill's

Who lets no spark of mercy rise,
For crimes, by which men lose their eyes:
Nor her, who with an equal hand
Weighs tea and sugar in the Strand;
Nor her, who, by the world deem'd wise,
Deaf to the widow's piercing cries,
Steel'd 'gainst the starving orphan's tears,
On pawns her base tribunal rears;
But her, who after death presides,
Whom sacred truth unerring guides,
Who, free from partial influence,
Nor sinks nor raises evidence,
Before whom nothing's in the dark,
Who takes no bribe, and keeps no clerk)
Justice, with equal scale below,
In due proportion weighs out woe,
And always with such lucky aim
Knows punishments so fit to frame,
That she augments their grief and pain,
Leaving no reason to complain.

time, was the administration of the police of London. This task was intrusted to the conduct of a set of vulgar, ignorant men, called trading justices; they were in the commission of the peace for the county of Middlesex and city of Westminster, which office they so degraded, that few gentlemen could be found to accept of it. These men, with clerks taken from the lowest stations, as the fit instruments of their rapacity, levied fines and annual tributes from those offenders who were rich enough to obtain exemption from punishment. A specimen of such a justice may be found in Foote's Minor. They had their stations in different districts of the town, but the head quarters was then, as now, both as regards the evil and its intended corrective, in Covent Garden.

Old maids and rakes are join'd together,
Coquettes and prudes, like April weather.
Wit's forced to chum with Common Sense,
And Lust is yoked to Impotence.
Professors (Justice so decreed)
Unpaid, must constant lectures read;
On earth it often doth befall,
They're paid, and never read at all:
Parsons must practise what they teach,
And bishops are compell'd to preach.
She, who on earth was nice and prim,
Of delicacy full and whim;
Whose tender nature could not bear
The rudeness of the churlish air,
Is doom'd to mortify her pride,
The change of weather to abide,
And sells, whilst tears with liquor mix,
Burnt brandy on the shore of Styx.
Avaro, by long use grown bold

[457] In the Conclave, (a poem written by Churchill, but deemed too personal and virulent for publication,) Dr. Pearce, the eminently learned and pious prelate here vilified, under the name of Avaro, was one of the principal personages under the name of Longinus. The poem opened with these lines:—

"The Conclave was met, and Longinus the Pope,
Who leads a great number of fools in a rope,
Who makes them get up, and who makes them sit still;
Who makes them say yea or nay, just as he will;
Who a *critic* profound does all critics defy,
And settles the difference 'twixt *Beta* and *Pi;*
Who forgiveness of faults preaches up to another,
But forbids it to come near himself or his brother."

In every ill which brings him gold,
Who his Redeemer would pull down,
And sell his God for half-a-crown;
Who, if some blockhead should be willing
To lend him on his soul a shilling,
A well-made bargain would esteem it,
And have more sense than to redeem it,
Justice shall in those shades confine,
To drudge for Plutus in the mine,

460 A painted window, representing the crucifixion, was put up over the altar in St. Margaret's Church, Westminster. Dr. Pearce, then Bishop of Rochester and Dean of Westminster, thought it savoured of popery, and therefore made the most strenuous exertions to have it removed. The following epigram was circulated on the occasion:—

Our Saviour, as scripture informs us, in Jewry
The changers of money drove out in a fury;
Now Rochester's bishop, what can he do more,
Returns the affront, and kicks Christ out of door.

The painted glass window which gave rise to this controversy was originally designed as a present to Henry VII. to be put up in his celebrated chapel. By what means this design was prevented from taking place, and through what various changes of fortune this curious piece of workmanship passed, before it took its station in St. Margaret's Church, is related in a very learned and elegant tract published at the period, under the title of "Embellished Ornaments of Churches considered, with a particular view to the late decoration of the Parish Church of St. Margaret's, Westminster; to which is subjoined an account of the altar piece and stained glass window erected over it, 4to. 4*s*. Dodsley:" from which it appears that the Churchwardens of that parish made a purchase of the window and fixed it up without a proper license for that purpose; and that a prosecution was instituted against them in consequence.

All day long to toil and roar,
And, cursing, work the stubborn ore
For coxcombs here who have no brains,
Without a sixpence for his pains:
Thence, with each due return of night,
Compell'd, the tall, thin, half-starved sprite
Shall earth re-visit, and survey
The place where once his treasure lay,
Shall view the stall where holy Pride,
With letter'd Ignorance allied,
Once hail'd him mighty and adored,
Descended to another lord:
Then shall he, screaming, pierce the air,
Hang his lank jaws and scowl despair;
Then shall he ban at Heaven's decrees,
And, howling, sink to hell for ease.
  Those, who on earth through life have past
With equal pace from first to last,
Nor vexed with passions nor with spleen,
Insipid, easy, and serene;
Whose heads were made too weak to bear
The weight of business or of care,
Who, without merit, without crime,
Contrive to while away their time;
Nor good nor bad, nor fools nor wits,
Mild Justice with a smile permits
Still to pursue their darling plan,
And find amusement how they can.
  The beau, in gaudiest plumage drest
With lucky fancy o'er the rest
Of air a curious mantle throws,

And chats among his brother beaus;
Or, if the weather's fine and clear,
No sign of rain or tempest near,
Encouraged by the cloudless day,
Like gilded butterflies at play,
So lively all, so gay, so brisk,
In air they flutter, float, and frisk.
 The belle (what mortal doth not know
Belles after death admire a beau?)
With happy grace renews her art
To trap the coxcomb's wandering heart;
And, after death as whilst they live,
A heart is all which beaux can give.
 In some still, solemn, sacred shade,
Behold a group of authors laid,
Newspaper wits and sonneteers,
Gentleman bards and rhyming peers,
Biographers, whose wondrous worth
Is scarce remembered now on earth,
Whom Fieldings humour led astray,
And plaintive fops, debauch'd by Gray,
All sit together in a ring,
And laugh and prattle, write and sing.
 On his own works, with laurel crown'd,
Neatly and elegantly bound,
(For this is one of many rules,
With writing lords and laureat fools,
And which forever must succeed
With other lords who cannot read,
However destitute of wit,
To make their works for bookcase fit)

Acknowledged master of those seats,
Cibber his Birth-day Odes repeats.
  With triumph now possess that seat,
With triumph now thy Odes repeat;
Unrivall'd vigils proudly keep,
Whilst every hearer 's lull'd to sleep;
But know, illustrious Bard! when Fate,
Which still pursues thy name with hate,
The regal laurel blasts, which now
Blooms on the placid Whitehead's brow,

530 Colley Cibber, the hero of the Dunciad, and Whitehead's predecessor in the Laureate's chair. Few persons ever suffered more severity of censure from their contemporaries, or more unmerited neglect from posterity, than Cibber. His plays for many reasons ranked high in the acting list, and "The Apology for his Life" forms one of the most amusing specimens of autobiography in our language, and at the same time comprises the best history of the English stage during the long period he was connected with it. Some natural defects prevented his ever attaining excellence as an actor, and he ingenuously states the disadvantages resulting from them. He in 1757, at the advanced age of 86, concluded an inoffensive life passed in the utmost ease, gayety, and good humour. A retentive memory, accompanied by an equable flow of spirits, and a vivacity which extreme age and infirmity could not repress, rendered him, to the last moment of his existence, the life of every circle he frequented. To these qualifications nature had added one which should have thrown a protecting lustre over all his foibles; he possessed a truly good heart, which prompted him to the continued exercise of acts of charity and of every social virtue. The unjustifiable attacks of Pope in the Dunciad, who from private pique substituted his name for that of Theobald, he encountered with the keenness of his raillery, and with that peculiar ease and flow of native humour, which pervades all his prose writings.

Low must descend thy pride and fame,
And Cibber's be the second name."
  Here Trifle cough'd, (for coughing still
Bears witness of the speaker's skill,
A necessary piece of art,
Of rhetoric an essential part,
And adepts in the speaking trade
Keep a cough by them ready made,
Which they successfully dispense
When at a loss for words or sense)
Here Trifle cough'd, here paused—but while
He strove to recollect his smile,
That happy engine of his art,
Which triumph'd o'er the female heart,
Credulity, the child of Folly,
Begot on cloister'd Melancholy,
Who heard, with grief, the florid fool
Turn sacred things to ridicule,
And saw him, led by whim away,
Still farther from the subject stray,
Just in the happy nick, aloud,
In shape of Moore, addressed the crowd:
  "Were we with patience here to sit,
Dupes to the impertinence of wit,
Till Trifle his harangue should end,
A Greenland night we might attend.
Whilst he, with fluency of speech,

560 The Rev. Mr. Moore, then curate of St. Sepulchre's. The share he took in the Cock Lane conspiracy, and the legal conviction that ensued, have been noticed in the preliminary note to the first book of this poem.

Would various mighty nothings teach.
(Here Trifle, sternly looking down,
Gravely endeavour'd at a frown,
But Nature unawares stept in,
And, mocking, turn'd it to a grin)
And when, in Fancy's chariot hurl'd,
We had been carried round the world,
Involved in error still and doubt,
He'd leave us where we first set out.
Thus soldiers (in whose exercise
Material use with grandeur vies)
Lift up their legs with mighty pain,
Only to set them down again.
  Believe ye not (yes, all I see
In sound belief concur with me)
That Providence, for worthy ends,
To us unknown, this Spirit sends?
Though speechless lay the trembling tongue,
Your faith was on your features hung;
Your faith I in your eyes could see,
When all were pale and stared like me:
But scruples to prevent, and root
Out every shadow of dispute,
Pomposo, Plausible, and I,
With Fanny, have agreed to try
A deep concerted scheme—this night
To fix or to destroy her quite.
If it be true, before we've done,
We'll make it glaring as the sun;
If it be false, admit no doubt,

Ere morning's dawn we'll find it out.
Into the vaulted womb of death,
Where Fanny now, deprived of breath,
Lies festering, whilst her troubled sprite
Adds horror to the gloom of night,
Will we descend, and bring from thence
Proofs of such force to common sense,
Vain triflers shall no more deceive,
And Atheists tremble and believe."
He said, and ceased; the chamber rung
With due applause from every tongue:
The mingled sound (now let me see—
Something by way of simile)
Was it more like Strymonian cranes,
Or winds low murmuring when it rains,
Or drowsy hum of clustering bees,
Or the hoarse roar of angry seas?
Or (still to heighten and explain,
For else our simile is vain)
Shall we declare it like all four,
A scream, a murmur, hum, and roar?
Let Fancy now, in awful state
Present this great triumvirate,
(A method which received we find
In other cases by mankind)
Elected with a joint consent,
All fools in town to represent.
The clock strikes twelve—Moore starts and swears,
In oaths, we know, as well as prayers,
Religion lies, and a church brother

May use at will or one or t'other;
Plausible from his cassock drew
A holy manual, seeming new;
A book it was of private prayer,
But not a pin the worse for wear:
For, as we by the bye may say,
None but small saints in private pray.
Religion, fairest maid on earth!
As meek as good, who drew her birth
From that bless'd union, when in heaven
Pleasure was bride to Virtue given;
Religion! ever pleased to pray,
Possess'd the precious gift one day;
Hypocrisy of Cunning born,
Crept in and stole it ere the morn;
Whitfield, that greatest of all saints,
Who always prays and never faints,
(Whom she to her own brothers bore,
Rapine and Lust, on Severn's shore)
Received it from the squinting dame;
From him to Plausible it came,
Who, with unusual care opprest,
Now, trembling, pull'd it from his breast;
Doubts in his boding heart arise,
And fancied spectres blast his eyes,
Devotion springs from abject fear,
And stamps his prayers for once sincere.
  Pomposo, (insolent and loud,

653 Dr. Johnson, whose Tory politics rendered him particularly obnoxious to Churchill notwithstanding their common

Vain idol of a scribbling crowd,
Whose very name inspires an awe,
Whose every word is sense and law,
For what his greatness hath decreed,
Like laws of Persia and of Mede,
Sacred through all the realm of Wit,
Must never of repeal admit;
Who, cursing flattery, is the tool
Of every fawning, flattering fool;
Who wit with jealous eye surveys,
And sickens at another's praise;
Who, proudly seized of learning's throne,
Now damns all learning but his own;
Who scorns those common wares to trade in,
Reasoning, convincing, and persuading,
But makes each sentence current pass
With puppy, coxcomb, scoundrel, ass;
For 'tis with him a certain rule,

prejudices against the Scotch, affected to hold our Author in great contempt. The character of Pomposo was much extolled by Johnson's enemies, but the only reply that the Doctor made to the satire was, "That he thought Churchill a shallow fellow in the beginning, and had seen no reason for altering his opinion." "Highly (says Dr. Kippis) as we reverence this eminent writer's character and abilities, we must express ourselves to be of a different opinion. However inferior Churchill might be in many respects to Dr. Johnson, he certainly did not deserve the appellation of a shallow fellow. He was undoubtedly possessed of a sound and vigorous understanding, though it might not always be applied happily or prudently. The contemptuous terms in which men of real genius are apt to speak of each other we have often had occasion to observe and lament."

The folly's proved when he calls fool;
Who to increase his native strength,
Draws words six syllables in length,
With which, assisted with a frown
By way of club, he knocks us down;
Who 'bove the vulgar dares to rise,
And sense of decency defies;
For this same decency is made
Only for bunglers in the trade,
And, like the cobweb laws, is still
Broke through by great ones when they will—
Pomposo, with strong sense supplied,
Supported, and confirmed by Pride,
His comrades' terrors to beguile
"Grinn'd horribly a ghastly smile:"
Features so horrid, were it light,
Would put the devil himself to flight.

Such were the three in name and worth,
Whom Zeal and Judgment singled forth
To try the sprite on reason's plan,
Whether it was of God or man.

Dark was the night; it was that hour
When terror reigns in fullest power,
When, as the learn'd of old have said,
The yawning grave gives up her dead;
When Murder, Rapine by her side,
Stalks o'er the earth with giant stride;
Our Quixotes (for that knight of old
Was not in truth by half so bold,
Though Reason at the same time cries,
Our Quixotes are not half so wise,

Since they, with other follies, boast
An expedition 'gainst a Ghost)
Through the dull deep surrounding gloom,
In close array, towards Fanny's tomb
Adventured forth; Caution before,
With heedful step, the lanthorn bore,
Pointing at graves; and in the rear,
Trembling, and talking loud, went Fear.
The church-yard teem'd—th' unsettled ground,
As in an ague, shook around;
While, in some dreary vault confined,
Or riding on the hollow wind,
Horror, which turns the heart to stone,
In dreadful sounds was heard to groan.
All staring, wild, and out of breath,
At length they reached the place of death.
A vault it was, long time applied
To hold the last remains of Pride:
No beggar there, of humble race,
And humble fortunes, finds a place;
To rest in pomp as well as ease,
The only way's to pay the fees.
Fools, rogues, and whores, if rich and great,
Proud even in death, here rot in state.
No thieves disrobe the well-dress'd dead;
No plumbers steal the sacred lead:
Quiet and safe the bodies lie;
No sextons sell, no surgeons buy.
Thrice, each the ponderous key applied,
And thrice to turn it vainly tried,
Till taught by Prudence to unite,

And straining with collected might,
The stubborn wards resist no more,
But open flies the growling door.
  Three paces back they fell amazed,
Like statues stood, like madmen gazed;
The frighted blood forsakes the face,
And seeks the heart with quicker pace;
The throbbing heart its fears declares,
And upright stand the bristled hairs;
The head in wild distraction swims,
Cold sweats bedew the trembling limbs;
Nature, whilst fears her bosom chill,
Suspends her powers, and life stands still.
  Thus had they stood till now; but Shame
(An useful though neglected dame,
By Heaven design'd the friend of man,
Though we degrade her all we can,
And strive, as our first proof of wit,
Her name and nature to forget)
Came to their aid in happy hour,
And with a wand of mighty power
Struck on their hearts; vain fears subside,
And, baffled, leave the field to Pride.
  Shall they, (forbid it, Fame!) shall they
The dictates of vile Fear obey?
Shall they, the idols of the Town,
To bug-bears, fancy-formed, bow down?
Shall they, who greatest zeal exprest,
And undertook for all the rest,
Whose matchless courage all admire,
Inglorious from the task retire?

How would the wicked ones rejoice,
And infidels exalt their voice,
If Moore and Plausible were found,
By shadows awed, to quit their ground?
How would fools laugh, should it appear
Pomposo was the slave of fear?
"Perish the thought! though to our eyes
In all its terrors, hell should rise,
Though thousand Ghosts, in dread array,
With glaring eyeballs, cross our way;
Though Caution, trembling, stands aloof,
Still we will on, and dare the proof."
They said; and, without farther halt,
Dauntless march'd onward to the vault.
 What mortal men, who e'er drew breath,
Shall break into the house of Death,
With foot unhallow'd, and from thence
The mysteries of that state dispense,
Unless they, with due rites, prepare
Their weaker sense such sights to bear,
And gain permission from the state,
On earth their journal to relate?
Poets themselves, without a crime,
Cannot attempt it e'en in rhyme,
But always, on such grand occasion,
Prepare a solemn invocation,
A posy for grim Pluto weave,
And in smooth numbers ask his leave.
But why this caution? why prepare
Rites needless now? for thrice in air
The spirit of the Night hath sneez'd,

And thrice hath clapp'd his wings well-pleased.
Descend then, Truth, and guard thy side,
My Muse, my patroness, and guide!
Let others at invention aim,
And seek by falsities for fame;
Our story wants not, at this time,
Flounces and furbelows in rhyme;
Relate plain facts; be brief and bold;
And let the poets, famed of old,
Seek, whilst our artless tale we tell,
In vain to find a parallel.
Silent all three went in; about
All three turn'd silent, and came out.

797 There is a fortuitous resemblance between this invocation to Truth and that in the opening of the Henriade:

Descends du haut des cieux, auguste Vérité,
Répand sur mes écrits ta force et ta clarté.

The goddess was apparently more propitious to Voltaire in poetry than in prose, his epic story of Henri Quatre being much more veracious than his prose accounts of Peter the Great and the Russian Empire; yet although the wilful misstatements of Voltaire have been noticed and exposed by every subsequent historian and traveller, it is painful to observe that in a work recently published under the superintendence of the *Useful* Knowledge Society, Voltaire is repeatedly quoted as the staple authority for the information communicated on the subject of Russia, its history and constitution; it is needless to add that a more unsafe guide could not have been consulted, nor one less entitled to credence.

SUPPLEMENTAL NOTE.

As german to the matter of this poem we extract from a very scarce Treatise on Ghosts and Demonology, the following authentic process of consigning a Spirit to the Red Sea, that universal limbo for all contumacious interlopers into the precincts of light and life.

The Form and Manner of Laying a Ghost; communicated by Master William Peterson, Minister of Hartburn in Lancashire.

In the reign of our good lady, Queen Elizabeth, of blessed memory, when this country had war with Spain, there was a fearful appearance of a Ghost at Cockerill Hall, in my parish of Hartburn. The Lord was with me, and I was not fearful of it; howbeit, it did cause great troublement and disturbance to many worthy people in my parish. Master Hugh Johnson, the Lord of Cockerill Hall, desired me to come and pray by the lady Bridget, his wife, and if I were not fearful, to sit up in the house and confer with the Ghost. Now I had been documented by an ancient man, of wonderful knowledge in Astrology, how to lay a Ghost; and in this I offered my humble service to Master Hugh, who kindly accepted of the same. Then I went up into the room where the Ghost was most minded to come, and with my consecrated chalk I made a circle, in the centre of which I took my stand. The Ghost at his own time did come forth; and I said unto him,

From whence comest thou?

He answered—

From home, now.

I said—

Where is thy home?

He answered—

Where thou shalt not come.

Then I said unto him—

Thou shalt go home again.

He answered—

When we've conquer'd Spain.

Then said I—

I will lay thee in the Red Sea.

He replied—

No, that cannot be!

I said—

Why so?

He answered—

The Spaniards will take me as I go.

I said—

Thou shalt have a convoy.

He answered—

Then I will begone, boy!

Then I threw five grains of salt into the fire, and turning my face towards the East, I said—

There shalt thou lay
For ever, and a day.

But sporting with my words, of which I was very well aware, he made answer—

There will I lay
For never, any day.

When he had said thus he attempted to go; but I restrained him, for had he escaped with these words, he would not have been laid. The method I took to withhold him, was by casting some 6 o'clock dew, which I had gathered for that purpose, upon his skirts. He then seemed very angry, and said in a somewhat harsh tone,

Take away thy dew,
Or thy ranting thou may rue.

I nothing heeded his braggarding; but told him that I would not take it off till he should say:

There will I lay
For ever, and a day.

He then seemed to be mighty angry, and mischievously inclined, making strange howlings and grimaces, and seeking me harm: but he could not come within my circle of consecrated chalk.

At last being forced to it by necessity of time, it drawing near to the crowing of the cock, he repeated the words, so I took off the 6 o'clock dew, and he flew away.

As he was going, I repeated the following latin verses, which I had composed for the business; and by the time that they were finished, I suppose he was got to the bottom of the Red Sea, for he never appeared more at Cockerill Hall.

Spiritus tuum non est stare,
Ibis nunc ad Rubrum mare:
Nam, si tibi fiat standum,
Tibi tunc est verber dandum.
Fuge jam celerior vento,
Et non abi pede lento;
Nam, si stares in itinere,
Tibi nulla parcam in re.
Te dimittam in avernum:
Et ligabo in æternum;
Semper ibi cruciaberis,
Ad supplicia damnaberis.
Juro hic per omnes deos,
Quos nunc voco testes meos,
Quod ad lucem non redibis,
Si non nunc ad mare ibis,
Fuge jam celerior vento,
Et non ibi pede lento.

Owing probably to the efficacy of the foregoing form, the appearance of ghosts has of late years been less frequent, and in the same proportion haunted houses have diminished in number; of the few remaining ones Holland house approaches nearest to the metropolis, and according to a tradition prevalent in Kensington, that favourite of fortune, Sir Stephen Fox, who died in 1716 at the age of 89, and of an obscure origin himself, was the father and founder of the two Peerages of Ilchester and Holland, as also Addison, and the first Lord Holland still occasionally revisit the chamber in which each of them died, and which within memory was shut up, as no servant would ever venture to go into it alone.

THE GHOST.*

BOOK III.

It was the hour, when housewife Morn
With pearl and linen hangs each thorn;
When happy bards, who can regale
Their Muse with country air and ale,
Ramble afield, to brooks and bowers,
To pick up sentiments and flowers;
When dogs and squires from kennel fly,
And hogs and farmers quit their sty;

* The monthly reviewers passed the following judgment on this book:—"Poetry, wit, humour, ridicule, satire, ill-nature, gross abuse, and low scurrility, are the characteristics of the digressive incoherent production now before us, which may not improperly be termed a kind of Tristram Shandy in verse.

"This undisciplined, irregular bard, this pandour in poetry, may, at the rambling rate in which he has hitherto proceeded, extend his *no* plan to the compass of the Iliad, and give us as many books on the imposture of Cock-lane, as Homer employed to sing the dire effects of the wrath of Achilles.

"With a slight alteration, and some latitude, the following lines, parodied from lines 1221, and sqq. of this poem, may be applied to the ingenious author himself:

"Here Churchill's rough ungovern'd soul,
Despising decency's control;
Despising French, despising Erse,
Pours forth the plain old English verse;
And bears aloft with terrors hung
The honours of the vulgar tongue."

When my Lord rises to the chace,
And brawny chaplain takes his place.
These images, or bad or good,
If they are rightly understood,
Sagacious readers must allow
Proclaim us in the country now;
For observations mostly rise
From objects just before our eyes,
And every lord, in critic wit,
Can tell you where the piece was writ;
Can point out, as he goes along,
(And who shall dare to say he's wrong?)
Whether the warmth (for bards, we know,
At present never more than glow)
Was in the town or country caught,
By the peculiar turn of thought.
It was the hour,—though critics frown,
We now declare ourselves in Town,
Nor will a moment's pause allow
For finding when we came, or how.
The man who deals in humble prose,
Tied down by rule and method goes;
But they who court the vigorous Muse
Their carriage have a right to choose.
Free as the air, and unconfined,
Swift as the motions of the mind,
The poet darts from place to place,
And instant bounds o'er time and space;
Nature (whilst blended fire and skill
Inflame our passions to his will)

Smiles at her violated laws,
And crowns his daring with applause.
  Should there be still some rigid few
Who keep propriety in view,
Whose heads turn round, and cannot bear
This whirling passage through the air,
Free leave have such at home to sit,
And write a regimen for wit;
To clip our pinions let them try,
Not having heart themselves to fly.
  It was the hour, when devotees
Breathe pious curses on their knees;
When they with prayers the day begin
To sanctify a night of sin;
When rogues of modesty, who roam
Under the veil of night, sneak home,
That free from all restraint and awe,
Just to the windward of the law,
Less modest rogues their tricks may play,
And plunder in the face of day.
  But hold,—whilst thus we play the fool,
In bold contempt of every rule,
Things of no consequence expressing,
Describing now, and now digressing,
To the discredit of our skill,
The main concern is standing still.
  In plays, indeed, when storms of rage
Tempestuous in the soul engage,
Or when the spirits, weak and low,
Are sunk in deep distress and woe,

With strict propriety we hear
Description stealing on the ear,
And put off feeling half an hour
To thatch a cot, or paint a flower;
But in these serious works, design'd
To mend the morals of mankind,
We must for ever be disgraced,
With all the nicer sons of taste,
If once, the shadow to pursue,
We let the substance out of view.
Our means must uniformly tend
In due proportion to their end,
And every passage aptly join
To bring about the one design.
Our friends themselves cannot admit

70 The powerful and masculine tone of Churchill's mind well qualified him to appreciate at their true value the mawkish tragedies and sentimental comedies which about this period began to supersede the pathetic and witty but licentious productions of Otway, Southern, Congreve, and Vanburgh. The vapid school of Whitehead, Dodsley and Murphy, poorly continued the series of the legitimate acting English drama until it terminated in the rant and splendid scenery of Pizarro and the broad farce of O'Keefe and Reynolds.

The latest modern acting tragedies, although of very different calibre, are Douglas and the Revenge, while the comedies of Cumberland and Mrs. Inchbald, however inferior in wit and stage effect to those of their predecessors, have not since been equalled, the nearest approach being by Tobin in his nondescript dramas of the Curfew and the Honeymoon.

The preceding observations apply of course only to plays professedly intended for the stage and not to the dramas or rather mysteries of Lord Byron, while the Rev. Dr. Croly in

This rambling, wild, digressive wit;
No—not those very friends, who found
Their credit on the self-same ground.
  Peace, my good grumbling Sir—for once,
Sunk in the solemn, formal dunce,
This coxcomb shall your fears beguile—
We will be dull—that you may smile.
  Come, Method, come in all thy pride,
Dullness and Whitehead by thy side;
Dullness and Method still are one,
And Whitehead is their darling son:
Not he whose pen, above control,
Struck terror to the guilty soul,
Made Folly tremble through her state,

his classical and beautiful play of Catiline, has at once shown what a good tragedy should be, and that he is fully equal to the task of producing one.

95 Paul Whitehead, a man of notoriously profligate private character, author of several satires, now deservedly forgotten, in which he unsparingly lashed the vices and follies of the age, and carried his pseudo patriotism almost to republicanism: they were respectively entitled, "The State Dunces"; Honour"; and "Manners"; for the last of which he was ordered by the House of Lords to be taken into custody. He also wrote some other poems of little merit. His companionable qualities, or rather vices, procured him the friendship of Sir Francis Dashwood, who, when Chancellor of the Exchequer, conferred on him a patent place of £800 a year, which he enjoyed till his death in 1774, and which operated as a most convincing argument of the purity of the times, and of the folly of his former principles. By his will, Paul Whitehead bequeathed his heart to his patron Lord Le Despencer, who caused it to be enclosed in an urn, and deposited in the church erected by him at High Wycombe.

And villains blush at being great;
Whilst he himself, with steady face,
Disdaining modesty and grace,
Could blunder on through thick and thin
Through every mean and servile sin,
Yet swear by Philip and by Paul
He nobly scorn'd to blush at all;
But he, who in the Laureat chair,
By grace, not merit planted there,
In awkward pomp is seen to sit,
And by his patent proves his wit:
For favours of the great, we know,
Can wit as well as rank bestow;
And they who, without one pretension,
Can get for fools a place or pension,
Must able be supposed of course
(If reason is allowed due force)
To give such qualities and grace
As may equip them for the place.

105 William Whitehead, tne poet laureate, an account of whom is given in a note on the Prophecy of Famine. In 1762, he published "A Charge to the Poets," throughout which there reigns a considerable portion of "humble insolence," and affected candour. He ridiculously assumed a degree of consequence as Laureate, which that situation in its best estate could never confer, and dealt out his dictates with a tone of superiority which his abilities could not support.

"Then since my king and patron have thought fit
To place me on the throne of modern wit,
My grave advice, my brethren, hear at large,
As bishops to their clergy give a charge."

But he—who measures, as he goes,
A mongrel kind of tinkling prose,
And is too frugal to dispense,
At once, both poetry and sense;
Who, from amidst his slumbering guards,
Deals out a charge to subject bards,
Where couplets after couplets creep
Propitious to the reign of sleep;
Yet every word imprints an awe,
And all his dictates pass for law
With beaus, who simper all around,
And belles, who die in every sound:
For in all things of this relation,
Men mostly judge from situation,
Nor in a thousand find we one
Who really weighs what's said or done;
They deal out censure, or give credit,
Merely from him who did or said it.
  But he—who, happily serene,
Means nothing, yet would seem to mean,
Who rules and cautions can dispense
With all that humble insolence
Which impudence in vain would teach,
And none but modest men can reach;
Who adds to sentiments the grace
Of always being out of place,
And drawls out morals with an air
A gentleman would blush to wear;
Who, on the chastest, simplest plan,
As chaste, as simple, as the man

Without or character, or plot,
Nature unknown, and art forgot,
Can, with much raking of the brains,
And years consumed in letter'd pains,
A heap of words together lay,
And smirking, call the thing a play;
Who, champion sworn in virtue's cause,
'Gainst vice his tiny bodkin draws,
But to no part of prudence stranger,
First blunts the point for fear of danger.
So nurses sage, as caution works,
When children first use knives and forks,
For fear of mischief, it is known,
To others' fingers or their own,
To take the edge off wisely choose,
Though the same stroke takes off the use.
  Thee, Whitehead, thee I now invoke,
Sworn foe to Satire's generous stroke,
Which makes unwilling conscience feel,
And wounds, but only wounds to heal.

152 Alluding to Whitehead's comedy of the School for Lovers, a servile copy from le Testament of Fontenelle. The following affected inscription is prefixed to the play:— "To the memory of M. de Fontenelle, this comedy is inscribed by a lover of simplicity." This play has some merit in the reading but is too simple for representation. Whitehead's tragedies, like those of Murphy, were principally borrowed from the French, and proved equally unsuccessful on the stage. In an advertisement prefixed to his dramas, Whitehead observes that "most of the pieces had already met their fate with the public, and would probably never have been collected if the author had not imagined that *his character as Laureate* obliged him to revise and correct them."

Good-natured, easy ereature, mild
And gentle as a new-born child,
Thy heart would never once admit
E'en wholesome rigour to thy wit;
Thy head, if conscience should comply,
Its kind assistance would deny,
And lend thee neither force, nor art
To drive it onward to the heart.
O may thy sacred power control
Each fiercer working of my soul,
Damp every spark of genuine fire,
And languors, like thine own, inspire!
Trite be each thought, and every line
As moral, and as dull as thine!
  Poised in the mid-air—(it matters not
To ascertain the very spot,
Nor yet to give you a relation
How it eluded gravitation)—
Hung a watch-tower—by Vulcan plann'd
With such rare skill, by Jove's command,
That every word, which whisper'd here
Scarce vibrates to the neighbour ear,
On the still bosom of the air
Is borne, and heard distinctly there,
The palace of an ancient dame,
Whom men as well as gods call Fame.
  A prattling gossip, on whose tongue
Proof of perpetual motion hung,
Whose lungs in strength all lungs surpass,
Like her own trumpet made of brass;

Who with an hundred pair of eyes
The vain attacks of sleep defies;
Who with an hundred pair of wings
News from the farthest quarters brings;
Sees, hears, and tells, untold before,
All that she knows and ten times more.
  Not all the virtues which we find
Concenter'd in a Hunter's mind,

204 Miss Hunter, a young lady of family and fortune, and maid of honour to Queen Charlotte, eloped on the day of the coronation with the grandfather of the present Earl of Pembroke. On her table was found a paper containing the following lines from Pope:

"How oft when press'd to marriage have I said,
Curse on all laws but those which love has made.
Love, free as air, at sight of human ties,
Spreads his light wings, and in a moment flies.
Let wealth, let honour, wait the wedded dame,
August her deed, and sacred be her fame.
Before true passion all those views remove,
Fame, wealth, and honour! What are you to love?
The jealous God, when we profane his fires,
Those restless passions in revenge inspires,
And bids them make mistaken mortals groan,
Who seek in love for aught but love alone.
Should at my feet the world's great master fall,
Himself, his throne, his world, I'd scorn them all;
Not Cæsar's empress would I deign to prove,
No, make me mistress to the man I love."

The king, on learning the transaction, immediately deprived Lord Pembroke of his military commands, and with his own hand struck him out of the list of privy counsellors. Miss Hunter, after the death of Lord Pembroke, became the wife of General Clarke. She had a son by Lord Pembroke, who was allowed to assume the name of Montgomery, and was shot in a duel by Colonel Macnamaro several years ago.

Can make her spare the rancorous tale,
If, in one point she chance to fail;
Or if, once in a thousand years,
A perfect character appears,
Such as of late with joy and pride
My soul possess'd, ere Arrow died;
Or such as, envy must allow
The world enjoys in Hunter now;
This hag, who aims at all alike,
At virtues e'en like theirs will strike,
And make faults in the way of trade,
When she can't find them ready made.
  All things she takes in, small and great,
Talks of a toyshop and a state;
Of wits and fools, of saints and kings,
Of garters, stars, and leading-strings;
Of old lords fumbling for a clap,
And young ones full of prayer and pap;
Of courts, of morals, and tye-wigs,
Of bears and serjeants dancing jigs;
Of grave professors at the bar
Learning to thrum on the guitar,
Whilst laws are slubber'd o'er in haste,
And judgment sacrificed to taste;
Of whited sepulchres, lawn sleeves,
And God's house made a den of thieves;
Of funeral pomps, where clamours hung,

231 Alluding to the interment of George II., which took place the 11th of November, 1760; it was regulated according to the ceremonial usual on such occasions; but some impro-

And fix'd disgrace on every tongue,
Whilst Sense and Order blush'd to see
Nobles without humanity;
Of coronations, where each heart,
With honest raptures, bore a part;
Of city feasts, where Elegance
Was proud her colours to advance,
And Gluttony, uncommon case,
Could only get the second place;
Of new-raised pillars in the state,
Who must be good, as being great;
Of shoulders, on which honours sit
Almost as clumsily as wit;
Of doughty knights, whom titles please,
But not the payment of the fees;
Of lectures, whither every fool
In second childhood goes to school;
Of grey-beards, deaf to Reason's call,

prieties occurred in the procession, which was also rather scantily attended.

235 The coronation of George the Third, on the 22d of September, 1761. This great solemnity is amply noticed in the ensuing book.

237 Their majesties were entertained by the city in Guildhall, according to custom, on the first Lord Mayor's day after their coronation. The banquet was conducted in a style of splendour and elegance then unprecedented in the civic annals. The expense amounted to the sum of £6898, 5*s.* 4*d.*

247 Macklin and Sheridan, were at this time competitors in teaching elocution in its several departments of the senate, the stage, the pulpit, and the bar, and in some of their pupils in each, had to begin at the beginning, and to adapt their instruction to the level of the very meanest capacity.

From Inn of Court, or City Hall,
Whom youthful appetites enslave,
With one foot fairly in the grave,
By help of crutch, a needful brother,
Learning of Hart to dance with t'other;
Of doctors regularly bred
To fill the mansions of the dead;
Of quacks, (for quacks they must be still,
Who save when forms require to kill)
Who life, and health, and vigour give
To him, not one would wish to live;
Of artists who, with noblest view,
Disinterested plans pursue,
For trembling worth the ladder raise,
And mark out the ascent to praise;
Of arts and sciences, where meet,
Sublime, profound, and all complete,
A set (whom at some fitter time
The Muse shall consecrate in rhyme)

254 Hart was an eminent professor of the noble science of dancing; in his advertisements he undertook to teach grown gentlemen that elegant accomplishment on the easiest terms, and in the shortest period of time.

267 An invidious reflection on the Society for the encouragement of arts, manufactures, and commerce, founded in the year 1753. Previous to the institution of the Royal Academy, in 1765, the Society of Arts had an annual exhibition in its room of meeting, in Beaufort-buildings, of such paintings as had obtained the premiums proposed within the year. From this Society have branched the Royal Academy and several literary and scientific Institutions, and numerous societies for improvements in agriculture. Divested

Who, humble artists to out-do,
A far more liberal plan pursue,
And let their well-judged premiums fall
On those who have no worth at all;
Of sign-post exhibitions, raised
For laughter more than to be praised,
(Though by the way we cannot see
Why praise and laughter mayn't agree)
Where genuine humour runs to waste,
And justly chides our want of taste,

of the pride, pomp, and circumstance of corporate dignity, it unostentatiously pursues its course of usefulness, though from the nature of its constitution, the misplaced zeal and eloquence of some of its members has occasionally exposed it to ridicule. The meetings of the society are now held at their house in the Adelphi, the great room of which is decorated by a series of paintings by Barry, which are too generally known and admired to require any further notice of them here. The late Duke of Sussex was, during seventeen years, president of the Society, in which office he has been succeeded by Prince Albert, under whose patronage the most sanguine expectations of renovated funds and efficiency combined with public utility are entertained.

274 Bonnell Thornton thought the exhibition of the Society of Arts afforded a fair subject for ridicule, and, accordingly, previous to the annual opening of it on the 20th of April, 1762, advertised for the same day in the papers an intended exhibition, by the society of sign painters, of all the curious signs to be met with in town or country, together with such original designs as might be transmitted to them as specimens of the native genius of this country, but at the same time strongly reprobating the idea that any intention existed of injuring the Society of Arts. The public, considering it as a mere newspaper skit, enjoyed the joke, but the whole humour evaporated on the plan being actually carried into execution;

Censured, like other things, though good,
Because they are not understood.
 To higher subjects now she soars,
And talks of politics and whores;
(If to your nice and chaster ears
That term indelicate appears,
Scripture politely shall refine
And melt it into concubine)

a room in Bow-street, Covent-garden, was engaged, catalogues printed, and admission money taken to see this most senseless practical attempt at satire. The exhibition consisted of a number of wretched daubings, most of which had actually before been hung in irons, and were worn out in the service. Among so great a number there occurred some ludicrous combinations; and as the catalogue has become scarce, we shall extract the description of a few for the entertainment of our readers:

No. 9. The Irish Arms (a great clumsy pair of legs.) By Patrick O'Blaney. N. B. Captain Terence O'Cutter *stood* for them.

12. The Scotch Fiddle. By M'Pharson, *done from himself.*

19. Nobody. A man all legs.

20. Somebody. A man all belly.

27. The Spirit of Contradiction. Two brewers bearing a cask, the men going different ways.

30. The Dancing Bears. A sign for N. Duke or A. Hart, or any other dancing-master to grown gentlemen.

32. A Man struggling through the World. The sign of a pasteboard terrestrial globe with a man creeping through it, his head out at one end, and his heels at the other.

67. Death and the Doctor; *in Distemper.*

73. A Man loaded with Mischief. A fellow with a woman, a magpie, and a monkey on his back.

In the same breath spreads Bourbon's league;
And publishes the grand intrigue;
In Brussels or our own Gazette
Makes armies fight which never met,
And circulates the pox or plague
To London by the way of Hague;
For all the lies which there appear
Stamp'd with authority come here;
Borrows as freely from the gabble
Of some rude leader of a rabble,
Or from the quaint harangues of those
Who lead a nation by the nose,
As from those storms which, void of art,
Burst from our honest patriot's heart,
When Eloquence and Virtue (late

287 The family compact between France and Spain, having been concluded, in August, 1761, Mr. Pitt and Lord Temple alleging that they had certain information of the fact, proposed, in September, an immediate declaration of war against the latter, but were overruled in the cabinet, and immediately resigned their offices, as we have before had occasion to mention. In the ensuing session of parliament, upon Lord Temple's censuring administration for acting as they did with a knowledge of the existence of such a compact, Lord Bute rose and pronounced these words:—"My Lords, I affirm upon my honour, that there was no intelligence of such a fact so constituted at that time." This brought Lord Temple up again, who affirmed also upon his honour, "that there was intelligence of the highest moment; that he was not at liberty to publish that intelligence, but would refresh his Lordship's memory in private." He beckoned Lord Bute out of the house, and repeated to him the intelligence which had been laid before the cabinet. The dates confirmed Lord Temple's assertion; the family compact was signed on the 15th of

Remark'd to live in mutual hate)
Fond of each other's friendship grown,
Claim every sentence for their own;
And with an equal joy recites
Parade amours and half pay-fights,
Perform'd by heroes of fair weather,
Merely by dint of lace and feather,
As those rare acts which Honour taught
Our daring sons where Granby fought,
Or those which, with superior skill,
Sackville achieved by standing still.
This hag, (the curious, if they please,
May search, from earliest times, to these,

August 1761, ratified on the 8th of September, and the written advice to recall Lord Bristol from Madrid was given and dated on the 18th of the same month. War was declared in January, 1762.

[289] The Brussels Gazette was a notorious vehicle for the experiments of the continental diplomatists on the political credulity of the public.

[300] Mr. Pitt, who at this period, was generally known by the appellation of "the Great Commoner," a proud distinction poorly bartered for a coronet and a pension.

[310] The Marquis of Granby, the eldest son of the Duke of Rutland, distinguished himself in a conspicuous manner, during the seven years war, under Prince Ferdinand of Brunswick. He was second to Lord Sackville (whom he also succeeded) in the command of the English troops at the battle of Minden; and when the latter pretended not to comprehend Prince Ferdinand's orders, the Prince directed them to be repeated to the Marquis of Granby, as he was sure he would understand them. The Marquis died in 1770, in the 50th year of his age. Walpole relates of him that he was an honest open-hearted man of undaunted spirit, but no capacity, that he drank as profusely as a German, was honest and affable,

And poets they will always see
With gods and goddesses make free,
Treating them all, except the Muse,
As scarcely fit to wipe their shoes)
Who had beheld, from first to last,
How our triumvirate had past
Night's dreadful interval, and heard,
With strict attention, every word,
Soon as she saw return of light,
On sounding pinions took her flight.
  Swift through the regions of the sky,
Above the reach of human eye,
Onward she drove the furious blast,
And rapid as a whirlwind past,
O'er countries, once the seats of taste,
By time and ignorance laid waste;
O'er lands, where former ages saw
Reason and truth the only law;
Where arts and arms, and public love,
In generous emulation strove;

and of such unbounded good nature and generosity that it was impossible to say which principle actuated him in the distribution of the prodigious sums that he spent and flung away. He was thus celebrated by Sir C. H. Williams:

But of the clan there's not a man,
  For bravery that can be,
(Though Anstruther should make a stir)
  Compared with Marquis Granby.

His sword and dress both well express
  His courage most exceeding,
And by his hair, you'd almost swear,
  He's valiant Charles of Sweden.

Where kings were proud of legal sway,
And subjects happy to obey,
Though now in slavery sunk, and broke
To superstition's galling yoke;
Of arts, of arms, no more they tell,
Or freedom, which with science fell:
By tyrants awed, who never find
The passage to their people's mind;
To whom the joy was never known
Of planting in the heart their throne;
Far from all prospect of relief,
Their hours in fruitless prayers and grief
For loss of blessings they employ,
Which we unthankfully enjoy.
  Now is the time (had we the will)
To amaze the reader with our skill,
To pour out such a flood of knowledge
As might suffice for a whole college,
Whilst with a true poetic force,
We traced the goddess in her course,
Sweetly describing, in our flight,
Each common and uncommon sight,
Making our journal gay and pleasant,
With things long past, and things now present.
Rivers—once Nymphs—(a transformation

359 See tale of Lodona and Pan, as related by Pope in his Windsor Forest, and which also occurs in a more compressed form in the Carmin Quadragesimalia as the origin of the river Loddon.

In Windsor's plains, as fair Lodona stray'd,

Is mighty pretty in relation)
From great authorities we know
Will matter for a tale bestow:
To make the observation clear
We give our friends an instance here.
  The day (that never is forgot)
Was very fine, but very hot;
The nymph (another general rule)
Enflamed with heat, laid down to cool;
Her hair, (we no exceptions find)
Waved careless, floating in the wind;
Her heaving breasts, like summer seas,
Seem'd amorous of the playful breeze:
Should fond description tune our lays
In choicest accents to her praise,
Description we at last should find,
Baffled and weak, would halt behind.
Nature had form'd her to inspire
In every bosom soft desire:
Passions to raise, she could not feel,
Wounds to inflict, she would not heal.

The horned god surprised the wandering maid,
Swift flew the nymph, the god pursued the chace,
Wing'd with desire to share her soft embrace;
Panting o'er forests, hills, and dales they rove,
This urged by conscious fear and that by love,
Still doubtful is the chace, yet now more near
The lover's breath divides her parting hair;
Fatigued at length, she call'd on Cynthia's name,
And all dissolved into a purling stream.
Though changed yet mindful of her pristine woes,
She ever murmurs and for ever flows.

A god, (his name is no great matter,
Perhaps a Jove, perhaps a Satyr)
Raging with lust, a godlike flame,
By chance, as usual, thither came;
With gloating eye the fair one view'd,
Desired her first, and then pursued:
She (for what other can she do?)
Must fly—or how can he pursue?
The Muse, (so custom hath decreed)
Now proves her spirit by her speed,
Nor must one limping line disgrace
The life and vigour of the race.
She runs, and he runs, till at length,
Quite destitute of breath and strength,
To Heaven (for there we all apply
For help, when there's no other nigh)
She offers up her virgin prayer,
(Can virgins pray unpitied there?)
And when the god thinks he has caught her,
Slips through his hands and runs to water,
Becomes a stream, in which the poet
If he has any wit may show it.
  A city once for power renown'd
Now levell'd even to the ground,
Beyond all doubt is a direction
To introduce some fine reflection.
  Ah, woeful me! ah, woeful man!
Ah! woeful all, do all we can!
Who can on earthly things depend
From one to t'other moment's end?

Honour, wit, genius, wealth, and glory,
Good lack! good lack! are transitory;
Nothing is sure and stable found,
The very earth itself turns round:
Monarchs, nay ministers, must die,
Must rot, must stink—ah, me! ah, why!
Cities themselves in time decay;
If cities thus—ah! well-a-day!
If brick and mortar have an end,
On what can flesh and blood depend!
Ah, woeful me! ah, woeful man!
Ah! woeful all, do all we can!
England, (for that's at last the scene,
Though worlds on worlds should rise between,
Whither we must our course pursue)
England should call into review
Times long since past indeed, but not
By Englishmen to be forgot,
Though England, once so dear to Fame,
Sinks in Great Britain's dearer name.
Here could we mention chiefs of old,
In plain and rugged honour bold,
To virtue kind, to vice severe,
Strangers to bribery and fear,
Who kept no wretched clans in awe,
Who never broke or warp'd the law;

422 A happy parody of the declamatory style so frequently adopted by some of the minor poets when expatiating on the ravages of time, and contemplating its progressive influence on the labours of mankind.

Patriots, whom, in her better days,
Old Rome might have been proud to raise;
Who, steady to their country's claim,
Boldly stood up in Freedom's name,
E'en to the teeth of tyrant Pride,
And, when they could no more, they died.
There (striking contrast) might we place
A servile, mean, degenerate race;
Hirelings, who valued nought but gold,
By the best bidder bought and sold;
Truants from honour's sacred laws,
Betrayers of their country's cause;
The dupes of party, tools of power,
Slaves to the minion of an hour;
Lackeys, who watch'd a favourite's nod,
And took a puppet for their god.
Sincere and honest in our rhymes,
How might we praise these happier times!
How might the Muse exalt her lays,
And wanton in a monarch's praise!
Tell of a prince in England born,
Whose virtues England's crown adorn,
In youth a pattern unto age,
So chaste, so pious, and so sage;
Who, true to all those sacred bands
Which private happiness demands,
Yet never lets them rise above
The stronger ties of public love.

457 "Born and educated in this country, I glory in the name of Briton!"—George the Third's first Speech to his parliament, 18th of November, 1760.

With conscious pride see England stand,
Our holy Charter in her hand;
She waves it round, and o'er the isle
See Liberty and Courage smile.
No more she mourns her treasures hurl'd
In subsidies to all the world;
No more by foreign threats dismay'd,
No more deceived with foreign aid,
She deals out sums to petty states,
Whom Honour scorns, and Reason hates,
But, wiser by experience grown,
Finds safety in herself alone.
"Whilst thus," she cries, my "children stand
An honest, valiant, native band,
A train'd militia, brave and free,
True to their king, and true to me,
No foreign hirelings shall be known,
Nor need we hirelings of our own:
Under a just and pious reign
The statesman's sophistry is vain;

488 This period is at length arrived, and the safety of England is confided to the unconquerable spirit of its inhabitants. The voluntary exertions for the defence of the country in 1803, in the exhibition of which every political and religious difference was merged in a devoted love of country, will form the proudest epoch in the annals of British history. An energy has been displayed, and a spirit roused, which not even the irresolution of administration has been able to repress. Our obligations to government, however, are not of a nature to oppress us with their magnitude: as the subsidies profusely voted to foreign states for their hollow aid were only discontinued when no Power could be found who would accept them. [First Edition, 1804.]

Vain is each vile, corrupt pretence,
These are my natural defence;
Their faith I know, and they shall prove
The bulwark of the king they love."
These, and a thousand things beside,
Did we consult a poet's pride,
Some gay, some serious, might be said,
But ten to one they'd not be read;
Or were they by some curious few,
Not even those would think them true;
For, from the time that Jubal first
Sweet ditties to the harp rehearsed,
Poets have always been suspected
Of having truth in rhyme neglected,
That bard except, who from his youth
Equally famed for faith and truth,
By prudence taught, in courtly chime
To courtly ears brought truth in rhyme.
But though to poets we allow,
No matter when acquired or how,

502 Mallet addressed a contemptible poem, entitled "Truth in Rhyme," to the celebrated Lord Chesterfield, who suffered it to be published with the following extraordinary sanction prefixed:

"It has no faults, or I no faults can spy,
It is all beauty or all blindness I."

Imprimatur meo periculo.
CHESTERFIELD.

If this quotation from Conyngham was ironically applied, or really intended as a compliment, it in neither case does any credit to his lordship's taste. If modesty had found a

From truth unbounded deviation,
Which custom calls Imagination,
Yet can't they be supposed to lie
One half so fast as Fame can fly;
Therefore (to solve this Gordian knot,
A point we almost had forgot)
To courteous readers be it known,
That, fond of verse and falsehood grown,
Whilst we in sweet digression sung,
Fame check'd her flight, and held her tongue,
And now pursues, with double force
And double speed, her destined course,
Nor stops till she the place arrives
Where Genius starves and Dullness thrives;
Where riches virtue are esteem'd,
And craft is truest wisdom deem'd,
Where Commerce proudly rears her throne,
In state to other lands unknown;
Where, to be cheated and to cheat,
Strangers from every quarter meet;

place in the catalogue of Mallet's virtues, it would have induced him to suppress, instead of publicly exulting in, a testimony too extravagant for any poem ever to have deserved.

517 The Royal Exchange, a place where Churchill's genius was certainly not calculated to shine; his own failure in trade as a cider dealer seems to have tinctured him with a strong and unfounded prejudice against the most useful and liberal of men, the merchants of the city of London; whose unbounded donations, private as well as public, entitle them to the respect and gratitude of their countrymen.

Where Christians, Jews, and Turks shake hands,
United in commercial bands;
All of one faith, and that to own
No god but Interest alone.
When gods and goddesses come down
To look about them here in Town,
(For change of air is understood
By sons of Physic to be good,
In due proportion, now and then,
For these same gods as well as men)
By custom ruled, and not a poet
So very dull but he must know it,
In order to remain *incog.*
They always travel in a fog;
For if we majesty expose
To vulgar eyes, too cheap it grows;
The force is lost, and, free from awe,
We spy and censure every flaw;
But well preserved from public view,
It always breaks forth fresh and new;
Fierce as the sun in all his pride
It shines, and not a spot's descried.
Was Jove to lay his thunder by,
And with his brethren of the sky
Descend to earth, and frisk about,
Like chattering N*** from rout to rout,
He would be found, with all his host,
A nine days' wonder at the most.
Would we in trim our honours wear,
We must preserve them from the air;

What is familiar men neglect,
However worthy of respect.
Did they not find a certain friend
In novelty to recommend,
(Such we, by sad experience find
The wretched folly of mankind)
Venus might unattractive shine,
And Hunter fix no eyes but mine.
  But Fame, who never cared a jot
Whether she was admired or not,
And never blush'd to shew her face
At any time in any place,
In her own shape, without disguise,
And visible to mortal eyes,
On 'Change, exact at seven o'clock,
Alighted on the weathercock,
Which planted there time out of mind
To note the changes of the wind,
Might no improper emblem be
Of her own mutability.
  Thrice did she sound her trump, (the same
Which from the first belonged to Fame,
An old ill-favour'd instrument,
With which the goddess was content,
Though under a politer race
Bagpipes might well supply its place)
And thrice awaken'd by the sound,
A general din prevail'd around;
Confusion through the city pass'd,
And fear bestrode the dreadful blast.

Those fragrant currents which we meet,
Distilling soft through every street,
Affrighted from the usual course,
Ran murmuring upwards to their source:
Statues wept tears of blood, as fast
As when a Cæsar breathed his last:
Horses, which always used to go
A foot-pace in my Lord Mayor's show,
Impetuous from their stable broke,
And aldermen and oxen spoke,
Halls felt the force, towers shook around,
And steeples nodded to the ground;
St. Paul himself (strange sight!) was seen
To bow as humbly as the Dean:

585 The great and progressive improvements in the police and appearance of London had scarcely commenced so early as the publication of this poem. The kennels in the middle of the streets, the bad pavement and imperfect lighting, the sign posts and the water spouts having now been all removed or altered, Gay's admonitory cautions to walkers are become nearly obsolete:

"But when the swinging signs your ears offend
With creaking noise, then rainy floods impend,
Soon shall the kennels swell with rapid streams,
And rush in muddy torrents to the Thames.
On hosiers' poles depending stockings tied,
Flag with the slacken'd gale from side to side.
Ungrateful odours common sewers diffuse,
And dropping vaults distil unwholesome dews,
E'er the tiles rattle with the smoking shower,
And spouts on heedless men their torrents pour."

TRIVIA.

The Mansion House, for ever placed
A monument of City taste,
Trembled, and seem'd aloud to groan
Through all that hideous weight of stone.
  To still the sound, or stop her ears,
Remove the cause or sense of fears,
Physic, in college seated high,
Would any thing but medicine try.
No more in Pewterers' Hall was heard
The proper force of every word;
Those seats were desolate become,
A hapless Elocution dumb.
Form, city-born and city-bred,

599 The following note occurs on the subject of the Mansion House in an ingenious pamphlet entitled "Critical Observations on the Buildings and Improvements of London," published in 1771: "The bad taste of the city is a trite subject, and any strictures upon their former public management in those matters are hardly applicable at present. At least one would hope the season is now over when the citizens, before they approve of a plan, require to know if the author is of the livery, or if his creed is according to law; but the following anecdote of what happened forty years ago is told, and may not be unacceptable to the reader. When it was first resolved in Common Council to build a Mansion House for the Lord Mayor, Lord Burlington, zealous in the cause of the arts, sent down an original design of Palladio, worthy of its author, for their approbation and adoption. The first question in court was not, whether the plan was proper, but whether this same Palladio was a freeman of the city or no. On this great debates ensued, and it is hard to say how it might have gone, had not a worthy deputy risen up, and observed gravely, that it was of little consequence to discuss this point, when it was notorious that Palladio was a papist, and incapable of course.

By strict decorum ever led,
Who threescore years had known the grace
Of one dull, stiff, unvaried pace;
Terror prevailing over Pride,
Was seen to take a larger stride;
Worn to the bone, and clothed in rags,
See Avarice closer hug his bags;
With her own weight unwieldy grown,
See Credit totter on her throne;
Virtue alone, had she been there,
The mighty sound, unmoved, could bear,
  Up from the gorgeous bed, where Fate
Dooms annual fools to sleep in state,
To sleep so sound that not one gleam

Lord Burlington's proposal was then rejected nem. con. and the plan of a freeman and a protestant adopted in its room. Dance, the man pitched upon (who afterwards carried his plan into execution) was originally a shipwright, and, to do him justice, he appears never to have lost sight of his first profession. The front of the Mansion House has all the resemblance possible to a deep-laden Indiaman, with her stern galleries and gingerbread work. The stairs and passages within are all ladders and gangways, and the two bulkheads on the roof, fore and aft, not unaptly represent the binnacle and windlass on the deck of a great north country *Catt.*"

"Vous etes, je l'avoue, ignorant architecte,
Mais un habile charpentier."

607 Macklin's recitations and his lectures on elocution were delivered at Pewterers' Hall, in Lime Street. This hardy veteran evinced throughout his long life an extraordinary versatility of genius, as appeared by his performances in the several characters of actor, author, lecturer and tutor.

Of Fancy can provoke a dream,
Great Dulman started at the sound,
Gaped, rubb'd his eyes, and stared around.
Much did he wish to know, much fear,
Whence sounds so horrid struck his ear.
So much unlike those peaceful notes,
That equal harmony, which floats
On the dull wing of city air,
Grave prelude to a feast or fair:
Much did he inly ruminate
Concerning the decrees of Fate,
Revolving, though to little end,
What this same trumpet might portend.
  Could the French—no—that could not be
Under Bute's active ministry,
Too watchful to be so deceived—
Have stolen hither unperceived?
To Newfoundland, indeed, we know

627 Sir Samuel Fludyer, Bart. M. P. for Chippenham, Deputy-Governor of the Bank of England, and Lord Mayor of London for 1761–2. He was originally a clothier at Frome, in Somersetshire, in which business he acquired a considerable fortune, and died in 1768.

648 In May 1762 a French squadron escaped out of Brest in a fog, and captured the town of St. John's, in Newfoundland; the garrison surrendered themselves prisoners of war, and some vessels, and stores to a considerable amount, became the prey of the victors. Ministry were much blamed for their negligence; but farther inquiry was superseded by the recapture, in the September following, of the settlement by a British force under the command of Lord Colville and Colonel Amherst.

Fleets of war unobserved may go;
Or, if observed, may be supposed,
At intervals when Reason dozed,
No other point in view to bear
But pleasure, health, and change of air;
But Reason ne'er could sleep so sound
To let an enemy be found
In our land's heart, ere it was known
They had departed from their own.
  Or could his successor (Ambition
Is ever haunted with suspicion)
His daring successor elect,
All customs, rules, and forms reject,
And aim, regardless of the crime,
To seize the chair before his time?
  Or (deeming this the lucky hour,
Seeing his countrymen in power,
Those countrymen who, from the first,
In tumults and rebellion nursed,
Howe'er they wear the mask of art,
Still love a Stuart in their heart)
Could Scottish Charles——
                    Conjecture thus,
That mental *ignis fatuus*
Led his poor brains a weary dance
From France to England, hence to France,
Till Information (in the shape
Of chaplain learned, good Sir Crape,)

657 Beckford was the Lord Mayor elect for 1762-3.

A lazy, longing, pamper'd priest,
Well known at every City feast,
For he was seen much oftener there
Than in the house of God at prayer;
Who, always ready in his place,
Ne'er let God's creatures wait for grace,
Though, as the best historians write,
Less famed for faith than appetite;
His disposition to reveal,
The grace was short, and long the meal;
Who always would excess admit,
If haunch or turtle came with it,
And ne'er engaged in the defence
Of self-denying Abstinence,
When he could fortunately meet
With any thing he liked to eat;
Who knew that wine, on Scripture plan,
Was made to cheer the heart of man;
Knew too, by long experience taught,
That cheerfulness was kill'd by thought;
And from those premises collected,
(Which few perhaps would have suspected)
That none who, with due share of sense,
Observed the ways of Providence,
Could with safe conscience leave off drinking
Till they had lost the power of thinking;
With eyes half closed came waddling in,
And, having stroked his double chin,
(That chin, whose credit to maintain
Against the scoffs of the profane,

Had cost him more than ever state
Paid for a poor electorate,
Which, after all the cost and rout
It had been better much without)
Briefly, (for breakfast, you must know,
Was waiting all the while below)
Related, bowing to the ground,
The cause of that uncommon sound;
Related, too, that at the door
Pomposo, Plausible, and Moore,
Begg'd that Fame might not be allow'd
Their shame to publish to the crowd;
That some new laws he would provide,
(If old could not be misapplied
With as much ease and safety there
As they are misapplied elsewhere)
By which it might be construed treason
In man to exercise his reason,

702 The electorate of Hanover was the favourite possession of the two first Georges; and the many expensive wars in which the country was engaged during their reigns was the fruit of their partiality. These and subsequent events have unfortunately too clearly proved the want of foresight our ancestors displayed in not requiring the complete separation of the kingdom from the electorate as a constituent basis of the settlement of the crown upon the house of Hanover, and which has since been happily effected by the course of succession.

710 Application was made on behalf of these gentlemen to the Lord Mayor, for a prohibition against the hawking through the streets of London, "a full, true, and particular account" of their midnight visit to Fanny's tomb.

Which might ingeniously devise
One punishment for truth and lies,
And fairly prove, when they had done,
That truth and falsehood were but one;
Which juries must indeed retain,
But their effects should render vain,
Making all real power to rest
In one corrupted rotten breast,
By whose false gloss the very Bible
Might be interpreted a libel.
Moore (who, his reverence to save,
Pleaded the fool to screen the knave,
Though all, who witness'd on his part
Swore for his head against his heart)
Had taken down, from first to last,
A just account of all that pass'd;
But, since the gracious will of Fate,
Who mark'd the child for wealth and state
E'en in the cradle, had decreed
The mighty Dulman ne'er should read,

728 Lord Mansfield's interpretation of the law of libels though founded upon precedents made in the worst of times, was, with the exception of Lord Camden, universally adhered to by the bench. Juries were browbeaten and insulted, if they dared to find a verdict beyond the mere fact of publication; and that most absurd maxim, "the greater the truth, the greater the libel," influenced the discretion of the judge in the sentence he pronounced. To the patriotic exertions of Mr. Fox, we are indebted for the explanatory bill passed in 1791, which restored to the jury the power of deciding upon the law, as well as the fact, by returning a general verdict, [1803.] Some of the most obvious practical

That office of disgrace to bear
The smooth-lipp'd Plausible was there;
From Holborn e'en to Clerkenwell,
Who knows not smooth-lipp'd Plausible?
A preacher deem'd of greatest note
For preaching that which others wrote.
  Had Dulman now, (and fools, we see,
Seldom want curiosity)
Consented (but the mourning shade
Of Gascoyne hasten'd to his aid,
And in his hand, what could he more?
Triumphant Canning's picture bore)
That our three heroes should advance
And read their comical romance,
How rich a feast, what royal fare,
We for our readers might prepare!
So rich and yet so safe a feast,
That no one foreign blatant beast,
Within the purlieus of the law,
Should dare thereon to lay his paw,

remaining defects in the law of libel have been attempted to be remedied by a bill brought into parliament in a very crude and imperfect state by Lord Campbell, and somewhat improved in its passage through the two houses into an act; it is still however a very patch-work piece of legislation, leaving, as is the fashion of the times, its defects to be developed by a succession of expensive appeals to courts of justice, [1843].

740 The Rev. W. Sellon, in 1763, ostentatiously published a sermon which he had preached at St. Andrew's Holborn, at Clerkenwell, and at St. Giles's. On its publication, the critics discovered it to be as gross a piece of plagiarism as ever issued from the press.—See vol. i. p. 159, n.

And, growling, cry with surly tone,
Keep off—this feast is all my own.
  Bending to earth the downcast eye,
Or planting it against the sky,
As one immersed in deepest thought,
Or with some holy vision caught,
His hands to aid the traitor's art,
Devoutly folded o'er his heart:
Here Moore in fraud well skill'd, should go
All saint, with solemn step and slow.
O that Religion's sacred name,
Meant to inspire the purest flame,
A prostitute should ever be
To that arch-fiend Hypocrisy,
Where we find every other vice
Crown'd with damn'd sneaking cowardice.
Bold sin reclaim'd is often seen;
Past hope that man, who dares be mean.
  There, full of flesh, and full of grace,
With that fine round unmeaning face
Which Nature gives to sons of earth,
Whom she designs for ease and mirth,
Should the prim Plausible be seen,
Observe his stiff affected mien;
'Gainst nature, arm'd by gravity,
His features too in buckle see;
See with what sanctity he reads,
With what devotion tells his beads!
Now, Prophet, shew me, by thine art,
What's the religion of his heart:

Shew there, if truth thou canst unfold
Religion center'd all in gold;
Shew him, nor fear correction's rod,
As false to friendship, as to God.
  Horrid, unwieldy, without form,
Savage as ocean in a storm,
Of size prodigious, in the rear,
That post of honour should appear
Pomposo; fame around should tell
How he a slave to interest fell;
How, for integrity renown'd
Which booksellers have often found,
He for subscribers baits his hook,
And takes their cash—but where's the book?
No matter where—wise fear, we know,
Forbids the robbing of a foe;
But what, to serve our private ends,
Forbids the cheating of our friends?
No man alive, who would not swear

797 Dr. Johnson visited the Ghost in Cock Lane more than once, but it does not appear that he was of the subsequent party to the vault, being, however, fully satisfied of the imposture, he drew up the account of its detection, as published in the Gentleman's Magazine for February, 1762.

801 This passage reminded Dr. Johnson of the necessity of publishing his edition of Shakspeare, subscriptions for which had been received by him upwards of twenty years. Accordingly, in 1765, it appeared, and the extraordinary merit of the preface and critical observations, atoned for the meagreness of the notes; and for his deficiency in that spirit of persevering industry and indefatigable research, which distinguish the labors of a Theobald, a Malone, a Reed, and a Stevens; but to which Johnson could not or would not descend.

All's safe, and therefore honest there:
For spite of all the learned say,
If we to truth attention pay,
The word dishonesty is meant
For nothing else but punishment.
Fame, too, should tell, nor heed the threat
Of rogues, who brother rogues abet,
Nor tremble at the terrors hung
Aloft, to make her hold her tongue;
How to all principles untrue,
Not fix'd to old friends nor to new,
He damns the pension which he takes,
And loves the Stuart he forsakes.
Nature (who, justly regular,
Is very seldom known to err,
But now and then in sportive mood,
As some rude wits have understood,
Or through much work required in haste,
Is with a random stroke disgraced)
Pomposo form'd on doubtful plan,
Not quite a beast, nor quite a man;
Like—God knows what—for never yet
Could the most subtle human wit
Find out a monster which might be
The shadow of a simile.
These three, these great, these mighty, three,
Nor can the poet's truth agree,
Howe'er report hath done him wrong,
And warp'd the purpose of his song,
Amongst the refuse of their race,
The sons of Infamy to place,

That open, generous, manly mind,
Which we, with joy, in Aldrich find.
These three, who now are faintly shown,
Just sketch'd, and scarcely to be known,
If Dulman their request had heard,
In stronger colours had appear'd,
And friends, though partial, at first view,
Shuddering, had own'd the picture true.
But had the journal been display'd,
And their whole process open laid,
What a vast unexhausted field
For mirth must such a journal yield!
In her own anger strongly charm'd,
'Gainst hope, 'gainst fear, by conscience arm'd,
Then had bold Satire made her way,
Knights, lords, and dukes, her destined prey.
  But Prudence, ever sacred name
To those who feel not virtue's flame,
Or only feel it, at the best,
As the dull dupe of Interest,
Whisper'd aloud (for this we find
A custom current with mankind,
So loud to whisper, that each word
May all around be plainly heard;
And Prudence sure would never miss
A custom so contrived as this
Her candour to secure, yet aim

840 The Reverend Stephen Aldrich, Rector of St. John's, Clerkenwell, had too much good sense to be imposed upon by the Cock Lane Ghost, and actively contributed to its exposure.

Sure death against another's fame)
Knights, lords, and dukes—mad wretch, forbear,
Dangers unthought of ambush there;
Confine thy rage to weaker slaves,
Laugh at small fools, and lash small knaves,
But never, helpless, mean, and poor,
Rush on, where laws cannot secure,
Nor think thyself, mistaken youth!
Secure in principles of truth:
Truth: why shall every wretch of letters
Dare to speak truth against his betters!
Let ragged Virtue stand aloof,
Nor mutter accents of reproof;
Let ragged Wit a mute become,
When wealth and power would have her dumb;
For who the devil doth not know
That titles and estates bestow
An ample stock, where'er they fall,
Of graces which we mental call?
Beggars, in every age and nation,
Are rogues and fools by situation;
The rich and great are understood
To be of course both wise and good;
Consult then interest more than pride,
Discreetly take the stronger side;
Desert, in time, the simple few,
Who Virtue's barren path pursue;
Adopt my maxims—follow me—
To Baal bow the prudent knee;
Deny thy God, betray thy friend,

At Baal's altars hourly bend,
So shalt thou rich and great be seen,
To be great now, you must be mean.
  Hence, Tempter, to some weaker soul,
Which fear and interest control;
Vainly thy precepts are address'd
Where Virtue steels the steady breast;
Through meanness wade to boasted power
Through guilt repeated every hour;
What is thy gain, when all is done,
What mighty laurels hast thou won?
Dull crowds, to whom the heart's unknown,
Praise thee for virtues not thy own:
But will, at once man's scourge and friend,
Impartial Conscience too commend?
From her reproaches canst thou fly?
Canst thou with worlds her silence buy?
Believe it not—her stings shall find
A passage to thy coward mind:
There shall she fix her sharpest dart;
There shew thee truly, as thou art,
Unknown to those, by whom thou'rt prized,
Known to thyself to be despised.
  The man, who weds the sacred Muse
Disdains all mercenary views,
And he, who Virtue's throne would rear
Laughs at the phantoms raised by fear.
Though Folly, robed in purple, shines,
Though vice exhausts Peruvian mines,
Yet shall they tremble, and turn pale,
When Satire wields her mighty flail;

Or should they of rebuke afraid,
With Melcombe seek hell's deepest shade,
Satire, still mindful of her aim,
Shall bring the cowards back to shame.
  Hated by many, loved by few,
Above each little private view,
Honest, though poor, (and who shall dare
To disappoint my boasting there?)
Hardy and resolute, though weak,
The dictates of my heart to speak,
Willing I bend at Satire's throne;
What power I have be all her own.
  Nor shall yon lawyer's specious art,
Conscious of a corrupted heart,

928 George Bubb Doddington, the son of an apothecary at Weymouth, by his address in the electioneering management of that and its then sister borough, raised himself to the peerage under the title of Lord Melcombe. He was a retainer of the court of Frederick Prince of Wales, and on the accession of George the Third, became a devoted supporter of the measures of Lord Bute. Lord Melcombe was a man of shrewd sense and observation, and his diary of events, published by Mr. Penruddocke Wyndham, exhibits, amidst a heap of trivial details, a singular chain of gross venality and low intrigue, strongly illustrative of the influence of petty occurrences in the administration of public affairs. Political pamphleteers then reaped the harvest of corruption; a sort of open competition took place for the pen of a Ralph, a Mauduit, or a Guthrie; and his lordship's relation of the event of the biddings for their support is highly entertaining. Those who are ignorant of what materials courts and courtiers are composed, will profit by a perusal of the diary, which with the introductory lines to Thomson's Summer, and in Dr. Young's Universal Passion, will immortalize the noble name of Bubb, or Grub, as travestied by Sir C. H. Williams.

Create imaginary fear
To damp us in our bold career.
Why should we fear; and what? the laws?
They all are arm'd in virtue's cause;
And aiming at the self-same end,
Satire is always virtue's friend.
Nor shall that Muse whose honest rage,
In a corrupt degenerate age,
(When, dead to every nicer sense,
Deep sunk in vice and indolence,
The spirit of old Rome was broke
Beneath the tyrant fiddler's yoke)
Banish'd the rose from Nero's cheek,
Under a Brunswick fear to speak.
Drawn by conceit from reason's plan,
How vain is that poor creature, man!
How pleased is every paltry elf
To prate about that thing himself!
After my promise made in rhyme,
And meant in earnest at that time,
To jog, according to the mode,
In one dull pace, in one dull road,
What but that curse of heart and head
To this digression could have led?
Where plunged, in vain I look about,
And can't stay in, nor well get out.
Could I, whilst Humour held the quill,
Could I digress with half that skill;
Could I with half that skill return,
Which we so much admire in Sterne,

Where each digression, seeming vain,
And only fit to entertain,
Is found, on better recollection,
To have a just and nice connexion,
To help the whole with wondrous art,
Whence it seems idly to depart;
Then should our readers ne'er accuse
These wild excursions of the Muse;
Ne'er backward turn dull pages o'er
To recollect what went before;
Deeply impress'd, and ever new,
Each image past shall start to view,
And we to Dulman now come in,
As if we ne'er had absent been.
  Have you not seen when danger's near,
The coward cheek turn white with fear?
Have you not seen, when danger's fled,
The self-same cheek with joy turn red?
These are low symptoms which we find
Fit only for a vulgar mind,
Where honest features, void of art,
Betray the feelings of the heart:
Our Dulman with a face was bless'd,
Where no one passion was express'd;
His eye, in a fine stupour caught,
Implied a plenteous lack of thought;
Nor was one line that whole face seen in
Which could be justly charged with meaning.
  To Avarice by birth allied,
Debauch'd by marriage into pride,

In age grown fond of youthful sports,
Of pomps, of vanities, and courts,
And by success too mighty made
To love his country or his trade;
Stiff in opinion, (no rare case
With blockheads in or out of place)
Too weak, and insolent of soul
To suffer reason's just control,
But bending, of his own accord,
To that trim transient toy, my Lord;
The dupe of Scots, (a fatal race,
Whom God in wrath contrived to place
To scourge our crimes, and gall our pride,
A constant thorn in England's side;
Whom first, our greatness to oppose,
He in his vengeance mark'd for foes;
Then, more to serve his wrathful ends,
And more to curse us, mark'd for friends)
Deep in the state, if we give credit
To him, for no one else e'er said it,
Sworn friend of great ones not a few,
Though he their titles only knew,
And those (which envious of his breeding,
Book-worms have charged to want of reading)
Merely to shew himself polite
He never would pronounce aright;
An orator with whom a host
Of those which Rome and Athens boast,
In all their pride might not contend.
Who, with no powers to recommend,

Whilst Jackey Home and Billy Whitehead,
And Dicky Glover sat delighted,
Could speak whole days in nature's spite,
Just as those able versemen write;
Great Dulman from his bed arose—
Thrice did he spit—thrice wiped his nose—
Thrice strove to smile—thrice strove to frown—

1032 Richard Glover was originally an eminent merchant in the city of London, and distinguished himself by a remarkable speech he delivered at the bar of the House of Commons on behalf of the mercantile interest, previous to the breaking out of the Spanish war, in 1740. His zeal for the public interfering with his private concerns, his business decayed, and he became in 1751, an unsuccessful candidate for the city chamberlainship. For some years following he lived in perfect obscurity; but having surmounted his immediate difficulties, he again appeared in public in 1761, in the character of M. P. for Weymouth, under the patronage of Lord Melcombe and Frederic Prince of Wales. As a member of the House of Commons he took no active part, but confined himself to his literary pursuits. Of his principal performance, an epic poem entitled Leonidas, extravagant expectations were entertained, previous to the publication; but the ardour of the public quickly subsided, and though told in language highly classical and elegant, the fate of the Spartan hero excited but little interest. It was, however, translated into French, and has gone through four or five editions. Mr. Glover was also the author of two cold tragedies, founded on the interesting but exhausted histories of Medea and Boadicea. His amiable disposition and benevolence of mind, joined to manners the most elegant and captivating, rendered him the idol of a numerous circle. He died in 1785, at the age of 74. Some years since Mr. Duppa published a book stating the evidence on which he considered that the writer of Junius's Letters could be no other than Richard Glover; it is needless to add that he never obtained a single convert to his opinion.

And thrice look'd up—and thrice looked down—
Then silence broke—" Crape, who am I?"
Crape bow'd, and smiled an arch reply.
" Am I not, Crape?—I am you know
Above all those who are below.
Have I not knowledge? and for wit,
Money will always purchase it:
Nor, if it needful should be found,
Will I grudge ten, or—twenty pound,
For which the whole stock may be bought
Of scoundrel wits not worth a groat.
But lest I should proceed too far,
I'll feel my friend the Minister
(Great Men, Crape, must not be neglected)
How he in this point is affected;
For, as I stand a magistrate,
To serve him first, and next the state,
Perhaps he may not think it fit
To let his magistrates have wit.
" Boast I not, at this very hour,
Those large effects which troop with power?
Am I not mighty in the land?
Do not I sit, while others stand?
Am I not with rich garments graced,
In seat of honour always placed?
And do not Cits of chief degree,
Though proud to others, bend to me?
" Have I not, as a Justice ought,
The laws such wholesome rigour taught,
That Fornication, in disgrace,
Is not afraid to shew her face,

And not one whore these walls approaches
Unless they ride in their own coaches?
And shall this Fame, an old poor strumpet,
Without our license sound her trumpet;
And, envious of our City's quiet,
In broad day-light blow up a riot?
If insolence like this we bear,
Where is our state? our office where?
Farewell all honours of our reign,
Farewell the neck-ennobling chain,
Freedom's known badge o'er all the globe;
Farewell the solemn-spreading robe,
Farewell the sword, farewell the mace,
Farewell all title, pomp, and place;
Removed from men of high degree,
(A loss to them, Crape, not to me)
Banish'd to Chippenham or to Frome,
Dulman once more shall ply the loom."
   Crape, lifting up his hands and eyes,
"Dulman—the loom—at Chippenham"—cries;
"If there be powers which greatness love,
Which rule below, but dwell above,
Those powers united all shall join
To contradict the rash design.
   "Sooner shall stubborn Will lay down

1093 William Beckford, Esq., elected an Alderman June, 1752, and twice Lord Mayor of London, in 1762 and 1769. He was a West India merchant, possessed a princely fortune, and became highly popular by his strenuous opposition to the court: the memorable answer he made in 1770, to George the Third, on his refusal to grant the petition of the livery

His opposition with his gown;
Sooner shall Temple leave the road
Which leads to Virtue's mean abode;
Sooner shall Scots this country quit,
And England's foes be friends to Pitt,
Than Dulman, from his grandeur thrown,
Shall wander outcast, and unknown.
Sure as that cane, (a cane there stood
Near to a table made of wood,

for the dissolution of parliament, is inscribed under the monument erected to his memory in Guildhall. "Permit me, sire, farther to observe, that whoever has already dared, or shall hereafter endeavour, by false insinuations and suggestions, to alienate your majesty's affections from your loyal subjects in general, and from the city of London in particular, is an enemy to your Majesty's person and family, a violater of the public peace, and a betrayer of our happy constitution, as it was established at the glorious and necessary revolution." The king, who was accused of having smiled at the address, now reddened with anger and astonishment, and remained in profound silence; but when the Lord Mayor a short time afterwards went to St. James's, with the customary congratulations on the birth of a princess, he was informed "that as his lordship had thought fit to speak to his majesty after his answer to the late remonstrance, as it was unusual, his majesty desired that nothing of the kind might happen for the future." Mr. Beckford died in the year 1770, during his second mayoralty. His son is the distinguished author of Vathek and Letters from Portugal, &c.

1101 "Now by this sacred sceptre hear me swear,
Which never more shall leaves or blossoms bear;
Which, sever'd from the trunk, as I from thee,
On the bare mountains left its parent tree;
This sceptre, form'd by temper'd steel to prove
An ensign of the delegates of Jove,

Of dry fine wood a table made,
By some rare artist in the trade,
Who had enjoy'd immortal praise
If he had lived in Homer's days)
Sure as that cane, which once was seen
In pride of life all fresh and green,
The banks of Indus to adorn,
Then, of its leafy honours shorn,
According to exactest rule,
Was fashion'd by the workman's tool,
And which at present we behold
Curiously polish'd, crown'd with gold,
With gold well wrought; sure as that cane
Shall never on its native plain
Strike root afresh, shall never more
Flourish in tawny India's shore,
So sure shall Dulman and his race
To latest times this station grace."
Dulman, who all this while had kept
His eyelids closed as if he slept,
Now looking steadfastly on Crape,
As at some god in human shape—
"Crape, I protest, you seem to me
To have discharged a prophecy:

From whom the power of laws and justice springs,
Tremendous oath! inviolate to kings,
By this I swear, when bleeding Greece again
Shall call Achilles, she shall call in vain."
Pope's Iliad, B. 1. l. 309.

A similar passage occurs in the 12th book of the Æneid.

Yes—from the first it doth appear
Planted by Fate, the Dulmans here
Have always held a quiet reign,
And here shall to the last remain.
"Crape, they're all wrong about this Ghost—
Quite on the wrong side of the post—
Blockheads! to take it in their head
To be a message from the dead,
For that by mission they design,
A word not half so good as mine.
Crape—here it is—start not one doubt—
A plot—a plot—I've found it out."
"O God!"—cries Crape,—"how bless'd the nation,
Where one son boasts such penetration!"
"Crape, I've not time to tell you now
When I discover'd this, or how;
To Stentor go—if he's not there,
His place let Bully Norton bear—
Our citizens to council call—
Let all meet—'tis cause of all:
Let the three witnesses attend,
With allegations to befriend,
To swear just so much, and no more,
As we instruct them in before.
"Stay—Crape—come back—what, don't you see

1148 One of the law officers of the city of London, the general application of the character precludes our identifying the functionary immediately alluded to.

The effects of this discovery?
Dulman all care and toil endures—
The profit, Crape, will all be yours.
A mitre, (for this, arduous task
Perform'd, they'll grant whate'er I ask)
A mitre (and perhaps the best)
Shall, through my interest, make thee blest:
And at this time, when gracious fate
Dooms to the Scot the reins of state,
Who is more fit, (and for your use
We could some instances produce)
Of England's church to be the head,
Than you, a Presbyterian bred?
But when thus mighty you are made,

1165 Secker, Archbishop of Canterbury, was bred a Presbyterian, and his original profession was that of a man-midwife, at which period he was president of a free-thinking club; he was converted to the established church by Bishop Talbot whose relation he had married, and his faith settled by the good Bishop making him prebend of Durham, from whence he was transplanted, on the recommendation of Dr. Bland, to Queen Caroline, who had no objection to a medley of religions, to the Rectory of St. James on the death of the celebrated Dr. Samuel Clarke, and then successively filled the sees of Bristol and Oxford; his sermons were a kind of moral essays, clear from quotations of scripture; but what they wanted in gospel was made up by a tone of fanaticism; lastly, he in 1768, obtained the Primacy by the interest of Lord Hardwicke, out of gratitude for his having contrived a match between the Chancellor's son and Lady Arabella Gray, the grand daughter and heiress of the Duke of Kent. He died in 1788.—*Walpole.*

He, as is the usual course with proselytes, became so zealous an advocate for the church against his old associates, that he

Unlike the brethren of thy trade,
Be grateful, Crape, and let me not,
Like old Newcastle, be forgot.
"But an affair, Crape, of this size
Will ask from conduct vast supplies;
It must not, as the vulgar say,
Be done in hugger-mugger way:
Traitors, indeed, (and that's discreet)
Who hatch the plot, in private meet:

declared he would bestow the best living in his gift on any clergyman who would answer and confute the Confessional.

1168 The Duke of Newcastle, who died in 1768, had for more than fifty years filled the greatest offices in the state. The famous quadruple alliance was signed by him at Whitehall, July 22, 1718. He might, in the last years of his life, when out of office, and deserted by the minions he had raised to wealth and power, pathetically exclaim:—

"I've been so long remember'd I'm forgot."

This nobleman was the last minister of the whig school of 1688. His rank and fortune gave him great weight, and his princely establishment rendered him popular; after the death of his lamented brother, Henry Pelham, he was too weak to sustain his party, and though he continued nominally in office until 1762, he possessed but little influence. At this period finding it necessary to resign to make room for Lord Bute, and being offered a lucrative and dignified, but unimportant situation, he nobly replied, "that he would not contribute to burthen a country he was no longer permitted to serve." Smollett, in Humphrey Clinker, has given a just though caricatured account of the discarded minister, and of his levees at Newcastle House, the corner of Great Queen Street in Lincoln's-Inn-Fields. It was observed at the time, that though the whole bench of bishops were of his appointment, Warburton was the only one of the number who had the gratitude to visit a fallen patron. Lord Bute, principally

They should in public go, no doubt,
Whose business is to find it out.
  "To-morrow—if the day appear
Likely to turn out fair and clear—
Proclaim a grand processionade—
Be all the City-pomp display'd;

through the interest of the Duke of Newcastle, was made secretary of state on the removal of the Earl of Holderness. The Thane, as he was then called, soon forgot his obligations, and by seizing every opportunity to render the Duke's situation disagreeable, compelled him to resign his place of First Lord of the Treasury, of which Lord Bute possessed himself on May 29, 1762.

Had the Duke adhered to his political engagement with Lord Temple and Mr. Pitt, Lord Bute would have been defeated, and the empire might not have been so soon dismembered, but the old man's love of place prevailed, he compromised his party, and was the first victim of his own duplicity and of the superior craft of his colleague. Sir Robert Walpole is reported to have said of the Duke of Newcastle, His name is perfidy. Horace Walpole avenged his father's wrongs by designating Newcastle as a Secretary of State without intelligence, a Duke without money, a man of infinite intrigue, without secrecy or policy, and a minister despised and hated by his master, by all parties and administrations, without being turned out by any.

1178 The purpose of this solemn preparation was for the address of thanks to his majesty on the conclusion of the peace with France. That peace of which Lord Bute said that he desired no other epitaph to be inscribed upon his tomb than that he was the man who had made the peace of 1763, which occasioned the following epigram:

Say, when will England be from faction freed,
  When will domestic quarrels cease!
Ne'er till that wished for epitaph we read,
  Here lies the man that made the peace.

Let the Train-bands"—Crape shook his head—
They heard the trumpet, and were fled—
"Well"—cries the Knight—"if that's the case,
My servants shall supply their place—
My servants—mine alone—no more—
Than what my servants did before—
Dost not remember, Crape, that day
When, Dulman's grandeur to display,
As all too simple and too low,
Our City friends were thrust below,
Whilst, as more worthy of our love,
Courtiers were entertain'd above?
Tell me, who waited then? and how?
My servants—mine—and why not now?
In haste then, Crape, to Stentor go—
But send up Hart, who waits below;
With him, till you return again,
(Reach me my spectacles and cane)
I'll make a proof how I advance in
My new accomplishment of dancing."
  Not quite so fast as lightning flies,
Wing'd with red anger through the skies;
Not quite so fast as sent by Jove,
Iris descends on wings of love;
Not quite so fast as Terror rides
When he the chasing winds bestrides,
Crape hobbled—but his mind was good—
Could he go faster than he could?
  Near to that tower, which, as we're told,
The mighty Julius raised of old;

Where, to the block by Justice led,
The rebel Scot hath often bled;
Where arms are kept so clean, so bright,
'Twere sin they should be soil'd in fight;
Where brutes of foreign race are shown
By brutes much greater of our own;
Fast by the crowded Thames, is found
An ample square of sacred ground,
Where artless eloquence presides,
And nature every sentence guides.
Here female parliaments debate
About religion, trade, and state;

1218 Near London-bridge once stood a gate
Belinus gave it name,
Whence the green Nereids oysters bring;
A place of public fame.
Here eloquence has fix'd her seat;
The nymphs here learn by heart,
In mode and figure still to speak
By modern rules of art.
To each fair oratress this school
Its rhetoric strong affords,
They double and redouble tropes
With finger, fist, and words.
Both nerves and strength and flow of speech,
With beauties ever new,
Adorn the language of these nymphs
Who give to all their due.
O happy seat of happy nymphs,
For many ages known;
To thee each rostrum's forced to yield,
Each forum in the town.
Let other academies boast
What titles else they please,
Thou shalt be call'd the gate of tongues,
Of tongues that never cease.

Here every Naiad's patriot soul,
Disdaining foreign base control,
Despising French, despising Erse,
Pours forth the plain old English curse,
And bears aloft, with terrors hung,
The honours of the vulgar tongue.
Here Stentor, always heard with awe,
In thund'ring accents deals out law:
Twelve furlongs off each dreadful word
Was plainly and distinctly heard,
And every neighbour hill around
Return'd and swell'd the mighty sound,
The loudest virgin of the stream,
Compared with him would silent seem;
Thames, (who enraged to find his course
Opposed, rolls down with double force,
Against the bridge indignant roars,
And lashes the resounding shores)
Compared with him, at lowest tide,
In softest whispers seems to glide,
Hither directed by the noise,
Swell'd with the hope of future joys,
Through too much zeal and haste made lame,
The reverend slave of Dulman came.
Stentor—with such a serious air,
With such a face of solemn care,
As might import him to contain
A nation's welfare in his brain—
" Stentor"—cries Crape—" I'm hither sent
On business of most high intent,

Great Dulman's orders to convey:
Dulman commands, and I obey;
Big with those throes which patriots feel,
And labouring for the commonweal,
Some secret, which forbids him rest,
Tumbles and tosses in his breast;
Tumbles and tosses to get free,
And thus the Chief commands by me:
"To-morrow, if the day appear
Likely to turn out fair and clear—
Proclaim a grand processionade—
Be all the City-pomp display'd—
Our citizens to council call—
Let all meet—'tis the cause of all!"

1261 This repetition may be vindicated upon the same principle that the adoption of it by Homer is defended by Pope. "The repetition is not ungraceful in those speeches where the dignity of the speaker renders it a sort of insolence to alter his words." There can be no doubt therefore that a Lord Mayor must be considered as coming within the canon so laid down. Were other authority wanting, in support of the claim of that distinguished functionary, his brother justice Midas would supply it, as recorded in the amusing Burletta bearing his name:—

"Jove, in his chair,
Of the sky Lord Mayor."

END OF VOL. II.